PHILOSOPHERS AND PHILOSOPHIES

PHILOSOPHERS AND PHILOSOPHIES

BY

FREDERICK COPLESTON, S.J.

*Professor Emeritus of History of Philosophy
in the University of London*

SEARCH PRESS LONDON

BARNES & NOBLE BOOKS NEW YORK
(a division of Harper & Row Publishers, Inc.)

SEARCH PRESS LIMITED
2–10 Jerdan Place, London SW6 5PT
Great Britain
First published 1976
Copyright © Frederick Copleston 1976
ISBN 0 85 532370 8

Published in the USA 1976 by
Harper & Row Publishers, Inc.
BARNES & NOBLE IMPORT DIVISION

ISBN 0 06 491278 7

PRINTED AND BOUND IN GREAT BRITAIN BY
Billing & Sons Ltd,
Guildford, London and Worcester

CONTENTS

ACKNOWLEDGMENTS: Chapter I appeared first in *Contemporary British Philosophy: Third Series*, ed. H.D. Lewis (London, Allen & Unwin, 1956). Chapter II was given as an inaugural lecture in the University of London and appeared in the *Heythrop Journal* in 1973. Chapter III was given as an unpublished paper to the Aquinas Septcentennial Conference at the University of Calgary, Canada, in 1974. Chapter IV was originally presented as the Suarez lecture at Fordham University in 1967 and published in *Thought*. Chapter V was given as a lecture at Westfield College, University of London. Chapter VI is an unpublished talk to the London Society for the Study of Religion. Chapter VII is a paper given originally to the Aristotelian Society in 1974 and published in the *Proceedings* of that Society. Chapter VIII was published first in *Spinoza: Essays in Interpretation*, ed. M. Mandelbaum & E. Freeman (Open Court, LaSalle, Ill., 1975). Chapter IX appeared in *New Studies in Hegel*, ed. W. E. Steinkraus (Holt, Rinehart & Wilson, N.Y., 1971). Chapter X was published first in *The Review of Metaphysics* in 1968. Chapter XI was given as the Dawes Hicks lecture on philosophy to the British Academy in 1955 and was published first in the *Proceedings* of the Academy. Chapter XII was given as an unpublished talk to the Philosophical Society of Birkbeck College, University of London. The publishers thank the Editor of the *Heythrop Journal*, the Principal of Westfield College, Professor A. Parel of the University of Calgary, the Editor of *Thought*, the Secretary of the Aristotelian Society, the Open Court Publishing Company, Messrs Holt, Rinehart & Wilson, the Editor of the *Review of Metaphysics*, and the Secretary of the British Academy for their kind permission to reprint these chapters.

CHAPTER 1

PHILOSOPHICAL KNOWLEDGE

I T IS TAKEN FOR GRANTED, and with good reason, that astronomers, biologists, physicists, historians and so on possess a great deal of factual knowledge which other people do not possess. And it is possible to delimit with sufficient clarity the special field of knowledge of, for example, the astronomer or the historian. 'But it is not at all so clear what it is that the philosopher as philosopher knows or can know. Is it possible for him by philosophical reflection to attain factual knowledge about reality?[1] If so, are the propositions in which this knowledge is expressed capable of imparting fresh information about reality to at least some people? Or are they simply and always pompous ways of saying what everyone already knows? In the latter case we should have to say that the philosopher, unlike the astronomer, cannot increase our factual knowledge of reality. And we might then be inclined to say that philosophical knowledge, provided that we are willing to admit that there is such a thing, is concerned with the meaning of terms and propositions. Here, we may think, we are on safe ground. Even though we may abandon all claims that the philosopher can increase our factual knowledge about things, we can at least maintain the claim that he is capable of increasing our knowledge about the meaning of terms and propositions. 'Speculative' philosophy having been rejected, logical analysis or analysis of language still remains, and it is capable of resulting in what can properly be called philosophical knowledge.

Yet although it is easy to state that philosophical knowledge is concerned with the meaning of terms and propositions, it is not at all so easy to say what is meant by this statement. Does it mean that the philosopher clarifies the meaning of terms and propositions for those who have been suffering from logical and linguistic confusion, so that it is only to these latter that information can be said to be imparted? Or does it mean that the philosopher can impart knowledge about the meaning of terms and propositions to those who have been suffering not from linguistic confusion but simply from ignorance? If so, the information imparted is presumably not simply the sort of information imparted by philologists and lexicographers. For if it were, we might prefer to turn directly to them for our information. There does not seem to be any adequate reason for supposing that the philosopher can do the philologist's work better than the philologist himself can do it. Is, therefore, the information provided by the philosopher information about the 'objective' meaning of terms and propositions? If it is, it would seem to be difficult to avoid the conclusion that the philospher can in some sense at least impart information about reality. We might then be inclined to

1

conclude that the statement that philosophical knowledge is concerned with the meaning of terms and propositions is a way of saying that though the philosopher cannot increase the number of contingent facts which we know, he can give us a better understanding of the facts which we come to know in other ways than by philosophical reflection. But the question then arises what is meant by this and how precisely the philosopher gives us this 'better understanding'. Further, if the philosopher can in some sense give us a better understanding of reality, is not the way reopened to 'speculative' philosophy? All that would then seem to be excluded would be the claim that the philosopher as philosopher can do the work either of the explorer or of the scientist.

The treatment of these questions seems to be complicated by the fact that the word 'philosophy' covers a variety of subjects and questions and discussions which have been traditionally grouped together under one heading.[2] It is possible for different people to recommend different definitions or descriptions of philosophy; and it is very difficult to find a formula which will fit all the branches of 'philosophy' in a wide understanding of the term. However, in this essay I wish to avoid discussion based on pre-selected definitions; and I do not pretend to offer any slick statement about the nature of philosophical knowledge. I intend to proceed in an empirical manner by selecting for examination certain discussions and inquiries which are generally thought of as pertaining to 'philosophy' with a view to seeing whether this examination throws any light on my main theme. If by doing this I succeed in making some slight contribution to the solution of the problem which I have raised, so much the better. But it may be, of course, that I shall merely succeed in illustrating the complexity of the problem. But this itself would not be an altogether despicable result. For simple solutions to problems are sometimes accompanied by failure to see the complexity of the problems at issue.

2

It seems to me to be true that certain philosophical discussions have resulted in the clarification of the meaning of terms and propositions for those who have been suffering from linguistic confusion. The discussion of the reference of universal terms is a fairly obvious case in point. Those who thought that to a universal term like 'man' there must correspond some sort of universal entity, whether a subsistent universal essence distinct from individual men or, as with some ultra-realists of the early Middle Ages, one essence existing simultaneously in different men under different accidental modifications,[3] can reasonably be said to have been suffering from linguistic confusion. They did not properly understand the meaning and function of universal terms. And those who, like Abelard, pointed out how the strange conclusions which follow from such theories can be avoided by means of a different analysis of the meaning of universal terms were engaged in clearing up a linguistic confusion in the minds of others. The latter can thus be said to have received information about the meaning and function of terms. Furthermore, they can be said, in some sense at least, to have received information about reality. For they were told that there are no such things as universal entities, that is, things existing independently of the mind. This does not mean that they were told simply that there is no empirical evidence in favour of the statement that there are universal entities, just as a man might be told that there is no adequate empirical evidence in favour of the statement that there are elves or fairies. For it was pointed out to them that a universal thing is intrinsically impossible. To say of anything that it is a thing is to say that it is an individual existent; and there can no more be an universal thing than there can be a round square. Hence they can be said to have received the information that reality is such that it cannot comprise universal entities.

But who received this information? Certainly not the ordinary man.[4] When Antisthenes remarked that he perceived horses but not horseness, he may have laid himself open to the retort that anyone who is not blind can perceive horses whereas it requires a mind to perceive horseness, but none the less he was speaking for the ordinary man. The latter would never dream of looking for a universal horseness as an entity alongside individual horses. And the fact that it never occurs to the ordinary man to think that there are universal entities corresponding to universal terms seems to show that in some sense of the word 'know' he knows that there are no such things. In other words, the linguistic confusion which was dissipated by the opponents of ultra-realism was a confusion in the minds of philosophers, not in the mind of the ordinary man. Abelard cleared up a confusion of the mind of William of Champeaux, not in that of the contemporary man in the street. And the confusion was able to arise in the first place because philosophers are the sort of people who notice peculiarities about terms which the ordinary man does not notice. The latter uses universal terms correctly in the concrete propositions of everyday speech, but he does not reflect upon them in an abstract manner. The ultra-realists, being philosophers, did so; and thus it was possible for them to fall into the confusion into which they did fall. And their opponents helped to dissipate a confusion in the minds of their colleagues, not of those of non-philosophers.

3

But though it can reasonably be said that the discussion about universal terms resulted in clearing up a linguistic confusion, it does not follow that the whole discussion can be accurately labelled as an example of the dissipation by some philosophers of confusion in the minds of other philosophers. In the first place the discussion does not necessarily begin with logical or linguistic confusion. To ask, for example, what is the meaning of the term 'beautiful' or what is objectively connoted by the term is not by itself a sign of linguistic confusion. To put such questions is, indeed, to ask for clarification; but the questions can very well precede any answers which might reasonably be regarded as the result of confusing one kind of term with another. If an answer is given which depends on or involves linguistic confusion, this confusion will have to be cleared up by further analysis. But though a question about the meaning of universal terms might be so formulated as to give evidence from the start of logical confusion, this is not necessarily the case.

In the second place, when any linguistic or logical confusion which may have occurred in the course of the discussion has been cleared up and the right answer, whatever it may be, has been given to the question raised, the philosopher does not find himself in precisely the same position as the ordinary man. The latter may use words like 'beautiful' and 'just' quite correctly in everyday speech, and in so far as he uses them correctly he can hardly be said to be altogether ignorant of their meaning; but it by no means follows that he can give an abstract analysis of the meanings of these terms. If he can do so, he is not an 'ordinary' man but a philosopher. If we suppose, therefore, that the philosopher can in principle give such an analysis, we can say that he can in principle attain knowledge which is not possessed by the ordinary man, even though this knowledge does not involve knowing entities which are unknown by the ordinary man. And in this case we can hardly reduce philosophy to the dissipation by some philosophers of linguistic or logical confusion in the minds of some of their colleagues, though this may very well be, as an empirical fact, one of the useful results of philosophical analysis.

4

To say, however, that philosophy cannot be reduced to the dissipation of linguistic confusion in the sense indicated above is not to say what it is that the philosopher knows or is capable of knowing that the ordinary man does not know. And in attempting to throw some light on this matter I take for consideration the philosophical analysis of causality.

We are all aware that there are causal relations, and this awareness finds expression in the concrete propositions of everyday speech. What the philosopher knows, as distinct from the ordinary man, is certainly not the fact that there are causal relations. Awareness of some concrete causal relation is presupposed by the philosopher when he sets about analyzing the causal relation. Further, philosophical analysis of the causal relation cannot result in the discovery of hitherto unknown particular causes of particular events. We cannot, for example, discover the cause or causes of cancer of the lung by philosophical analysis.

This is, of course, one reason why philosophical analysis is often spoken of as linguistic analysis. In his analysis of causality the philosopher is not pursuing physical or chemical analysis: he is concerned with the meaning of a term. He does not pretend to discover that X caused Y, where X is a particular cause and Y a particular event: he asks rather what it means to say that X is the cause of Y. In this sense he is concerned with language. And if theoretical, as distinct from practical, problems are problems of what to say rather than of what to do, we can say, if we like, that his problem is a problem of language.

At the same this way of speaking can be misleading. For it may suggest that the philosopher is concerned with a problem of lexicography or of philology. And this is patently not the case. When he analyses the meaning of the term 'cause' or 'causality', he is concerned with the real or objective meaning of the term. That is to say, in the case of the proposition 'X is the cause of Y' he asks what is the relationship to which the proposition refers: he tries to state explicitly and abstractly the meaning of the proposition in the light of the facts which the proposition purports to exhibit. He is concerned with language, but he is not concerned merely with words in the sense that he makes no reference to the facts exhibited by or described in the propositions in which the relevant terms occur.

Now, I have admitted that the ordinary man knows that there are causal relations. He may know very well that the banging of the door is caused by the wind. He doubtless knows very well how to stop the banging of the door. He requires no enlightenment from a philosopher on such matters. Nor, indeed, could the philosopher, as a philosopher, give him enlightenment about these matters. We must say, therefore, that the ordinary man knows, in some sense of the word 'know', what causality is. At the same time I have maintained that the philosopher, when he applies himself to the analysis of terms like 'cause' and 'causality', is concerned with the objective meaning of the terms. And this seems to imply that the analysis, if successful, yields a better understanding in some sense than the understanding of causality possessed by the ordinary man. But what is this 'better understanding'? What is it that the philosopher discovers or can discover by analysis which the ordinary man does not know?

We cannot legitimately say, I think, that the ordinary man is aware of some features of the causal relation and that the philosopher discovers other features, of which the ordinary man is unaware. An experienced diagnostician can frequently tell what is wrong with a patient by observing him, asking him questions, using a stethoscope and so on. But for the discovery of some maladies the use of X-rays or of some other comparatively exceptional means may be necessary. Again, while all can see some characteristics of an insect simply by using their eyes without the employment of any mechanical instrument, a microscope may be required for discovering other characteristics. But I do not think that the function of a philosophical analysis is analogous to that of X-rays and microscopes in the cases just mentioned. It is not that the ordinary man

has an explicit knowledge of some features of the causal relationship
while the philosopher has explicit knowledge of other features. It seems
to me that explicit knowledge of any of the features of the causal
relationship considered as such, in abstraction, that is to say, from this or
that particular causal relation, is philosophical knowledge. The ordinary
man certainly experiences concrete causal relations. I am aware that I am
now causing the typing of these words. But in so far as I am a non-
philosopher I have no explicit and abstract knowledge of any features of
the causal relation as such. And in so far as I possess a reflective and
explicit awareness of any of these features I am a philosopher.

But this is not to say that the non-philosopher is completely ignorant
of all the features of the causal relation. For awareness of concrete and
particular causal relations comprises an implicit knowledge of all the
features of the relation. This is shown by the fact, or what appears to me
to be the fact, that we have only to reflect on our awareness of concrete
particular causal relations in order to make explicit the peculiar features
or characteristics of the causal relation considered as such. Indeed, on
what else could we reflect in order to attain this explicit knowledge? And
if explicit knowledge of the nature of the causal relation considered as
such is obtained by reflective analysis on particular causal relations, it
seems to follow that awareness of the latter comprises an implicit knowledge of the characteristics of the relation.

This suggests that philosophical analysis consists, in great part at
least, in making explicit a knowledge already possessed implicitly by the
ordinary man. The philosopher notices features of a situation, which the
ordinary man does not notice but of which he cannot be said to be
entirely ignorant. If someone returns from a journey of exploration and
tells me of hitherto unknown butterflies which he has discovered, he
gives me a fresh item of information which I could not have discovered
by reflecting on the knowledge of butterflies which I may already
happen to possess. But if a philosopher informs me that *a, b* and *c* are
features of the causal relation, he is, if he is telling the truth, drawing my
attention to and making me explicitly aware of true propositions which I
could in principle have discovered for myself by reflecting on the knowledge which I already possess of concrete particular causal relations. Philosophical knowledge of the objective meaning of causality cannot be
simply equated with awareness of particular causal relations. We can
justifiably say that the knowledge attained by an adequate analysis is
something different from the knowledge of particular causal relations
possessed by the ordinary man. And if causal relations are features of
reality and not simply mental constructions, we can justifiably say that
an adequate analysis increases our knowledge of reality. At the same time
it does not increase it by adding another item of factual information
similar to the statement that delirium tremens is brought about by
prolonged over-indulgence in alcohol. It increases our knowledge by

making explicit an awareness of the features of the causal relation as such which is implicitly comprised in awareness of particular causal relations. Or we can say that it increases our knowledge by drawing attention to features of a situation which are not 'noticed' by the ordinary man. It seems to me, therefore, that we can quite well admit that the philosopher as philosopher is neither an explorer nor an analytical chemist without being thereby compelled to say that there is no sense in which he knows, or can know, more than the ordinary man.

5

I have mentioned the activity of 'drawing attention to'. And I think that this activity has played and plays an important part in philosophy. We can see examples of it in political philosophy. Consider, for instance, the organic theory of the State. It is, indeed, obvious that the State is not an organism in the sense in which a plant or an animal is an organism. But to call the State an organism might serve to draw attention to the facts that the State, in the sense of political society, is an organization in which different members co-operate for the fulfilment of a certain end or for certain ends, that it survives the death of individual members, that it possesses a continuity of tradition, language, and culture, and so on. Facts of this kind are not, of course, discovered by the political philosopher in the sense in which a scientist may discover hitherto unknown facts; but the political philosopher can draw attention to a certain set of facts which he has not discovered for the first time but which he underlines and so makes us notice. The analogy which he uses in describing the State helps to underline and draw attention to these facts.

The matter is not, of course, as simple as all that. If a political philosopher draws attention to certain features of the State, he presumably does so because he thinks that they are worth drawing attention to. And by the use of certain descriptive terms or analogies he endeavours to make the rest of us value what he values. A man who calls the State an 'organism' may very well wish to encourage in our minds a certain attitude of reverence towards the State as towards a quasi-transcendent entity to which individual human beings are subordinated and apart from which their lives and activities lose their significance. And the man who rejects this organism-analogy and substitutes some other descriptive term or analogy may do so because he regards this reverence towards the State as a quasi-transcendent entity as being highly undesirable and because he wishes to facilitate instead a view of the State as one among other forms of social organization, a form which possesses no pre-eminent sacredness. In his opinion the use of the organism-analogy encourages people to exalt the State 'beyond good and evil' and to neglect the value of the individual person.

In so far as terms and analogies are used to express a feeling about the State and to promote a similar feeling in others they can be said to have emotive and evocative functions. But we cannot justifiably conclude that a term which possesses an emotive function possesses no more than emotive significance. For its power to exercise an emotive function may depend on its power to draw attention to certain real features of political society. Thus the organism-analogy draws attention to certain real features of political society. At the same time, of course, it draws attention to certain features at the expense of others. Moreover, it may suggest features which are not in fact features of political society, or features which can be features of certain types of State but which many of us regard as undesirable. In the language of political theory descriptive and emotive functions may frequently go together and interpenetrate one another. And an important task of the clear-sighted political philosopher is to sort out and distinguish carefully these various functions. However, though I have mentioned the emotive function of terms like 'organism' when used in political theory because it is important not to forget it, my main point for present purposes is that terms used in political theory can also exercise the function of drawing attention to facts which the political philosopher is not the first to discover but which he wishes to underline and to make us notice.

Similar remarks can, I think, be made about the writings of a number of philosophers belonging to the 'existentialist' movement. If an existentialist writes, for example, of the radical insecurity and instability of human existence, he can hardly be said to be giving us fresh factual information of which we were hitherto completely ignorant. But it may very well be true that he draws attention to features of human existence on which we normally and for most of the time do not focus our attention. He may also think it important and desirable for various reasons that we should pay attention to these features of the human situation, and his language may be partially designed, by the selection of emotively charged terms, to facilitate breaking through the so-called crowd-mentality and relating these features to oneself personally.

It may, indeed, appear that concepts like 'noticing' 'drawing attention to' and 'making explicit' are inapplicable to a form of philosophizing such as phenomenological analysis. If a philosopher, it may be asked, gives a phenomenological analysis of being-conscious-of, of perceiving, of loving or of awareness of values, does he only draw attention to what we already know? Does he not in some sense increase our knowledge?

We could hardly maintain successfully that the philosopher who gives a descriptive analysis of being-conscious-of opens up a new world in the same sense in which the European discoverers of America opened up a new world to their fellow Europeans. No doubt, even before the discovery of America some people thought that there was probably land 'out there'; but this was not the same thing as knowing the existence of America. It scarcely needs saying that before its discovery both the existence and the natural features of the American continent were un-

known by Europeans. Being-conscious-of was not, however, an unknown
activity in this sense until a phenomenologist discovered it. All human
beings are conscious of something at some time. Similarly the philosopher who attempts to give a descriptive analysis of an activity like
loving or hoping does not discover love or hope in the sense in which
Christopher Columbus discovered America.

Yet it is one thing to be conscious, attention being riveted on the
object of consciousness, and it is another thing to reflect on being-
conscious-of, attention being focused on this activity itself and not on
the object. Similarly it is one thing to love somebody, and it is another
thing to reflect on the activity of loving. This bending-back of the mind
on the activity itself, without the normal absorption in the particular
concrete object of the activity, is obviously a necessary condition for a
descriptive analysis of being-conscious-of or loving or of perceiving. And
if it is carried out, the structural features of an activity may be brought
to light of which we were formerly not explicitly aware. In this sense our
knowledge is increased; and to this extent we can speak of 'discovery'.
But the new world which is opened up is simply the old world revealing
itself to a mind which achieves the necessary change of direction in the
focusing of attention. This enables the implicit to be made explicit. When
we read an adequate phenomenological analysis we 'recognize' features of
an already familiar activity, features which we had perhaps not
previously noticed because our attention was directed towards the object
of the activity rather than towards the activity itself. We are more in the
position of a man who under the guidance of an art-expert appreciates
hitherto unappreciated features of a familiar picture than in that of a
man who listens to Professor Challenger telling him that he has discovered a living dinosaur in South America.

Another example. Let us suppose that a metaphysician concerns himself with beings as beings or with things as things and that he attempts to
lay bare in explicit statement the fundamental and all-pervasive
ontological structure of things. He must obviously start with reflection
on the things with which we first become acquainted by other means
than by philosophical reflection. And what he does is to focus his
attention on what is in a sense most familiar, on what is so familiar that
we normally do not notice it. And the results of this focusing of
attention are propositions which are both familiar and unfamiliar. They
are unfamiliar or strange because they state truths which we do not
normally advert to in explicit, abstract and universal form. But once we
understand the propositions we can see that they state in explicit,
abstract and universal form truths which find implicit expression in the
concrete particular propositions of everyday speech. Of course, a
proposition which really does state an essential feature of a thing considered as a thing does not state a truth which could possibly be refuted.
If, for example, a finite thing is essentially capable of change, it could

never be true to say that there was a finite thing which was incapable of change. And in this respect a proposition which states any essential feature of a thing as a thing certainly differs from propositions like 'there are men on Mars' or 'all sheep on X's farm are white'. For even if these propositions were in fact true, they might conceivably be false. Nevertheless, a proposition about things as things can be informative in the sense that it states something of which we may not be explicitly aware in the abstract and universal form in which it is stated in the proposition in question. Hence the proposition can be said to contribute to a clearer understanding of reality, and in this sense it increases knowledge.

6

I have maintained that there is a sense in which the philosopher can be said to increase our knowledge or understanding of reality, even though he does not play the part of the explorer. I have maintained, for example, that though we do not owe to the philosopher our knowledge that there are causal relations, the latter's analysis of what it means to say that one thing is the cause of another can increase our understanding of reality. The ordinary man's knowledge of causality may be called first-level knowledge. It is knowledge of particular causal relations without reflection on the causal relation as such. The philosopher's knowledge can be called second-level knowledge. It presupposes the ordinary man's awareness of particular causal relations and is the result of explicit reflection on the causal relation as such, the change from one level to the other being effected by a shift of attention. The philosopher has not at his disposal material which is not at the disposal of the ordinary man, but he adopts a different point of view. And the adoption of this point of view enables him to make explicit the metaphysic which is implicitly contained in the concrete propositions of everyday speech.

This last sentence should not be taken to mean that in my opinion the whole of what is customarily called logical or linguistic analysis can properly be called metaphysical analysis. But if I am right in thinking that the philosophical analyst, when he considers a theme such as the causal relation, is concerned with what I have called the objective or real meaning of terms and propositions, he appears to be engaged in the same sort of activity that many philosophers have regarded as metaphysical analysis. And when I speak about a metaphysic being implicitly contained in the concrete propositions of ordinary speech, I do not mean that by merely inspecting a set of words like 'Brown was killed by Jones' we can elicit a philosophical analysis of causality: the proposition has to be considered both in the light of the concrete relation referred to and from a particular point of view, a point of view which is not, for example, that of the detective. One can equally well talk about a metaphysic implicit in common experience. But inasmuch as this experience must be given verbal expression if we are able to discuss it, it is convenient to speak of a metaphysic implicit in the concrete propositions of everyday speech.

But if one believes, as I believe, that the philosopher can make positive affirmations about the human soul and about God it is necessary to ask whether such affirmation can in any sense be considered as the result of making explicit what is implicitly contained in propositions of ordinary speech or in common experience. At first sight at least a claim that they can be so considered appears to lack even the slightest degree of plausibility. Nobody denies, for example, that there are causal relations. The point at issue is not whether there are causal relations or not but what the causal relationship is or what it means to say that X is the cause of Y, the demand being for a general definition and not for the act of pointing out a concrete example. But there are plenty of people who deny that there is any soul in man, at least if by 'soul' one means a spiritual principle; and there are many who doubt or deny the existence of a being possessing attributes which make it proper to call the being 'God'.

7

In spite of all that has been said to the contrary, it seems to me perfectly reasonable to claim that the ordinary man has implicit awareness of the soul, which finds expression in everyday speech. I do not mean that either the philosopher or the non-philosopher enjoys a direct intuition of the soul. What I mean is this. On the one hand, the pronoun 'I' is used in such a way in ordinary speech that it cannot be taken to refer to an occult immaterial substance which happens to be situated in a certain body. I quite agree that an examination of ordinary language does not support the idea that man consists of an immaterial mind which happens to find itself in a body to which it has only extrinsic relation. On the other hand, any attempt to substitute 'the body' in every case in which we use the pronoun 'I' would certainly appear forced and strange to the ordinary man. The latter would think it very odd if in sentences like 'I think democracy is the most desirable form of political constitution' or 'I believe in God' or 'I consider that Tolstoy was a greater novelist than Edgar Wallace' we attempted to substitute for the pronoun 'I' exclusive reference to the body. We should have in any case to say, for instance, 'my body', a phrase which rather gives the show away. It is not unreasonable, therefore, to maintain that the ordinary man has an awareness of the self as something which neither excludes the body nor is simply identifiable with it without residue. This awareness is implicit in the sense that it finds expression in the concrete propositions of everyday speech, though the ordinary man does not focus his attention upon it or attempt to analyse it. And this implicit awareness forms the basis for philosophical reflection about the nature of the soul and about the relationship between soul and body. The philosopher does not enjoy privileged access to an occult entity; but he can reflect on the nature of man as revealed in human activities and in the concomitant awareness of those activities as 'mine'. He thus attempts to make explicit what is implicitly contained in the concrete propositions of everyday speech, provided that we add that the meaning of the propositions has to be interpreted in the light of the experiences to which they refer. I cannot within the compass of this essay discuss divergent explicit interpretations. The point which I wish to make is that positive affirmations about the human soul do not necessarily involve the philosopher in the claim that he is the privileged discoverer of an occult entity. The reflections of the philosophical psychologist who is neither a materialist nor a phenomenalist are not so remote from the level of everyday speech as they are sometimes depicted as being. By saying this I do not mean to suggest that the problem of a man's psychophysical constitution is an easy problem; for I do not think that it is anything of the kind. At the same time I do not consider that a solution is brought any nearer by insisting on the necessity for analysing the propositions of everyday speech and then interpreting them in a way which seems to me to make nonsense of what the ordinary man is accustomed to say about himself. It may be said that it is naïve and uncritical to take the ordinary man's utterances at their face value. But the question is whether these utterances are themselves naïve and uncritical in a pejorative sense. I do not think that they are.

8

Any view according to which there is a natural intuition of God seems to me untenable. For present purposes I use the word 'God' to mean a transcendent Being (identifiable neither with any finite thing nor with the aggregate of finite things) on which finite things are conceived as depending existentially. And I thus prescind from a more clearly Christian specification of the meaning of the term. But, even so, if one understands by 'intuition' a positive mental seeing, analogous to perception, of a present object, one cannot, I think, successfully maintain that there is a natural and universal intuition of God. Apart from the difficulty of adopting the heroic course of saying that atheists do in fact intuit what they declare that they do not intuit, I do not see, for epistemological and psychological reasons, how trancendent Being could be a direct natural object of the human mind. By saying this I do not mean to deny the possibility of mystical experience, nor its philosophical relevance. For though I do not think that mysticism is philosophy, one can philosophize about mysticism, as, for example, Bergson did. But the question which I am asking is what is the relation between ordinary common experience and the affirmation of God's existence, not between the latter and a comparatively exceptional experience.

It seems, however, to be true that some people[5] who are not philosophers at all in the academic sense of the word raise such questions as whether the complex of finite changing things which we call 'the world' is co-extensive with reality, whether human history is simply a chance episode in a physical cosmos which is synonymous with reality or whether it has some purpose and significance given it from outside. And to ask such questions is to raise the problem of the Transcendent. One can, indeed, try to interpret a question such as whether human history has a goal or purpose in such a way that it is capable of receiving, at least in principle, an empirically verifiable answer. For one can interpret the question as equivalent, for example, to the question what purposes or goals different individuals or groups have in point of fact set before themselves. But if it is interpreted in this way, it becomes a different question: it is no longer the question which was originally asked. For the questioner did not intend to ask what purposes human beings have as a matter of fact set before themselves, but what, if any, is the purpose of human existence and human history, whatever ideals different individuals and groups may have set before themselves. And to ask this question is necessarily to raise the problem of the Transcendent. For human existence and history can have no goal or purpose unless it is determined from outside, that is to say, by a Being which transcends history.

In my opinion these questions arise out of man's existential situation, not out of linguistic confusion on the part of philosophers. They are questions which any human being can raise simply because he is a human being. I do not say that every human being necessarily asks such questions; what I have asserted is that 'some people' who are not philosophers ask them. It is possible, for example, to become submerged in the everyday practical concerns of life. But it is a peculiarity of the human being, as distinct from other living things, that, though involved in the world and in the changing historical process, he is capable of standing-back, as it were, and of apprehending his involvement in the changing world of finite things. And it is in the context of this standing-back that the so-called ultimate questions arise as questions of vital concern to the questioner.

I have said that to raise these questions is to raise the problem of the Transcendent. At the same time the very questions themselves seem to imply some apprehension of the Transcendent, if, that is to say, they are seriously asked. If, for instance, I seriously ask whether the changing historical process (I do not refer here simply to human history) is co-extensive with reality, some marginal awareness of an undescribed background or ground of finite existence seems to be involved.[6] It appears to me that the focusing of attention on finitude and change produces an immediate inference to the Transcendent as the undefined and undescribed complement of the finite and changing. If, however, I speak of 'inference', I do not refer to syllogistic argument or, indeed, to any reflective argument at all. I use the word to show that I do not postulate any intuition of the divine being in itself or any direct apprehension of the Transcendent as a thing among things. Indeed, it is precisely because the

Transcendent is not apprehended as a thing among things, an object among objects, that even when the questions of which I have been speaking have been seriously raised, agnosticism is still possible.

The questions are, I think, in some cases requests for a clear rational justification for this immediate inference or movement of the mind. And the traditional proofs of God's existence are so many attempts to meet this demand. The proof is an attempt to make explicit an implicit awareness which is involved in seeing the question as a real question. But it is sufficiently obvious that no such proof is an infallible instrument for compelling assent to God's existence. The metaphysician can help us to focus our attention on what in some sense is already familiar to us (finitude, for example, with all that it involves) and to see its significance; but he cannot compel us to do so. In other cases the questions are requests for light about the nature of the Transcendent. I cannot discuss this matter here. But it is perhaps worth while pointing out that 'speculative' metaphysicians have differed rather in their respective characterizations of ultimate reality than in their answer to the question whether finite things are co-extensive with reality. And, without wishing to subscribe to agnosticism, I would add that this is only to be expected. The situation of the metaphysician can be said perhaps to prolong on the reflective level the situation of the ordinary man who has noticed and paid attention to those features of empirical reality with which the reflections of the metaphysician, as I conceive him, begin.

9

It might perhaps be reasonably expected that I should end this essay with a summary statement of what I take to be the nature of philosophical knowledge and of the way in which it is attained. But I doubt whether a single comprehensive formula can be found; and, even if it can, I do not pretend to have found it. However, some sort of a summary must, I think, be attempted.

In the first place, while admitting that one of the useful results of philosophical discussion can be, and sometimes has been, the dissipation by more clear-sighted philosophers of linguistic or logical confusion in the minds of their more muddled colleagues, I have argued that philosophy cannot be reduced to this activity, however beneficial the activity may be. For this dissipation of confusion may occur in the course of a philosophical inquiry which does not necessarily start with 'confusion', though it may be undertaken in response to a desire for clarification.

In the second place, that about which clarification is desired may often be the meaning of terms and propositions. And where this is the case philosophical knowledge can legitimately be said to consist in the knowledge of the meaning of terms and propositions. But I have argued that this should not be understood in a sense which is incompatible with

saying that the philosopher aims at a better understanding of reality and
that philosophical knowledge includes a clearer understanding of reality.
For if there are, as I think there are, cases in which the philospher can
properly be said to be concerned with the real or objective meaning of
terms and propositions, with what a term 'really' means or what we
'ought' to mean by it, reflection shows, in my opinion, that these are
cases in which the philosopher is concerned, not with giving us new items
of factual information of a kind which cannot be discovered by philosophical analysis, but with attaining a clearer understanding of the world
already presented to us in experience and about which we speak in
everyday discourse.

Thirdly, if one admits the truth of this contention, the way to
metaphysics seems to me to be reopened. As I have already indicated, I
should regard the analysis of causality, for instance, as a metaphysical
inquiry. And those inquiries which are perhaps more commonly thought
of as 'metaphysical' are due to the same desire for understanding which
lies at the root of all philosophical inquiry. True, the questions raised will
not meet with sympathetic consideration unless they are felt to be real
questions. And it may well be that the more important ones will not be
seen as real questions unless they are seen in the context of man's
existential situation. But they are seen and raised as real questions before
the philosopher applies himself to them. And I have suggested in the case
of one particular problem at least that the very raising of the question
implies an implicit awareness of the answer. The philosopher therefore
tries to make the implicit explicit. But the fact that he is not in a
position analogous to that of a privileged visitor to Mars helps to explain
his limitations, which are indeed abundantly evident from the history of
metaphysics.

A final remark. In this essay I have spoken of 'everyday speech' or
'discourse' or of 'ordinary language'. This is indeed a term, the meaning
of which cannot be precisely determined. And its use may suggest a
much sharper distinction between the 'philosopher' and the 'ordinary
man' than I should wish to make. Nearly everyone philosophizes to some
extent, even if it is only to the extent of from time to time asking himself philosophical questions. Metaphysics is not, I think, simply the
hobby of a few eccentric individuals. The asking of metaphysical
questions, at least of questions of vital concern to the questioner, is a
widespread and sometimes very powerful tendency of the human mind.
But my reason for using terms such as 'ordinary language' is my
conviction that the philosopher in his reflections is confronted with the
same world that is revealed to the non-philosopher or 'ordinary man' in
his experience, an experience which, as expressible and communicable,
forms the basis of philosophical reflection. How sharp one makes the
distinction between the philosopher and the non-philosopher depends, of
course, on the meanings one gives to the terms. In one sense com-

paratively few human beings are philosophers; in another sense a very great number can be said to philosophize from time to time.

Notes

[1] I use the word 'reality' in preference to the word 'world' because I do not wish to use a term which might appear to confine the scope of the question to material things.

[2] Bertrand Russell has remarked that philosophy is the No Man's Land between theology and science. The retort might be made, of course, that it is the philosopher's land. But there does seem to be some uncertainty about its frontiers.

[3] I have pointed out elsewhere that the early medieval ultra-realists were not victims simply of linguistic confusion as this is ordinarily understood. They were partly influenced by a mistaken notion of what was required in order to safeguard the theological doctrine of original sin and its transmission.

[4] By the term 'ordinary man' I do not mean a moron; I mean simply the non-philosopher.

[5] I use the vague phrase 'some people' because I am obviously not in a position to say how many people raise questions of this sort. But some non-philosophers certainly do so.

[6] Many people perhaps simply ask themselves in a half-articulate manner some such question as, 'what is it all about?' But I think that the same observations apply even here.

CHAPTER 2

THE HISTORY OF PHILOSOPHY:
RELATIVISM AND RECURRENCE

I PUBLISHED the first volume of my *History of Philosophy* in 1964. In this first volume I claimed the right 'to compose a work on the history of philosophy from the point of view of a scholastic philosopher'.[1] The question of right is irrelevant. One is entitled to compose a history of philosophy from any standpoint one chooses. Whether one will find a publisher and readers is another question. At the same time, if someone announced that he was writing a history of Europe from the point of view of a patriotic Englishman or of a loyal citizen of the Soviet Union, we might feel some misgiving.

What, however, did I mean by the vague phrase the standpoint of a scholastic philosopher'? My original intention, as stated in the preface to the first volume, was that of providing Catholic ecclesiastical seminaries with an ampler work than the textbooks then commonly in use. And by scholasticism I clearly meant Thomism. So much was this the case that in the introduction to the second volume which appeared in 1950, I referred to fourteenth-century philosophy as a 'decline'.[2] This remark greatly annoyed one reveiwer, though most of them, knowing little of fourteenth century philosophy, remained unruffled.

At the same time I clearly wished to allow for the development of Aquinas's thought and the application of his principles to problems which he did not himself envisage. This is obviously one reason why I identified the perennial philosophy with 'Thomism in a wide sense',[3] rather than with Thomism simply in the sense of the thought of Aquinas in the thirteenth century.

On the surface at any rate I was flying the Thomist flag. But it seems to me that another line of interpretation is visible even in my first volume. On the page just quoted it is stated that the perennial philosophy developed 'in and through modern philosophy', not alongside or apart from it. And though I criticized Hegel in both the first and the second volumes, I have no doubt that I hoped to be able to show *a posteriori* that the historical development of philosophy was in fact what Hegel believed it to be, namely a dialectical advance, the advance of the one perennial or true philosophy evolving through successive stages.

It may indeed be possible to reconcile these two points of view by taking Thomism in so wide a sense that the term is pretty well evacuated of all definite historical reference. I prefer, however, not to play this particular game but rather to recognize two tendencies, on the one hand an attempt to present Thomism as the perennial philosophy, on the other a hankering after an Hegelian interpretation of the history of philosophy which would represent Thomism as simply one stage in the dialectical development of philosophical truth.

2

What do I now think of these two lines of interpretation? In the publisher's blurb to a work which appeared in 1972 with the title *A History of Medieval Philosophy* it is stated that in the author's view the critical and analytic philosophy of the fourteenth century cannot be seen simply as representing a decline in creative vigour. 'On the contrary, logical studies in this period were of a quality not equalled until the nineteenth century.' As I was the author in question, and as I wrote this paragraph of the blurb, these remarks are sufficient comment on what I said in 1950 about the fourteenth century.

As for the dream of finding in the history of philosophy a continuous dialectical advance, perhaps I may quote briefly from the seventh volume of my *History of Philosophy*, which was published in 1963. I there drew the conclusion that: 'There is no very good reason to suppose that we shall ever reach a universal and lasting agreement even about the scope of philosophy . . . We can hardly expect anything else but a dialectical movement, a recurrence of certain fundamental tendencies and attitudes in different historical shapes. This is what we have had hitherto, in spite of well-intentioned efforts to bring the process to a close. And it can hardly be called undue pessimism if one expects the continuation of the process in the future'.[4]

This passage scarcely suggests that by 1963 I was still thinking of the historical development of philosophy as a continuous triumphant march of reason through the centuries, a progress in which each successive system or movement constituted an advance on what had gone before.

To aggravate matters, in the early nineteen-sixties I published a number of light-hearted articles (space fillers to oblige an editor) which incited a pious layman to denounce me for abandoning the perennial philosophy and embracing historical relativism. As far as I am aware, the good man did not attempt any philosophically argued rebuttal of my views. His main concern was with an alleged incompatibility between the articles in question and Pope Pius XII's encyclical letter *Humani Generis* (1950). Leaving aside, however, this aspect of the matter, I wish to make some remarks about historical relativism which will, I hope, clarify my present ideas on the subject. I then propose to return briefly to the topic of the recurrence of tendencies and attitudes, to which I refer in the passage quoted from the seventh volume of my *History of Philosophy*.

3

In one of the articles to which I have alluded I wrote that: 'No philosopher is an external spectator of all time and existence. He does not see the whole of reality. And in so far as he tries to conceive it, he does so from a particular situation in space and time, from a particular historical situation. It is only natural that world-views should be one-sided and partial'.[5]

My critic concluded, rightly of course, that this statement was intended to be a universal statement. Thinking therefore that St Thomas Aquinas was being put on a par with such undesirables as Hegel and Marx, he reached for the faggots.

What I said in this passage, however, seems to me simply a pompous way of stating what is obviously true. We can of course form some idea of, for instance, human history as a whole. If I think of history as moving towards a goal, whether through the operation of divine providence or through the working out of dialectical laws of change, I obviously have a totalizing idea of history, irrespective of the question whether it is well-founded or not. But I do not form this idea because I have seen the whole course of history from outside. I form it from inside the historical process. And my view of history, as also of course of the world as a whole, is limited by my particular situation. It is perspectival, even if I have a belief which goes beyond my field of vision.

In regard to the use of the word 'situation', I have no wish to deny that it makes sense to speak, as existentialists are inclined to do, of a human situation in general. But a human situation in general is an abstract concept. What man actually lives in is a particular concrete historical situation. People living in ancient Greece, medieval Christendom and twentieth-century Europe are all human beings. And we can prescind from differentiating factors and speak of a common human situation. But this does not alter the fact that there are specifiable ways in which the world of the ancient Greek differed from that of the medieval Christian and from that of the twentieth-century European. And these differences affect the construction of comprehensive world-views, not in the sense that they are deprived of all objective reference, but rather in the sense that they are inevitably limited and inadequate. That is to say, no one of them can be completely adequate and final.

This may appear to be an excellent reason for abandoning the construction of world-views. It seems to me, however, quite natural that some minds at any rate should feel the urge to obtain conceptual mastery over a wide range of human experience by means of a synthesis which extends further than the scope of any particular science. But I have no wish to discuss this matter here. Instead I wish to emphasize the point that it is not only would-be comprehensive world-views which are affected by the fact that man's vision and perspective are influenced by his historical situation. It is hardly possible to study the development of philosophical thought without noticing examples of the ways in which philosopher's minds have been influenced not only by past and contemporary philosophy but also by a variety of extra-philosophical factors. A hackneyed example is the conditioning by Greek political life of the

social and political theories of Plato and Aristotle. Another obvious
example is the conditioning of Marx's thought by the social circumstances of his time. It is not, however, simply a matter of social and
political theory. For instance, it would be absurd to deny the influence
of theology and of religious interests on medieval philosophical
thought. Again, the development of the formal and empirical sciences has
influenced philosophy in a variety of ways, sometimes by suggesting a
paradigm of method, sometimes by conditioning problematics, sometimes by influencing theory.

This state of affairs is of course simply what one might expect. Philosophy does not pursue an isolated path of its own. It is one of man's
cultural activities, and there are naturally interrelations between philosophy and other cultural factors. An ideal history of philosophy would, I
suppose, exhibit them. In practice historians of philosophy have to
economize by concentrating their attention on the development of
philosophical thought itself, with little more than passing references to
the general cultural background and to extra-philosophical influences.
Though understandable, however, this procedure can be misleading; in so
far, that is to say, as it tends to represent philosophy as an enclosed
world of its own. In point of fact philosophy is pursued by philosophers,
each of whom thinks within the context of a definite historical and
cultural situation.

4

It is not of course my intention to suggest that philosophy is simply an
ineffective reflection of the influence of extra-philosophical factors of
one kind or another. The traffic is not, so to speak, all one-way. There is
a complex web of interrelations between philosophy and other cultural
factors. And philosophical ideas can certainly exercise an influence
through the activities of the people who accept them. Marxism is an
obvious case in point.

In spite of this remark, what I have been saying may very well have
given the impression that my critic was quite justified in describing me as
a relativist. We need something more, however, than a general impression.

In the first place, recognition of pretty obvious facts, such as the
influence of the social conditions of their times on the thought of Plato
and Marx, should not, in my opinion, be described as adherence to relativism. For if recognition of pretty obvious facts is sufficient to justify an
accusation of relativism, it seems to follow that rejection of relativism
involves a refusal to recognize obvious facts.

Suppose, however, that a philosopher were to claim that no philosophical proposition could be more than relatively true, relative, that is to
say, to a certain historical situation or context, and that there could be
no perennially true philosophical proposition, in the sense of a
proposition which could be true whensoever and by whomsoever it was

enunciated. Would this be an expression of historical relativism? I presume that it would be. And I proceed to make some remarks about this claim.

(*i*) First, what is to count as a philosophical proposition? in *Language, Truth and Logic* Professor A. J. Ayer maintained that the propositions of philosophy were 'linguistically necessary and so analytic'.[6] If this thesis were accepted, historical relativism, in the sense defined, would have to be rejected. In a footnote, however, Professor Ayer says that when philosophers use empirical propositions 'as examples, to serve philosophical ends',[7] the propositions in question can be counted as philosophical. I do not feel altogether happy about regarding the scientific statements made by Schopenhauer in *The World as Will and Idea* as acquiring the status of philosophical propositions because they are used to support a philosophical world-view. But I recognize that a case can be made out for doing so. And if an empirical statement such as 'Mr Brezhnev is now sitting at his desk in his Moscow office' can count, in certain circumstances, as a philosophical proposition (which I doubt), and if it happens to be a true statement, then I am prepared to admit that there can be philosophical propositions which are only relatively true. For this particular statement would cease to be true if Mr Brezhnev went and stood on the Lenin mausoleum to watch a march-past.

This admission, however, would not entail historical relativism, as I have defined it. For to admit that *some* philosophical propositions are or can be only relatively true is not the same thing as saying that *all* are.

(*ii*) Secondly, if we assume that historical relativism should be understood as claiming that no philosophical proposition can be more than relatively true, there seems to be some difficulty in seeing precisely what this claim entails. Consider, for example, F. H. Bradley's statement that the Absolute 'has no history of its own'.[8] If someone were to maintain that the statement was true but only relatively true, what could this thesis mean? It would be odd to hold that in the period in which Bradley lived the Absolute had no history of its own but that in other periods it had, or might have had, a history of its own.

There are of course other possibilities. One might wish to regard Bradley's statement as a definition, as stating part of the meaning which he gave to the term 'the Absolute'. But in what sense can a stipulative definition be described as true or false?

Or we might mean that Bradley's statement was true only in relation to Bradley's desires or deep-seated needs and in relation to anyone who shared the same desires or needs. In this case, however, it might be better if we openly adopted the logical positivist thesis that a statement such as Bradley's possesses only emotive significance and is literally neither true nor false.

My point is simply that if we assume with Bradley that his statement about the Absolute is a true statement about Reality with a capital letter, it becomes very difficult to see what could be meant if we then go on to claim that the statement is true only in relation to a particular historical situation or context. It would be much simpler to claim that it is neither true nor false, either because it is a stipulative definition or because it is a meaningless proposition. I do not think that historical relativism, as I have defined it, can cope with such a case, unless it is united with logical positivism.

(*iii*) Thirdly, I should wish to maintain that there can in fact be perennially true philosophical propositions in the sense of statements which are true whenever and by whomsoever they are enunciated. I see no reason, for example, why a philosopher should not make statements about finite things which must be true, if there are any finite things at all.

Perhaps I may be permitted to make use of an analogy which I have employed elsewhere. Imagine a man swimming in a river. He sees, let us suppose, other people swimming nearby, a passing boat, the trees on the bank and so on. But he cannot see the whole of the river. He can form an idea of it, of course. But he would be mistaken if he believed that throughout its course the river must possess the same characteristics of breadth and depth and speed of current which it has at the place where he is swimming. At the same time, if he is so inclined, he can make statements which must be true of the river throughout its course, if there is a river at all.

We are faced of course with the question of the logical status of such statements. Some people might perhaps wish to claim that the statements simply illustrate the ways in which we use certain terms or words. Though, however, I think that the statements are in fact the result of conceptual analysis and perform the function just mentioned, I do not like the word 'simply'. Not, that is to say, if 'simply' is taken to imply that the statements in the question are 'only about words'. Suppose that I say with the phenomenologists that consciousness is intentional, that all consciousness is a consciousness *of*. This statement does not indeed assert that there are conscious beings. And we can say that it illustrates our use of the word 'conscious'. But surely it is not simply about a word. Am I not saying that *what* we call consciousness is intentional, that it is consciousness *of*? True, if this were not the case, we would not use the words 'consciousness' or 'conscious'. At the same time it is *consciousness* which is intentional, not the *word* 'consciousness'. Again, if I say that a finite thing is in principle capable of some change, I am not explicitly stating that there are finite things. But it seems to me misleading to suggest that the statement is simply about the *words* 'finite thing'. For I intend to say something about *finite things*, if there are any.

5

It will be noted that I have not made use of the stock refutation of relativism to be found in scholastic textbooks of the traditional type, namely that relativism is self-contradictory. For it is not clear to me that in the present context at any rate relativism is self-contradictory.

Suppose that I say that no philosophical proposition can be more than relatively true. It might be argued that this statement is not itself a philosophical proposition, but that it is a meta-philosophical statement which stands outside the class which is the subject of the statement. In this case no self-contradiction is involved.

It might of course be argued that any statement of historical relativism expresses a philosophical stance and must therefore be a philosophical statement. The conclusion may then be drawn that a contradiction is involved if it is asserted as an absolute truth that no philosophical proposition is true in an absolute sense. For this conclusion to follow, however, a proposition would have to be able to refer itself. Perhaps it can. In the Middle Ages Buridan maintained that every proposition refers to itself by implying its own truth. Ockham, however, dealt with logical paradoxes by maintaining that no proposition could refer to itself. And modern logicians, too, have held different views. As I have no wish to dogmatize on this matter, I prefer not to have recourse to the traditional refutation of relativism, but rather to argue that there are in fact philosophical propositions which are perennially true.

6

To be sure, propositions which are necessarily true do not tell us how things are when they could be otherwise. And in this sense they do not convey exciting news. But this aspect of the matter is irrelevant to the point at issue. The point is that if there can be perennially true philosophical propositions, historical relativism, as I have defined it, cannot be accepted. Further, if such perennially or necessarily true propositions could be arranged in such a way as to form what could reasonably be described as a system, I would be prepared to allow that there could be a perennially true philosophical system. But it seems to me that a system in this sense would be concerned with what might be called the 'logical scaffolding' of the world, to borrow a phrase from Wittgenstein. It would not be a system in the same sense as the comprehensive world-views which, in my opinion, are inevitably limited and perspectival. In terms of the analogy which I have used above it would be analogous to a set of statements about the river which must be true if there is a river at all, rather than to a comprehensive picture of the whole of the actual river in which the swimmer is immersed at one point.

7

At this point I wish to return to the passage which I quoted from the seventh volume of my *History of Philosophy*. In this passage I referred to 'a dialectical movement, a recurrence of certain fundamental tendencies and attitudes in different historical shapes'. And I propose to comment, though in an inevitably sketchy manner, on this picture of the history of philosophy as a combination of an element of continuity, expressed in the idea of recurrence, and an element of discontinuity, expressed in the idea of 'different historical shapes'.

(*i*) In the first place it might be argued that talk about recurrence is an expression of mental laziness or of the bewitching effect of general terms. Consider idealism. It is easy to say that idealism recurs in different forms or shapes. But what recurs? The idealism of Berkeley is one thing and that of Hegel another. Each thing is what it is and not something else. 'Idealism' is a portmanteau-word, a label for a number of quite distinct philosophies. So is the term 'monism'. The philosophies of Parmenides, Spinoza and Bradley are distinct. Each is what it is, not a recurrence of something else.

Again, people talk about the recurrent problems of philsophy, as though philosophers were always discussing the same old problems and solving none of them. But in what sense do problems recur? Consider the problem of human freedom, in a psychological sense. There was a time when the problem was raised in a theological context. If God is the universal cause, how can man be properly described as free? Later the problem was raised in the context of the classical scientific view of the world as a mechanical system. If the world is governed by causal laws, how can human action constitute an exception? Later still the problem was raised in the context of depth psychology. How can we know that the actions which we believe to be the expression of free choice are not really the effect of infra-conscious factors? Have we here one problem taking three shapes? Or have we three distinct problems? There is surely a good case for saying that the problems are relative to and specified by the contexts in which they are raised. After all, when a so-called recurrent problem arises in a new context, people feel that it needs fresh treatment. They are not satisfied by the solutions offered when the problem was raised in a different context. And this suggests that it is better to speak of distinct problems than to talk about one recurrent problem.

(*ii*) There is obviously some truth in this line of thought. But I do not think that the idea of recurrence can be simply eliminated. If, for example, we consider human behaviour .in general, we can easily see grounds in man himself for the recurrence of hedonistic theories. The philosophies of Epicurus, Helvetius and Jeremy Bentham are of course distinct. It is not a case of sheer repetition. Nor is it a case of the inevitable recurrence of a type of ethical theory. For philosphers might conceivably limit their attention to meta-ethics. If, however, we assume the continuation of moral theories of the traditional type, it is reasonable to expect the recurrence of hedonistic lines of thought, not because of some inherent defect in philosophy but because there are persistent aspects of human behaviour which give rise to such theories. Equally of course we can expect such theories to be subjected to criticism and objection. For there are other aspects of human behaviour which militate against hedonism.

This is indeed the sort of thing to which I was referring at the close of the seventh volume of my *History of Philosophy*. I wrote there of two aspects of man in his relation to his environment, one of which impels him to raise metaphysical problems, while the other inclines him to regard such problems as empty and profitless. I was not claiming that the same philosophy recurs. I was referring to 'two tendencies or attitudes based on the dual nature of man',[9] basic tendencies or attitudes which express themselves in different historical shapes, in different philosophies that is to say. And I still think that this view is correct.

(*iii*) Though however I do not believe that the idea of recurrence can be simply jettisoned, I would certainly not wish to claim that the whole of the history of philosophy can be described in terms of this concept. For one thing, it seems evident to me that fresh problems can arise, those, for instance, which can arise out of the development of a particular science. For another thing, if the historical development of philosophical thought could be adequately described solely in terms of the recurrence of basic tendencies and problems, we should presumably have to conclude that there was no advance or progress in philosophy. And the conclusion seems to me false.

(*a*) One reason for thinking this is that I agree with Antony Flew when in his work *An Introduction to Western Philosophy* he claims that advances can be assessed in terms of the formal validity or invalidity of arguments.[10] To be sure this is a pretty modest claim. For, as Flew is well aware, the conclusion of a formally valid argument might be false, while the conclusion of a formally invalid argument might in fact be true, though its truth would not of course have been proved. None the less it is reasonable to claim that if one philosopher exposes logical fallacies in another's arguments or if he substitutes a good argument for a bad one, this is an example of progress in the philosophical area.

(*b*) It is not however my intention to imply that I regard philosophy as consisting simply of arguments. In my opinion there can be degrees of what might be described as insight. For instance, one philosopher can have a greater insight than another into the complexities of language in general or of one particular area of language, such as religious discourse. Again, there can be insight in the field of philosophical anthropology. In some cases we may indeed be able to suggest historical reasons why a given insight occurred at one time rather than another. In this sense the insight can be described as historically conditioned. But it by no means follows necessarily that it is so tied to the relevant set of historical circumstances that it possesses no permanent validity or value. There is no reason, for example, why Aristotle should not have made statements about the voluntary and the involuntary, the truth of which transcends the specific forms of Greek social and political life. Similarly, if a twentieth-century philosopher recognizes features of religious language which were not clearly recognized in previous centuries, we can find reasons why this insight should have occurred when it did. We can refer, for instance, to the contemporary interest in language in general; and we can relate the development of this interest to other historical factors. But it by no means follows that the insight does not possess a validity transcending the historical circumstances which can reasonably be regarded as occasioning or facilitating it.

8

The upshot of these remarks is that though I can still feel the seductive attraction of simple overall interpretations of the historical development of philosophical thought in terms of one unifying idea, I have come more and more to mistrust them. The attraction seems to me natural enough. For the mind naturally seeks conceptual mastery over the multiplicity of phenomena. But unification in terms of one key-idea seems to me to involve over-simplification of what is extremely complex. The key-idea may be determined *a priori*, by a previously accepted metaphysics, that is to say. Hegel, for example, approached the history of philosophy with the conviction that it expressed the self-unfolding of absolute Spirit or Mind and so must represent a continuous dialectical advance. But this approach, though perhaps flattering to philosophers, involved a process of accommodating the facts to fit a preconceived theory, not indeed by inventing or denying the facts but rather by determining selection and emphasis. Or the key-idea may be suggested *a posteriori*, by consideration of the data, by fixing one's attention, for instance, on examples of the historical conditioning of philosophical thought or on the similarities which give rise to the concept of recurrence. It is not a question of such ideas as those of historical conditioning and of recurrence having no application. For in my opinion they are exemplified. It is a question of so emphasizing one idea that it is converted into a key to unlock all doors. We cannot, for instance, give an adequate description of the history of philosophy simply in terms of the concept of recurrence. For this procedure does not allow for novelty and the possibility of advance.

It can be objected of course that I seem to envisage the historian of philosophy as occupying a position of complete neutrality, and that complete neutrality is a myth. Or, if it is attainable at all, it is attainable only at the cost of reconstructing the history of philosophy in a purely utilitarian spirit, by producing a potboiler, for instance, to enable students to pass examinations, or by summarizing philosophers' views, when 'views' is equivalent to 'conclusions'. After all, in the preface to the first volume of my *History of Philosophy* I maintained that no historian of philosophy can write without some philosophical standpoint which acts as 'a principle of selection, guiding his intelligent choice and arrangements of facts.[11] Have I abandoned this view in favour of a myth of Olympian neutrality?

In the first place the historian is not compelled to choose between summarizing conclusions and arranging the data to confirm a preconceived overall interpretative scheme. For example, one does not need to be a Thomist or an Hegelian or a Marxist or a logical positivist to be able to exhibit not simply the conclusions of Immanuel Kant but also the problems with which he grappled, their historical context and the ways in which they arose. To put the matter in another way, the historian is not compelled to choose between superficiality on the one hand and propaganda for a certain system on the other. And it is misleading to suggest that he is so compelled.

In the second place, if the historian passes judgement on the philosophies of which he treats he will obviously do so from his own philosophical standpoint. He has every right to do so, if he wishes, provided that he makes sufficiently clear what he is doing. Indeed, as historians of philosophy are likely to be philosophers, they can be expected to pursue some philosophical discussion, even if the need for economizing in space severely limits such discussion.

These two points seem to me matters of common sense. I admit, however, that problems arise which can hardly be solved simply by referring to obvious truths. For example, it is certainly arguable that the construction of an intelligible account of the historical development of philosophical thought expresses principles of selection and judgements of value which themselves imply a philosophical stance. In practice, of course, convention has a part to play, conventional ideas, for instance, of what is philosophically important. But to appeal simply to the part played by convention would constitute an evasion of a genuine objection against the possibility of complete neutrality. And once we dispose of complete neutrality as a myth, we are faced with the question whether the historian's reconstruction of the history of philosophy is not part of the expression of what Hegel called the *Zeitgeist*, the spirit of the time. Was Hegel perhaps right after all in claiming that no philosophy could transcend 'its contemporary world'?[12] If so, would not Hegel's statement be applicable also to the historian of philosophy? Every reconstruction of the past is of course a reconstruction in the present and subject to a variety of influences.

These remarks may give the impression that after I have attacked pure historical relativism I have fallen back into it, succumbing to the temp-

tation which is likely to beset any historian of philosophy who does not
set out to illustrate the superior value of a particular system. It is not
however my intention to recant at the end of this lecture what I have
said during its course. My aim is rather to show that I am aware of meta-
historical problems which arise not so much when one is actually writing
history of philosophy as when one reflects on the nature and
implications of this activity. It is problems of this kind that I should like
to consider at length in a projected volume on the philosophy of the
history of philosophy, if I have both the time and the mental energy to
write it. Whether or not such reflection will bring me back to the Hegel-
inspired hopes of some thirty years ago remains to be seen. But at
present I think not. This, however, may well be an expression of the
influence of the *Zeitgeist* and, to this extent, a confirmation of one of
Hegel's theses.

Notes

[1] *A History of Philosophy* (hereafter HP) I, p. v.

[2] HP II, p. 9.

[3] HP I, p. 7.

[4] HP VII, p. 441.

[5] 'No Honest Woman: The Nature of Philosophy', *The Month,*   CCXV (1963) p. 354.

[6] *Language, Truth and Logic,* 2nd ed. (London, 1946), p. 31.

[7] Ibid., p. 26, n. 2.

[8] *Appearance and Reality* 2nd ed. (London, 1897), p.449.

[9] HP VII, pp.440–1.

[10] London, 1971, pp. 18–34.

[11] HP I, p. v.

[12] *Sämtliche Werke*, ed. H. Glockner (Stuttgart, 1928–56), VII, p. 35.

CHAPTER 3

PHILOSOPHY AND RELIGION
IN JUDAISM AND CHRISTIANITY

I T MIGHT seem appropriate to begin this chapter by defining the terms 'philosophy' and 'religion'. If however I were to offer such definitions, I would probably be doing one of two things. Either I would be indicating how the terms are used in ordinary language. And I take it that you know this already. Or I would be explaining in what sense I myself intend to use the terms. This exercise would be necessary if I intended to give to the terms meanings which differed from the meanings which they have in ordinary language, or if I intended to use them in a sense which was narrower than the broad range of meaning which they have in ordinary language. But I do not intend to use the terms in some peculiar sense of my own. So there is no need for me to get involved in the notoriously difficult task of trying to define philosophy and religion. I simply offer one or two introductory remarks with a view to avoiding possible initial misunderstanding.

In the first place, by 'religion' I do not mean simply theology. A theological system arises, I suppose, within a definite religion and is obviously related to it. But we hardly need a Thomas-à-Kempis to tell us that a theologian need not necessarily be a religious person, and that a religious person need not be a theologian. I do not exclude theology from the sphere of religion. For systematic reflection on the content of faith can very well be pursued in a religious spirit. But I do not identify religion with theology.

In the second place, by using the phrase 'philosophy *and* religion' I do not intend to imply that I regard them as necessarily antithetical. A philosopher may of course adopt a polemical and hostile attitude towards religion. Or he may try to preserve an attitude of neutrality. But there can perfectly well be a religiously-orientated philosophy. This may not be a feature of modern academic philosophy in this country. But that there can be religious philosophy is obvious from the fact that there has been such philosophy. The philosophy of Plotinus is a case in point. So was the philosophy of Vladimir Solovyov. So is the philosophy of Martin Buber.

With these presuppositions in mind, namely that there can be religiously-orientated philosophy and that religion cannot be simply identified with theology, I propose to make some inevitably sketchy and inadequate remarks about the interrelations between philosophical thought and religion in Judaism and Christianity. By the terms 'Judaism' and 'Christianity' I mean of course two historic religions. Some Christian theologians may like to say that Christianity is not a 'religion' but rather 'the truth of all religion', or something of that sort. But this way of speaking presupposes the point of view of Christian faith. From the historical or empirical point of view Christianity is one of the world-religions. And it is from the historical point of view that I approach my theme.

I am well aware that what I have been saying gives rise to questions which I am leaving unanswered. But this is unavoidable if I am to say something concrete about the subject on which I have undertaken to speak.

2

When we consider the relations between philosophy and religion in Judaism and Christianity, we can of course find clear similarities. As any historic religion exists in a cultural situation, it cannot avoid adopting some definite attitude to other factors in its situation. Philosophy is not necessarily one of them. The various peoples encountered by the Jews when they entered Palestine were not noted for philosophical speculation. Or, if they were, we have, as far as I know, no record of their achievements in this field. In the Hellenistic world however philosophical thought was obviously a prominent cultural factor. Moreover, the philosophy of the time bore little resemblance to the sort of activity pursued by, for example, the late Professor J. L. Austin, the meticulous mapping-out of ordinary language. In Neoplatonism and in Stoicism philosophy embodied a religious world-view and a way of life. It could thus appear, and indeed present itself as an intellectually superior rival to historic religions such as Judaism and Christianity. And Jews and Christians could hardly avoid adopting some attitude towards it. It is arguable, I suppose, that an attitude of indifference was easier on the part of the Jews than on that of the Christians. That is to say, it was easier for the Jews to regard themselves as a people apart, with their age-old traditions. The Christians were not a people in the same sense. Moreover, even if the Jews accepted proselytes, they were not so intent as the Christians on universal conversion. Again, in the case of Judaism great stress was laid on practical obedience, on observance of the Law that is to say, whereas in the case of Christianity emphasis was laid on faith or belief. I do not mean to imply of course either that Jews emphasized observance of the Law to exclusion of faith in God, or that Christians emphasized faith in such a way as to minimize the value of living in accordance with one's faith. I mean simply that if one lays the emphasis chiefly on the observance of Law, one need pay less attention to the clash of beliefs than if one lays the emphasis on the acceptance of certain doctrines. Such considerations however do not alter the fact that in a cosmopolitan city such as Alexandria the more intellectually minded Jews were naturally impelled to adopt some definite attitude towards Greek philosophy, precisely because of the nature of the dominant philosophies of the time.

It was possible of course to adopt a hostile attitude. Even if Tertullian, the second-century Christian writer, developed philosophical themes and was influenced to some extent by the Stoics, his general attitude to Greek philosophy was that between Athens and Jerusalem, as he put it, there was nothing in common. It was also possible however to adopt a much more favourable attitude by seeing in Greek philosophy one way in which truth was imparted to man, and by making use of Greek thought in the interpretation of the Biblical writings.

This positive attitude was manifested, as we are doubtless all aware, by the famous Jewish writer Philo of Alexandria. Philo regarded the same truth as having been expressed in both Greek philosophy and the Jewish Scriptures and tradition. True, he seems to have thought that a philosopher such as Plato had borrowed ideas from the Scriptures. But this obviously does not affect the fact that he recognized positive truth-value in Greek thought. It is also clear that Philo made considerable use of ideas taken from the Platonic and Pythagorean traditions in his interpretations of the Scriptures. His use of the concept of the divine Logos is an example, a concept which he connected with the idea of the divine Wisdom as found in the Scriptures. It might perhaps be argued that Philo's use of the notion of allegory in interpreting the Scriptures and his distinction between 'higher' and 'lower' meanings would lead naturally to the conclusion that literal observance of the ceremonial precepts of the Law was not required by those who were capable of discerning higher sense of the Biblical text. But here Philo was able to maintain that as man is both body and soul, and not simply the latter, he is not entitled to disregard the literal sense of the sacred texts. In other words, Philo had no intention of jettisoning Jewish orthodoxy in favour of Greek philosophy. He wished to reconcile them, to exhibit a harmony.

It is doubtless possible to exaggerate the influence of Philo on Christian thought. But he lived well before the Christian thinkers at Alexandria, such as Clement and Origen, who are notable for their positive attitude towards Greek thought. And he certainly exercised some influence on Christian thought, even if it is difficult to determine its extent in any very precise way. In any case, just as Philo tried to come to terms with Greek thought, so did Clement and Origen and other early Christian writers after him. We can say that he set a pattern, which they subsequently followed.

It is obvious however that in important respects the attitude of the Christian writers was different from that of Philo. It has been said of philo that he interpreted the Scriptures in the light of Greek philosophy and that he revised Greek philosophical ideas in the light of Scriptural teaching. This is doubtless true. And much the same can be said of some early Christian writers. For the Christians however there was another factor, namely the Incarnation. There had been a twofold preparation for the coming of Christ. God had prepared the Jewish people by the revelation of his will through Moses and the prophets; and he had prepared the pagan world through Greek philosophy, which embodied man's search for God and for the way of salvation. We can of course say that both Philo and the early Christian writers such as Clement and Origen tried to come to terms with the philosophical factor in the cultural situation, an attempt which was made easier by the fact that in the Hellenistic world the dominant philosophical traditions were religiously orientated. But the Christian thinkers looked on both the Jewish religion and Greek philosophy as having been fulfilled in the Christian revelation.

3

Now if Greek philosophy is viewed as embodying man's search for God and for the way of salvation, the road to happiness, it is easily understandable that a Christian theologian such as St Augustine could see in the Christian religion itself the true philosophy or wisdom inasmuch as it fulfilled man's need and so superseded pagan philosophy. Needless to say, Augustine did not think that the coming of Christ rendered any further intellectual effort superfluous. His programme however was that of understanding the content of faith, working out its implications and developing an overall Christian vision of the universe. Philosophy as distinct from Christian thought had fulfilled its historical function. It had sought, and what was sought had been found.

In the Middle Ages the situation underwent a marked change. In the second half of the twelfth century and the first part of the thirteenth a much more extensive knowledge of Greek thought became available to the Christian West. When we look back on the medieval scene from a much later date, it is natural to see in this increased knowledge of Greek philosophy, especially of Aristotle, an influx of knowledge of the past, a stage in the process which was to be carried further at the time of the Renaissance. To look at the matter in this way however, as analogous, that is to say, to the discovery in 1891 of part of the text of Aristotle's *Constitution of Athens,* is to miss the significance which the situation had for the medieval mind. The Christian medieval thinkers were confronted for the first time with what appeared to them as a comprehensive world-view, a system of thought which owed nothing to Christianity and which could and did seem to some minds as a naturalistic rival to the Christian faith. In other words, Aristotelianism appeared as a contemporary challenge, not as a philosophy which had passed into history and was no longer relevant.

The Christian thinkers of the thirteenth century were thus forced to adopt definite attitudes towards the Aristotelian philosophy. Some were hostile; and for a time the ecclesiastical authorities made efforts to check the growing enthusiasm for the new learning. Others, believing that Aristotelianism was, in the main, true and that it represented a large part of what we might describe as secular knowledge, endeavoured to integrate the philosophy of Aristotle into a Christian world-view. Notable among them was St Thomas Aquinas. Shortly after his death however there was a marked conservative reaction, a swing away from the pagan philosophers to the wisdom of Augustine and Anselm.

In brief, the Christian theologians of the thirteenth century were faced with the problem of the relations between philosophy and religion or, more generally, between reason and faith. This was a problem which had been already faced by Jewish thinkers. Indeed it is a problem which is bound to arise when claims are made to a revelation embodied in sound texts. It thus arose in Islam too. But here I am concerned simply with Jewish thinkers. These thinkers lived for the most part in the Islamic world, where they enjoyed a greater freedom; and intellectual movements in Islam were influential in Jewish intellectual circles. But the Jewish thinkers naturally translated into their own terms the problems which confronted the Moslem philosophers and theologians.

4

With some Jewish thinkers of the Middle Ages there is little sign of any sense of a clash between philosophy and Biblical teaching. This is the case with the leading Jewish Neoplatonist in Islamic Spain, Solomon ibn Gabirol, who lived in the eleventh century. His main work, *The Fountain of Life*, was translated into Latin and exercised some influence on Christian scholars. The Christians however believed that the author, whom they called Avicebron or Avicebrol, was a Moslem. The main reason for this was doubtless the fact that *The Fountain of Life* had been originally written in Arabic. But as the author simply expounded a metaphysical system, in the form of a dialogue between master and pupil, without making any overt references to the Bible or the Talmud, the Christians had little ground for thinking that he was in fact a Jewish writer, Gabirol did indeed write Hebrew poetry; but it was only in the nineteenth century that Solomon Munk identified the author of *The Fountain of Life* with the poet.

For a critical attitude towards philosophy we have to turn to Yehuda Halevi, who flourished in the first part of the twelfth century and whose attack on the philosophers parallels that made by al-Ghazali in defence of Islam. Halevi imagines a discussion between a philosopher, a Christian, a Moslem and a Jewish rabbi, each of whom hopes to convert a certain king to his own beliefs. The philosopher is a follower of Islamic Aristotelianism, of a neoplatonized Aristotelianism that is to say. And in the discussion the Jewish rabbi successfully rebuts the claim of metaphysics to provide a basis for religion. Metaphysics cannot provide genuine knowledge of God. Religious truth comes through God's revelation of himself. As for the moral life, reason certainly suggests lines of conduct which are desirable from the utilitarian point of view. But man cannot by his own efforts live a life which is truly pleasing to God. In other words, when philosophers claimed to establish knowledge of God and to teach the genuinely good life, the way of salvation, their claims were bogus. Philosophical religion, so to speak, is a sham.

Halevi's attitude can be paralleled both in Islam and in Christianity. But for a much more complex and sophisticated view of the relation between philosophy and the Jewish religion we have to turn to Moses Maimonides, the most celebrated Jewish philosopher of the Middle Ages, who died in 1204. In his *Guide of the Perplexed* he makes it clear that he is addressing Jews who have studied philosophy and the sciences and who find themselves perplexed about the meaning of the Scriptures and put off by the external precepts of the Law. A man in this state may believe that intellectual integrity demands that he should renounce the Scripture and the Law. Or he may believe that he is obliged to stifle intellectual doubts and hold fast to his religion. Maimonides sets out to show that there is a third possibility, namely that of coming to understand the inner meaning of the Scriptures and the Law and of seeing that this inner meaning is in full accord with genuine philosophy. To exhibit this inner meaning Maimonides made systematic use of Greek and Islamic philosophy. And some Jewish writers attacked the work vehemently, on the ground that it represented the abandonment of true religion in favour of Graeco-Islamic philosophy. Maimonides however was the greatest authority of his time on the Jewish Law; and he had no intention of encouraging apostacy from the Jewish religion. He wanted to show that it was possible to be at the same time a devout Jew and also a philosopher and scholar. Incidentally, the *Guide of the Perplexed* was translated into Latin in the thirteenth century and exercised a considerable influence on Christian thinkers, including Aquinas.

5

In regard therefore to the handling of the problem of the relation between philosophy and religion we can find somewhat similar attitudes in Judaism and Christianity. In both there were writers who mistrusted philosophy and who maintained that religious faith should be purified from the contamination of Graeco-Islamic thought. In both religions however there were those who tried to show that there was no essential incompatibility between philosophy on the one hand and religious faith on the other. If this involved an interpretation of religious beliefs in the light of philosophical doctrines, it also involved a revision or rethinking of philosophical positions in the light of religious faith.

The presupposition of this second attitude was obviously that both philosophy and faith are concerned with truth, and that truth cannot contradict truth. In the seventeenth century however a very different way of reconciling philosophy and religion was expounded by the famous Jewish philosopher Baruch Spinoza. In the *Tractatus Theologico-*

Politicus Spinoza remarks that the chief aim of the treatise is 'to separate faith from philosophy'. 'between faith or theology and philosophy there is no connection, no affinity . . . Philosophy has no end in view save truth: faith looks for nothing but doctrine and piety'. What Spinoza is maintaining in effect is that religious faith is orientated entirely to action, to moral conduct, in particular to love of the neighbour. Obedience to God, in living a life of piety and love, presupposes indeed faith in God. For religion consists in acting with the idea of God. But the anthropomorphic pictures of God as given in the Scriptures are quite sufficient for this purpose. Indeed, they serve this purpose admirably, as they represent God as willing this, forbidding that, being pleased, displeased, and so on. These pictures should be left as they are. To start interpreting the Bible according to the criteria of reason is to philosophize the Bible, to introduce philosophy into the sphere of faith. And this procedure shows a radical misunderstanding of the nature of religious faith.

Spinoza does indeed admit that the Scriptures contain truth about God, for example that there is one God. But in his view Biblical talk about God has a pragmatic function, namely to stimulate to a way of life. If God is represented as ordering or forbidding this or that, the relevant statements cannot be true in the sense that God actually does issue orders and prohibitions. At the same time this way of speaking is precisely the way which is best suited to stimulate people to act or to refrain from acting in certain ways. To use a later terminology, the statements possess pragmatic or instrumentalist meaning rather than the truth of correspondence with fact. To set about interpreting such talk in accordance with the criteria of Neoplatonism or of Aristotelianism or any other philosophical system and then to proclaim that the philosophical interpretation is the inner meaning of the Scriptures is therefore to show a misunderstanding of the nature and function of Biblical talk about God. It is in fact to deprive the statements in question of their value, of their 'force' *(vis)* as Augustine put it.

As a matter of historical fact, one of Spinoza's chief motives in making this distinction between philosophy on the one hand and religious faith on the other was to justify and encourage a policy of toleration. If faith or 'theology' is concerned not with truth but with conduct, there is no good reason why people who hold one set of religious beliefs should regard people who have different beliefs as ungodly and proceed to persecute them. The only ungodly persons are those who hate others. Again, if the Biblical stories owe their value to their pragmatic function, ecclesiastical and civil authorities have no justification for molesting philosophers simply on the ground that what they say is inconsistent with or contrary to Bible teaching about God.

This preoccupation with condemning religious persecution is easily understandable in the light of the circumstances of the time. It is evident however that what Spinoza is saying in effect is that beliefs ordinarily held by Jews and Christians are suited, because of their pragmatic value, to those who are incapable of grasping the truth in the form in which it is presented in Spinoza's own philosophy. In the eighteenth century Moses Mendelssohn maintained, like Spinoza, that it was not the task of Judaism to lay down dogmatic beliefs which men are obliged to accept but rather to teach a way of life and observance of the Law. But Mendelssohn was largely concerned with contrasting Judaism with the Christianity of the creeds (Athanasian Christianity as he called it), whereas Spinoza spoke quite generally about Judaism and Christianity together. Further, whereas Mendelssohn was inclined to emphasize the inscrutable ways of God, Spinoza had, as we all know, a metaphysical system of his own in which he claimed to exhibit the truth about the nature of reality. It seems to me therefore that we can quite well say that Spinoza's position looks forward to the elaborately developed philosophy of Hegel in which religious beliefs are represented as pictorial ways of presenting the truth which philosophy presents in conceptual form. There is, to be sure, an important difference. For Spinoza maintained that whereas philosophy is concerned with truth, faith or theology is not, while Hegel maintained that philosophy and theology are both concerned with truth, though they present the same truth in different ways. At the same time it seems to me that if we bear in mind Spinoza's metaphysical system, it is reasonable to see his attitude to the relation between philosophy and theology as leading on to the position of Hegel.

We may indeed think that Spinoza's attitude is much better reflected in the thesis expounded by Professor R. B. Braithwaite in his famous 1955 lecture *An Empiricist's View of the Nature of Religious Belief*. For Braithwaite proposes the view that Christian beliefs are stories which should not be described as true or false but which have the function of serving as a background and psychological stimulus to the life of Christian love. In other words, such beliefs have a pragmatic function, as with Spinoza. Whereas however Spinoza was convinced that philosophy could establish genuine knowledge of the nature of God, Braithwaite has no such conviction. In fine, Spinoza was a metaphysician, a celebrated speculative philosopher, whereas Braithwaite writes from the point of view of a logical empiricist or positivist and is anxious to show how a logical positivist can claim to be a Christian without gross inconsistency. The approaches of the two men are quite different, even if on certain points their views are similar.

6

Spinoza was not of course an orthodox Jewish believer. He was only twenty-four years old when he was expelled from the synagogue. And whatever view we defend in the discussion about the extent to which his religious upbringing and his studies of Jewish writings influenced his philosophical ideas, it is clear that he came to take a pretty detached view of both Judaism and Christianity. He believed in the truth of a philosophical system which stands in the mainstream of European thought since the close of the medieval period. It may well be true that there is more reason for connecting his philosophical thought with Judaism than there would be in the case of, say, Bergson and Husserl, whom most people would regard as Jewish philosophers only in the sense that they were philosophers of Jewish origin. At the same time few people, I imagine, would venture to claim that Spinoza was a specifically Jewish thinker in the same sense in which this can be said of Maimonides.

If however we leap over the centuries and consider Martin Buber, we are turning to a man who, before Adolf Hitler came to power, occupied the chair of the Jewish religion and ethics at Frankfurt-am-Main and can certainly be regarded as a specifically Jewish thinker. He did not, like Spinoza, reflect on Judaism and Christianity from a detached philosophical position, external to them both. In his work *Two Types of Faith* he contrasted Jewish faith (*emunah*) in God's word as uttered in dialogue with his people and Christian faith (*pistis*) in the truth of propositions. And he did so from a position within Judaism, as one who saw the I-Thou relationship as expressed in Israel's dialogue with God. In other words, though both Spinoza and Buber reflect on Jewish religion, the latter does so from within this religion, whereas the former does so from the Olympian standpoint of a rationalist metaphysician.

When however I say that Martin Buber was a specifically Jewish thinker, I certainly do not mean to imply that his thought has significance and value only for his correligionists. For one thing, his distinction between the I-It and I-Thou relationships is either valid or invalid in itself; its validity does not depend on applications given to it in terms of a particular religion. For another thing, even if Buber's distinction between two types of faith was associated by him with the distinction between Judaism and Christianity, there are now a good many Christian theologians who would certainly wish to place the emphasis where Buber placed it, namely on personal faith in God rather than on acceptance of propositions. Even from Catholic theologians we can hear assertions about the difference between the God of faith and the God of the philosophers. I cannot say that I am altogether happy about such utterances. But they are common enough. It is not my intention to suggest that the theologians in question have all taken their ideas from Martin Buber. My point is rather that even if Buber is in one sense a specifically Jewish thinker, his thought has a much wider significance.

There is not of course anything odd in this. On the philosophical side Martin Buber's distinction between the I-It and I-Thou relationships can be regarded as reflection on the concepts of thing and person or, more properly perhaps, as an essay in phenomenology. It is concerned with what is human, not with what is specifically Jewish. His treatment is indeed religiously oriented. But the religious orientation and application is relevant to belief in God in quite a general way. On the theological side both Jews and Christians believe in God; and there is no reason why Christian theologians should not see in the Old Testament a dialogue of the kind which Buber finds there. Just as Philo and the early Christian writers could have common problems in regard to Biblical talk about God, so can Martin Buber and Christian theologians have common problems, in so far, that is to say, as they have common beliefs. Further, the greater the extent to which both Jews and Christians emphasize man's personal relationship to God rather than observance of ceremonial precepts on the one hand or acceptance of propositions on the other, so much the more evident does the common element become.

7

To say that both Jews and Christians believe in God is of course to make an extremely banal remark from the point of view of the imparting of information. As news, it is stale news. At the same time this common belief in one transcendent and personal God means that both Jews and Christians stand exposed together to the criticism of modern philosophy. As far as this country is concerned, philosophers do not attempt to offer a rival religion, a metaphysical system which claims to establish genuine knowledge of the divine reality and to point out the true way of life to man. Philosophers of science do not try to compete with scientists in their own field. They treat of metascientific questions. And philosophers of religion, except when they are clearly apologists or concealed theologians, tend to treat of problems which arise out of reflection on the historic religions. Such problems may be connected with the meaning or function of talk about God. It is true of course that traditional orthodox Christianity gives more hostages to fortune than Judaism does. To take a particular example the doctrines of the Trinity and the Incarnation give rise to particular problems which do not arise in the Jewish religion, for obvious reasons. This is simply an empirical fact. But we are doubtless all well aware that in the field of philosophy of religion discussion in recent years has tended to centre on talk about God. And here Jews and Christians are, so to speak, in the same boat.

On the Christian side a few writers have tried to reinterpret the Christian faith in such a way that belief in a transcendent God is no longer involved. Such writers naturally throw all the emphasis on the life of love as the essential element in Christianity. Talk about God can then be interpreted as a story or set of stories which are 'entertained', as R.B. Braithwaite puts it (ambiguously, in my opinion), as a background and stimulus to a way of life, a moral policy. Our talk about God can be reinterpreted in terms of talk about Jesus of Nazareth, when the precise status attributed to Jesus is left somewhat obscure, or as commands. For instance, 'God is love', which is, on the face of it, an assertion about a transcendent reality, is interpreted as having the force of an imperative, 'love one another'. This is the sort of thing which can be found in Professor Paul Buren's well known book *The Secular Meaning of the Gospel*. Or use can be made, as by Alistair Kee, of the existentialist concept of transcendence, of transcending the so-called 'natural' man or natural life towards a new life of love, in a secular setting, without, that is to say, belief in God being either presupposed or involved. We then get a kind of Christian atheism, resting on the assumption that, in Nietzsche's phrase, 'God is dead'. That is to say, belief in God is taken as something which modern man is increasingly unable to accept.

In view of the central position which belief in God occupies in traditional Christianity radical reinterpretations of the Christian religion in which this belief is eliminated or at any rate no longer appears as an essential element tend to appear to the external observer as extremely tortuous or as desperate attempts to save something from the wreckage. The explanation however seems to me simple enough. The writers in question all sincerely believe that the Christian message is of great value to man. But they do not think that belief in a transcendent God can stand up to criticism. They therefore try to reinterpret the Christian religion in such a way as not to involve this belief, not at any rate as an essential factor. There can of course be differences in approach. One writer may be primarily concerned with interpreting Christianity in a way which will be compatible with the implications of a certain philosophy and still allow him to adhere to Christianity. In other words, his approach is primarily personal. Another writer may approach the matter from the point of view of what 'modern man' can reasonably be expected to believe. But the first type of writer would not publish a reinterpretation of Christianity unless he thought that it would be of help to others besides himself. And the second type would hardly accept the attitude of 'modern man' as a criterion unless he himself shared this attitude. In other words, the differences are differences of emphasis. The results are basically similar.

To what extent, if any, presentations of a Christianity without God have an analogue in modern Judaism I do not know. And I had better express my ignorance frankly. The following remark however may be relevant. If a Christian is convinced that belief in God is essential to Christianity and that the Christian religion cannot exist without it, and if he then loses his own belief in God but still regards the belief as essential to Christianity, he will cease to call himself a Christian. He may claim, for example, that the ethical values of Christianity can perfectly well be maintained in the framework of secular humanism. If however a Jew loses belief in God, he does not cease to be a Jew. So he is perhaps less likely than the Christian to go in for ingenious reinterpretations of his religion. He simply becomes a secularized Jew, as indeed many Jews are in the State of Israel. If he wishes, he can of course lay emphasis on

observance of the law as a means of social cohesion. I have no wish to
imply that a Jewish thinker *cannot* reinterpret the Jewish religion in a
manner analogous to that in which some radical Christians have reinterpreted the Christian religion. It remains true however that the Jew does
not cease to be a Jew if he abandons belief in a transcendent God,
whereas a Christian who abandons belief in God ceases to be a Christian,
unless indeed he can find a plausible way of reconciling atheism with the
profession of Christianity. The Christian therefore has more incentive
than the Jew for pursuing a policy of reinterpretation.

Scuttling in face of philosophical criticism and of the *Zeitgeist* is not
however the only possible policy. It is possible to lift the whole matter
out of the sphere of philosophy by insisting that God is not an 'It', the
existence of which can be proved, but the absolute 'Thou', who is known
only through encounter, in the dialogue which lies at the heart of
religion. As for talk about God, it is possible to maintain that this makes
sense only in a religious context, in the context of the faith. In more
Wittgensteinian terms, it is possible to maintain that talk about God is
meaningful only to those who actually use the language. It is through
conversion, through self-relating to the living God, that the relevant
language comes to have meaning. It cannot be really understood from
outside. The believer can preach to the unbeliever, but he cannot convert
him by philosophical reasoning. For it is a matter of conversion, not of
philosophy.

Perhaps we can find a certain convergence towards this position both
in Jewish and in Christian thought. On the Jewish side this can be seen in
the thought of Martin Buber. And it is indeed evident that the Old
Testament is the story of a dialogue between God and his people, the
divine will being communicated through Moses and the prophets. On the
Christian side the theology of encounter has gained in popularity and
influence even among Catholic theologians. The Christian theologians
naturally lay emphasis on encounter with God and through Christ. But
the influence of Karl Barth, the famous Protestant theologian, and so
indirectly of Kierkegaard, seems to me to be pretty evident in Catholic
circles.

This attitude, with its mistrust or even denial of the competence of
philosophy in the religious sphere, is understandable. It may appear as a
properly religious reaction to the rationalism of philosophers such as
Spinoza and Hegel. To my mind however it gives rise to questions which
demand a philosophical treatment. It is all very well, for example, to talk
about encounter. But what, if any, are the criteria for believing that it is
God who is encountered? If someone claims to have encountered the
Queen in Woolworth's, there are presumably specifiable criteria for
deciding whether the claim is valid or invalid. Where are the criteria for
deciding whether what purports to be encounter with God is or is not
encounter with God? It may be said that the question is ridiculous. It is

a matter of faith, and any criteria are internal to faith. There are no neutral criteria. If this is the answer, we know where we are. But we cannot prohibit the raising of the question. Again, it is all very well to claim that talk about God can be understood only within the area of faith, by those who actually use the language, and that it naturally seems nonsensical to those who stand outside the area of faith. After all, the language used is public language, a means of social communication. And it can very well be asked whether there are not criteria of meaningfulness which cut across the boundaries between different types of language, scientific, ethical, aesthetic, religious and so on. Whatever the answer may be, the question is perfectly legitimate.

In this lecture I have obviously not attempted to solve any problems. The upshot of my remarks is simply the rather obvious conclusion that unless a religion withdraws into an enclosed garden of its own, cut off from its cultural situation and emerging only to preach to people in a language which is alien to them, it cannot avoid some dialogue with philosophy. The one really important old-style philosophical system in the world today, namely Marxism, regards religion as an expression of human alienation. And here any dialogue must involve what amounts to philosophical anthropology or interpretation of man. Apart from Marxism, philosophy is passing through a phase in which it has become either predominantly critical and analytic or predominantly phenomenological. Analytic philosophy does not of course offer any metaphysically-based religion to rival the historic religions. Nor does it offer, as Marxism does, an aestheistic world-view. But it does raise questions which have relevance in the area of religion. And they can be disregarded only by means of a complete, and in my opinion questionable, seperation of the sacred from the profane, of faith from reason. The questions, or some of them at least, are relevant to both Jews and Christians. And it might well be fruitful and profitable to both parties, if Jewish and Christian thinkers entered into more discussion about the ways in which they see the relevant problems and about the possible lines of solution. Indeed mutual discussion between Jewish and Christian thinkers and representatives of contemporary philosophical trends might well be a source of stimulus to all concerned. It is no longer simply a question of reconciling Neoplatonism or Aristotelianism with Judaism or Christianity. It is a question of the viability of basic religious beliefs. And this can hardly be a matter of indifference to either Jewish or Christian believers.

It would however be rash to assume that religiously-orientated philosophy has disappeared for good and all. In this connection I should like to refer to Franz Rosenzweig, author of *The Star of Redemption* (1912). As historians of Jewish thought have pointed out, Rosenzweig did not simply presuppose Judaism and then interpret it in terms of some ready-made philosophical reflection on his personal experience, on human existence. Provided that one is not thinking of existentialism in terms of certain fixed doctrines, one can say that his approach was existential. He conceptualized his own experience in terms of Judaism, while at the same time he recognized that others would conceptualize their experience in Christian terms. From the philosophical point of view one can of course raise a number of questions about the relation between 'experience' and conceptualization. But I cannot discuss such problems here. My point in mentioning Rosenzweig is to draw attention to the fact that there can be an approach to religious faith through philosophical reflection on man in his situation. On the Christian side we can find a philosophical approach to religious faith in the case of Gabriel Marcel, who was a philosopher before he became a committed Christian. Here once again, it seems to me, there is an area for fruitful discussion between Jewish and Christian thinkers.

CHAPTER 4

AQUINAS AND THE AUTONOMY OF RELIGIOUS LANGUAGE

W HEN WITTGENSTEIN points out in his *Philosophical Investigations*[1] that language can be used in a variety of ways (to assert, to command, to question, to exclaim, to pray, to thank, to curse, and so on) he is reminding us of familiar linguistic operations and is drawing attention to what is obviously true. It by no means follows of course that he has no good reason for making the point which he does make. For one thing, he is correcting his earlier one-sided picture-theory of the proposition. For another thing, emphasis on the variety of the functions of language serves as a useful antidote to neopositivist over-emphasis on the statement of fact and on the operation of describing. To say that Wittgenstein is labouring the obvious, if we mean by this that his remarks are superfluous, would be quite erroneous. At the same time, if Wittgenstein is drawing attention to a feature of ordinary language, a feature which can in principle be seen by anyone at any time, it is not surprising if glimpses of it at any rate were enjoyed in earlier centuries.

Let me take an example from Aquinas. When referring to the activity of praising God he remarks that our words are used not in order to give any information to God, or for his benefit but 'in order that we may arouse ourselves and others who are listening to reverence towards God' (*S.T.*, 22 *ae*, q, 91, a, 1). If, for instance, a man addresses God as almighty and all-loving, what he says should not be interpreted as a giving of superfluous information to God about his attributes or nature. His words have what is customarily described as an expressive-evocative function. They are used to express or to arouse and attitude in human beings, 'to arouse', as Aquinas puts it, 'the interior affection of the praiser and to stimulate others to the praise of God' (*Ibid.*, reply to second objection).

Obviously, to make such remarks in regard to a particular context, as Aquinas does, is not the same thing as to develop a general theory of language and of its manifold functions. Nor is it equivalent to the meticulous and sophisticated mapping-out of ordinary language at which J. L. Austin was so adept. But I am not trying to make out that recent developments in the philosophy of language were all anticipated by the medieval theologian. My point is rather that recognition of the varied functions of language is not excluded by what Aquinas has to say about the use of first-order religious language. He is doubtless much better known for his theory about the use of language in what he takes to be factual statements relating to God, his theory of analogical predication that is to say. But the example which I have given shows, I think, that he is prepared to recognize in first-order religious language functions or uses which could hardly be divined simply by inspecting the grammatical

43

forms of the relevant sentences. If I say to God 'thou art all-holy and all-loving', the sentence, taken by itself would suggest that I am engaged in telling God something about himself. And if God is omniscient, the information is presumably superfluous. According to Aquinas, the real function of the words, if uttered in sincere praise, is to express an attitude in myself or to arouse it, and, if others are listening, to stimulate a like attitude in them.

In general I think one can say this. If we mean by a plurality of language-games a variety of linguistic operations such as asserting, commanding, questioning and so on, there is nothing in the writings of Aquinas which would prevent him from accepting the idea of a plurality of language-games. Again, Aquinas could quite well accept in principle the contention that propositions can have functions which are different from those which mere inspection of the words or of the relevant grammatical forms would suggest.

2

The theory of a plurality of language-games is however often understood as referring to languages in the sense of the language of empirical science, the language of morals, religious language, and so on. This concept does not seem to me to be identical with the one mentioned above. For though such operations as praying, blessing, cursing and thanking hardly belong to the language of natural science, the operation of asserting can be found both in the language of science and in that of religion. Aquinas would obviously maintain, for instance, that there can be and are true assertions about God. In other words, if he accepted the idea of a plurality of language-games, in the sense of the languages of science, religion and so on, he would have to hold that distinctions between different linguistic operations can cut across the boundaries between these languages.

It hardly needs saying that Aquinas himself did not think in terms of a theory of language-games but rather in terms of the extension of ordinary language into a variety of spheres. He certainly recognized the existence of problems of meaning in regard to talk about God; and he saw them as arising out of the extension of language to talk about a transcendent reality surpassing the range of adequate conceptualization. Hence his theory of analogical predication, with its distinction between the 'mode of signifying', which reflects our experience of creatures, and 'that which is signified' or 'that to which a name is applied', which transcends human comprehension (cf. *S.T.*, 1*a*, q. 13, a. 3). It is not my intention to suggest that this theory is immune from criticism. I am simply drawing attention to the rather obvious fact that Aquinas thinks in terms of the extension of ordinary language into a sphere in which it is inevitably subject to strains and stresses. It may therefore seem that one is guilty of a glaring anachronism if one inquires into his attitude towards the theory of a plurality of language-games, especially as this theory presupposes, from the historical point of view, a situation which did not obtain in the Middle Ages, namely the tendency to elevate the language of physical science into a paradigm or model language. In so far as the idea of a plurality of language-games represents a reaction to positivism, it is a modern phenomenon. And to ask what a medieval thinker would say about it may very well appear to be anachronistic. The idea, it may be said, could hardly arise at a time when theology was regarded as the chief science and science in our sense existed only in a very rudimentary form.

It is indeed true that the theory of a plurality of language-games has actually arisen in a cultural situation which is different from that of St Thomas Aquinas. At the same time it could be argued that even at the time of Aquinas there was in effect a basis for recognizing a plurality of languages, and that Aquinas could prefectly well have admitted this, if the matter had been explicitly put to him. Consider medicine, for example, which Aquinas described as an 'art' rather than as a science, as having, that is to say, a practical rather than a theoretical end or goal. It is doubtless questionable whether in the medieval period medicine was of much use for the cure of diseases; but it existed none the less. And if the question had been put to him, could not Aquinas have admitted that the term 'God' belonged to the language of religion (and, in his view at any rate, to that of metaphysics) and not to that of medicine? Would not this have been in accordance with his view of the hierarchy of sciences, theoretical and practical? Again, can we really suppose that Aquinas would have found any insuperable objection to admitting that in what he regarded as the chief science, namely theology, a considerable number of concepts and terms had been developed which pertained to the language of theology and not to any other language, not even to first-order religious language? He may not actually have thought in this way; but if the matter had been put to him, he could surely have made allowance for the idea of a plurality of languages without being thereby compelled to make any change in his views as expressed in his writings.

This line of thought seems to me reasonable enough, as far as it goes. That is to say, if we understand the theory of a plurality of language-games as referring simply to the obvious fact that the use of language in a variety of spheres leads to the emergence of special concepts which have particular functions to perform in one context or sphere and not in another, I see no reason why Aquinas could not accept the theory. To be sure, if we understood the theory as implying that all *prima facie* assertions about God should be interpreted as really being something else (that 'God loves us', for instance, should be interpreted as an imperative, 'love one another'), Aquinas could not accept the theory without abandoning his evident conviction that we can make true assertions about God as the objectively existing ultimate reality. But we have already noted that Aquinas would wish to claim that distinctions between different linguistic operations can cut across the boundaries between distinguishable languages in the sense of religious language, scientific language and so on. And if we allow for this claim, I think that it would be possible for Aquinas to accept the idea of a plurality of languages, if the idea were understood simply in the way to which I have referred.

3

It should not be forgotten however that when Wittgenstein talks about language-games, he is thinking of the fact that each kind of game has its own rules, and that the playing of one game. To assess the merits of a footballer in terms of his following or not following the rules of cricket would be an abvious absurdity. Each kind of game is, to use a Moorean expression, what it is and not something else. Similarly, each language-game is what it is and not something else. It can be properly judged only in terms of itself and of its own intrinsic criterion of what can and cannot be said. Just as there are only games and not game-in-general in relation to which particular games have to be judged, so are there only distinct types of language. There is no paradigm or model language which can serve as a criterion for judging all particular languages. To be sure, in regard to a particular purpose there can be privileged games. If you are looking for physical exercise, tennis is obviously better suited for this purpose than bridge or halma. But there is no privileged game in an absolute, as distinct from a relative sense. Similarly there is no privileged language in an absolute sense. The language of chemistry, for example, cannot do the job of religious language or ethical language. And religious language cannot do the the job of scientific language. Each thing is what it is and not something else.

Could Aquinas accept this idea? Perhaps he might, up to a certain point. Though he conceived theoretical science according to a deductive model, one of the ways in which he distinguished between philosophy and theology was by claiming that whereas the philosopher's process of reasoning is based on premisses known by the natural reason, the theologian starts with revealed premisses. This idea certainly gives rise to difficulties or problems. But my point is simply that Aquinas looks on philosophy as exemplifying certain rules and on theology as following certain other rules. And though it would be much more natural for him to think in terms of distinguishable sciences than in terms of distinct language-games, it is conceivable at any rate that, if he were pressed, he might allow that one could speak of distinguishable languages with rules of their own. It might however be easier for him to do this, if we referred to distinctions between, say, Christian and Jewish discourse. For he could hardly avoid admitting, as an empirical fact that is to say, that in Christian discourse statements about God are permissible, or even obligatory, which are impermissible in Jewish or Moslem discourse. In other words, he could admit that in the Christian community there are in-built rules of what can and cannot be said which express the faith of that community, and that in the Jewish community or the Moslem community there are other rules.

It is perhaps worth remarking that the example which I have just given provides one reason why I do not think that Aquinas would show much enthusiasm for the theory of the plurality of language-games in the form in which it has often been presented to make the distinction which is sometimes drawn between the language of morals and the language of religion. For it is pretty obvious that the Christian religion comprises in-built judgments of value. If a man said that he was a convinced Christian because he believed in the Trinity and the Incarnation but that he thought that love between human beings was a silly ideal and that mutual hatred was a much sounder ideal, we might well comment 'my dear Sir, you have a very odd idea of the Christian religion'. We would surely wish to claim that certain ethical ideals were part of the Christian religion, and that Christian discourse or language includes ethical language. Whether the latter can exist on its own or not is another question. My point is simply that as the Christian religion includes, as an essential component, certain ideals and moral norms, I find it difficult to envisage Aquinas taking kindly to any theory of language-games which implied a sharp division between the language of morals and religious language.

However this may be, it seems clear to me that if language-games are interpreted in the sense of religious language, the language of ethics, poetic language and so on, and if the claim that such language-games are autonomous is understood as meaning that there are no general criteria of rationality and coherence, Aquinas could not accept this claim without becoming involved in a radical revision of his views as we know them from his writings. In the Middle Ages there were indeed some hints of this claim, in regard to the language of Christian faith. For example, in the first half of the fourteenth century, after Aquinas's death that is to say, Robert Holcot, a Dominican of Cambridge, maintained that ordinary logic was inapplicable in the sphere of faith and suggested that there was a logic of faith which transcended even the principles of identity and non-contradiction. Aquinas however would certainly not have admitted that the doctrine of the Trinity, for example, was incompatible with the principles of logic. He held indeed that the truth of this doctrine could not be demonstrated philosophically and that it could only be known through divine revelation. But to maintain that a doctrine could not be proved by natural reason and to maintain that it was contrary to reason were for him not at all the same thing. He makes this quite clear. (See for example, the *Summa Contra Gentes*, Bk. 1, ch. 7.) And when dealing explicitly with the doctrine of the Trinity, he tries to show that it does not contravene the principle of non-contradiction. In other words, he holds that there are general criteria of rationality which are applicable in diverse spheres or, if we can use the term, in different language-games. In this case of course he could not allow that the language of the Christian faith is completely autonomous, if this involved claiming that there are no, so to speak, neutral criteria of rationality or intelligibility by which it can be judged. After all, he says explicitly *(ibid.)* that what is contrary to the principles which natural reason sees to be true cannot come from God. There are truths which are above reason; but they are not contrary to reason.

4

It is open to anyone to comment that though this may be what Aquinas held, it by no means follows that his position is tenable. After the time of Aquinas, it may be said, there was a healthy reaction against the subordination of Christian faith to Greek philosophy. This reaction made its appearance in the fourteenth century and Robert Holcot exemplifies it. Theology and philosophy tended to fall apart, through the fairly radical criticism of the metaphysics which, with thinkers such as Aquinas, had formed or purported to form a bridge between them. This prepared the way for Martin Luther's insistence that it is only through God's self-revelation that we can know him, and that though philosophy has its own proper sphere it is powerless to reveal the divine nature but produces only caricatures or idols. If we express this point of view in terms of the line of thought inspired by Wittgenstein, we can say that the language of Christian faith is autonomous. If Christian beliefs give offence to the so-called natural reason, the reason of fallen man, this is only to be expected. It was the case in the time of St. Paul, and it is still the case today. The wisdom of God is folly to the wise of this world. Argument with them can achieve little. What is needed is conversion to the form of life which finds expression in the language of faith; and this language then acquires a meaning which it cannot have for the man who is alienated from God. From a purely intellectual point of view Aquinas's development of a synthesis between Christian theology and Greek philosophy was doubtless a remarkable achievement, showing great mental ability. But in the process he contributed to the introduction of a rationalism which some of his successors rightly rejected. And one of the chief merits of the modern theory of autonomous language-games is that it allows Christian faith to be itself. The neo-Wittgensteinian philosopher may not himself be a believer. But at any rate he sees that the language of Christian faith expresses and is rooted in a form of life, and that it can prossess real meaning only for those who participate in this form of life. It may be perfectly true that Aquinas could not consistently accept the theory of autonomous language-games. But it by no means follows that the theory has to be rejected.

No of course it does not follow. That is to say, the fact that positions held by Aquinas would militate against the theory of autonomous language-games does not by itself show that the theory is false. For the positions which are incompatible with it might themselves be untenable. The theory however seems to me to be open to serious objections. And I wish to draw attention to one or two of them. It is not, I hope, a case of my being unable to appreciate the attractiveness of the theory to some theologians. If a theologian is convinced that God reveals himself to man through Christ and that man either responds to the divine word in faith or rejects it. It is understandable if he also wishes to claim both that the divine word is its own justification and stands in no need of justification by the philosopher and also that any criticism of the divine word from an external standpoint expresses the limitations of fallen or alienated man. In this case the philosophical theory of autonomous language-games has an obvious attraction for the theologian. For it places religious language beyond the reach of external criticism, pursued in the name of alleged neutral or universal criteria of rationality and coherence. At the same time, if the fact that St Thomas Aquinas said something does not prove that what he said is true, no more does the fact that the theory of autonomous language-games can prove attractive to the theologian show that the theory is tenable.

5

In the first place I had better make it clear that I do not propose to discuss the problem of metaphysics. That is to say, I do not intend to criticize the theory of autonomous language-games on the ground that it presupposes a kind of linguistic positivism, according to which the philosopher can only describe the uses of language. More concretely, I do not intend to discuss the question whether the philosopher can justify the language of theistic belief by proving God's existence by meta-physical arguments. I propose to confine myself to a more logical, and less metaphysical approach.

As far as I know, nobody maintains that what people say *about* first-order religious language is immune from criticism. What the theory of autonomous language-games involves is the claim that first-order religious language, as expressing and indeed forming part of a way of life, cannot properly be judged or criticized in the name of neutral or universal criteria of rationality, intelligibility or coherence. So let us confine our attention to first-order religious language.

It is true to say, I suppose, that first-order religious language is characterized more by talk *to* God than by talk *about* him. At the same time the language of prayer and praise seems to me to imply assertions. If I pray to God, I imply that I believe that there is a God to pray to. In fact I imply a good many things, such as that God is personal and not say, an infra-conscious cosmic energy, a blind force as we might say. Such beliefs imply assertions. The assertions found in first-order religious language need not of course be regarded as 'flat constatives'. Nor need they be interpreted simply according to their surface appearance. If a man says, in the context of the Christian liturgy, 'I believe in one God the Father Almighty', it would hardly be appropriate to regard him as simply imparting autobiographical information about his private beliefs to any-one who happens to be within hearing. In the liturgical context the utterence clearly has an element of self-commitment. And it may have other elements too. None the less, the sentence implies the assertion that there is a God who is one, Father and Almighty. It may indeed be possible to interpret such utterances in the light, say, of Professor R. B. Braith-waite's theory about 'stories' which Christians tell themselves as a stimulus to a life of Christian love and for which no truth-claims are made. But this is a theory which is obviously designed to enable a man to combine a certain philosophical position, logical empiricism, with adherence to the Christian religion without laying himself open to the charge of inconsistency. Short of such interpretations, the natural way to understand such utterances as the one which I have mentioned is that they imply assertions which are believed to be true. In fine, I do not think that any interpretation of first-order Christian language which eliminates assertions on behalf of which truth-claims are made can be considered plausible. This is the point which I wish to make. Whether or not the truth of such assertions can be proved or supported by phil-osophical argument is an issue which I propose to disregard.

Now it seems to me reasonable to maintain that if anything is asserted, something is excluded. A putative statement of fact which excludes nothing at all may perhaps possess emotive significance, but I do not see how it can make good its claim to be a factual or informative statement, of which truth or falsity can be properly predicated. This does not seem to me to be an arbitrary rule or demand. In my opinion it is simply a case of our not understanding what is asserted unless something is excluded. Let me take an example which is rather hackneyed and which I have used elsewhere. Someone tells you that Jane is a good cook. Now what is required in order to qualify for being described as a good cook is doubt-less open to discussion. If you are satisfied with nothing less than first-class French-style cooking, you are unlikely to agree that Jane is a good cook if she can only cope with porridge and with fish and chips. At the same time, if the statement that Jane is a good cook is to have any definite meaning at all, it must exclude something. If it were compatible with Jane habitually serving up food totally unfit for human consump-tion, it is difficult to see how there would be any detectable difference between describing her as a good cook and describing her as a bad cook. Similarly, it seems to me that in his well known argument about 'death by a thousand qualifications' Professor Anthony Flew is justified in asking what is excluded by the assertion that God loves us as a father. If, that is to say, the assertion is to be taken as purporting to be a true statement about an existing reality and not simply as emotive utterence, it must surely exclude something. If it were held to be compatible with any imaginable state of affairs whatsoever, including, for example, God having created human beings with the express purpose of consigning them all to eternal torment, whatever their behaviour might have been, it would be difficult (in my opinion impossible) to see any difference between saying that God loves us and saying that he hates us. To have a definite meaning it must at any rate exclude what is incompatible with what is asserted.

It is not of course my intention to enter upon a debtate with Professor Flew. Nor am I concerned with arguing either for or against the truth of the statement that God loves us. I am concerned simply with arguing that there are in fact criteria of intelligibility which are applicable in distinct language-games, in the present context in all languages in which assertions or putative statements of fact occur. If this is correct, it militates against the claim that each language-game is completely autonomous. As I have already admitted, they can enjoy a certain measure of autonomy. For example, it would be absurd to judge a statement about the indwelling of the Holy Spirit as though it were a statement in nuclear physics. What should or should not be said about the Holy Spirit is presumably determined to a great extent by criteria which belong to the Christian faith of the Christian community. I should wish to argue however that even the statements of Christian faith must exemplify certain general criteria of intelligibility, if they are to be regarded as meaningful assertions. In this case of course the autonomy of Christian discourse, though real, is subject to limitations. And I see no good reason why the philosopher should not discuss the question whether statements of Christian belief do or do not fulfil the criteria required for intelligible discourse.

I trust that I have not been misunderstood. I am not concerned with denying that faith is a response to God and that the language of faith expresses this response. What I am suggesting is that the language of faith is none the less *language*, a human activity and subject to rules of human understanding. It has indeed its own rules, but these fall within a general framework of significant language. If language is a complex and many-sided activity of the one human being who can participate in a variety of forms of life and in corresponding language-games, it is only to be expected that language-games in the sense of asserting, commanding and so on, should cut across the boundaries of language-games in the sense of the language of science, religious language and so on, and that the logic of assertions, so to speak, should apply in more than one of the language-games in the second sense.

Let me put the matter in a slightly different way. I should not care to dogmatize on the subject of the relation between thought and language. But it seems reasonable to regard them not as two distinct entities but rather as standing to one another in a relation analogous to that between form and matter in the Aristotelian sense of these terms. This analogy allows, say, for translation, while it does not reify thought as an entity distinct from its expression. If one looks at the matter in this way, it is natural to think of general criteria of intelligibility as applicable throughout the area of what can be thought and said. The theologian may wish to emphasize the concept of God's word. But this word can hardly be grasped at all by man unless it is thought by him and thus expressed in human language. If God is to speak to man, he must use human language. What faith believes that God has said may not be provable by human reason. But if there is to be any communication at all, it must at any rate be intelligible by the human reason.

6

What I have been saying seems to have a bearing on the question whether or not a given language-game can be understood by the man who stands outside the form of life of which the language-game in question is an expression, and indeed a consituent part. If it is asked whether the man who stands outside religion can understand religious language, I do not think that the question can be appropriately answered by a simple 'yes' or 'no'. It seems to me that some distinctions have to be made. And I wish to make a few brief remarks on this topic.

From one point of view the contention that the man who does not participate in the religious form of life and who does not himself play the religious language-game is incapable of achieving any understanding of religious language seems to be untenable. The rules of the Russian language are presumably internal to that language. Though however it has its own rules and is a difficult language to learn, it is not impossible in principle to learn it. Analogously, one might learn to use Buddhist language correctly without either being or having any intention of becoming a Buddhist. And I fail to see any good reason why it should be impossible in principle that a non-Christian, given the readiness to take the requisite pains, would be incapable of learning how the Christian language-game is played. Presumably, this is the sort of thing which Wittgenstein had in mind when he said that in one sense he understood the word 'God'.[2] In earlier years he had learned what the word did not mean. He could ask questions relative to God . He could use the language according to the rules.

From another point of view however it seems reasonable to claim that the man who stands outside religion cannot understand religious language. There is, I think, an obvious sense in which the man who had, as we popularly say, no moral sense could not understand the language of morals. He might indeed learn to use the language, if he took the necessary trouble; but if he were devoid of any moral sense, he could hardly appreciate what the language 'means' to the man with strong moral convictions. Similarly, if a man stood outside a religion, in the sense that religion 'meant nothing' to him, he would hardly be in a position to understand the significance which the language of faith has for the believer in terms of its relevance to his life. To say this may indeed border on the tautological, in so far, that is to say, as it amounts to spelling out the statement that a man who stands outside a given form of life stands outside it and does not participate in it. It seems however to be true. We have indeed to allow for the class of persons who do not stand outside the area of religion to such an extent that it is a territory of which they have no experience at all but who, for various reasons, are not prepared to commit themselves to playing this particular language-game and embracing the beliefs which are associated with it. This is, I imagine, a pretty large class. Still, it seems to be true that there is indeed a sense in which the 'meaning' of the language of faith eludes the man who stands quite outside the relevant form of life or area of human experience.

These two points of view are not of course imcompatible. It is quite possible, for example, for a non-Christian to study Christian belief and literature and to learn how the language functions, even though the language of faith does not 'mean' to him what it does to the sincere believer. He may thus feel inclined to say that in one sense he understands the language and that in another sense he does not. Wittgenstein spoke in this sort of way in regard to use of the term 'God'. He may indeed have been thinking partly, or even primarily, of special characteristics or peculiarities attaching to talk about God and his activity. But I doubt whether this aspect of the matter is particularly relevant. For the semantic problems which arise in connexion with talk about God arise not only for the unbeliever but also for the believer, not indeed when the believer is actually using first-order religious language but when he reflects on it.

Such problems, it seems to me, can perfectly well be understood by both parties, believer and unbelievers, in such a way that they can carry on an intelligent discussion without necessarily being at cross-purposes. They differ of course inasmuch as the believer actually plays the language-game in question, whereas by definition the unbeliever does not. As I have already admitted, there is therefore a sense in which the unbeliever, who does not participate in the relevant form of life, does not appreciate what the language means to the believer. At the same time, when they reflect on the first-order language, both men can grasp the semantic problems which arise out of it. And this could not be the case if there were no sense in which the unbeliever is capable of understanding religious language.

It is doubtless the case that people have often talked about or dismissed religious beliefs without having taken the trouble to find out what the beliefs in question really are and how they are understood by

those who hold them. But understanding of a belief does not entail acceptance of it. At any rate this is what we assume in other areas, namely that
we can in principle understand beliefs without accepting them. And I find
it difficult to see why the religious area should constitute an exception. Is
religious language in general, or talk about God in particular, so idiosync-
ratic, so peculiar, that it can be understood only by those who actively play
this language-game? If this is the case, religious language is obviously
immune from external criticism. But immunity from criticism seems to be
purchased at the cost of communicability. Religious language becomes the
in-game of a limited circle which cannot be understood by anyone outside
the circle. And we are faced with the questionable concept of a language
which is not strictly a private language, inasmuch as a group of people
can understand it, but which is none the less not a public language in the
sense that it is in principle understandable by anyone.

7

It may appear that I have strayed far from the thought of the theologian
in whose honour I am supposed to be speaking, and that after some
references to Aquinas I have been putting forward my own views, for
what they may be worth. I have indeed been putting forward my own
views; but I think that they are consonant with the lines of thought
which Aquinas might be expected to pursue, if he were faced with the
theory of autonomous language-games and if he were not prepared to
undertake a revision of the positions which he adopted in the thirteenth
century. Indeed, this claim seems to me pretty obviously true. For
though, as I mentioned earlier in this lecture, Aquinas allowed for
utterances in first-order religious language the function of which, despite
their grammatical forms, is to express, evoke or confirm attitudes rather
than to convey information to anyone, he certainly believed that there
are statements which convey true information about God. And in cases
in which such statements appeared to contradict the principles of
reason, he tried to show that this was not in fact the case. Whether he
was successful or not is another question. My point is simply that his
procedure implies that there are in fact criteria of intelligibility which
cut across the boundaries of distinct language-games. I am doubtful
whether in point of fact Aquinas would show much enthusiasm for the
theory of language-games, though he might accept it, as I have suggested,
to a limited extent. I am convinced however that he could not consistently accept the theory of completely autonomous language-games in
the sense which I have been discussing. Further, I find it difficult to
suppose that he would have been prepared to agree that a man could
not understand a given language-game without participating in the
relevant form of life, unless of course this view were interpreted in such a
way as to make it true by definition.

If I am correct in thinking that Aquinas might be expected to react to the theory of autonomous language-games in the ways which I have suggested, I have not in fact strayed very far from my advertized theme. As Aquinas was obviously not explicitly confronted by neo-Wittgensteinianism in the thirteenth century, it would be impossible to say what he thought about it. One can only say what he might reasonably be expected to think about it, if he were at the same time to keep substantially to the other ideas expressed in his writings. At the same time it may seem extremely disingenuous if I claim the patronage of Aquinas for lines of thought in which I am clearly in agreement with a number of contemporary philosophers who would have little use either for Aquinas's metaphysics or for his religious faith.

In regard to metaphysics, Aquinas's rationalism can easily be exaggerated. It hardly needs saying that he believed as a Christian before he pursued any metaphysical reflections. Moreover, he thought of Christian theology as having the premisses of its own, which were revealed and not demonstrable by the philosopher. In this sense he might possibly be said to have looked on theology as a distinct language-game. At the same time he regarded the philosopher as capable of proving the so-called 'preambles' of faith, such as the existence of God. He makes it indeed clear enough that he did not mean to imply that people cannot or should not believe in God unless they have grasped metaphysical proofs of his existence. But he obviously regarded such proofs as possible. And this is admittedly not a popular position today, either with theologians or with philosophers. And while I should not care to dogmatize in any way about the matter, I confess to a feeling of perplexity in regard to this particular enterprise. A proof of the existence of a God as an additional item, so to speak, in the universe would hardly be a proof of the existence of *God*. This was seen by some thinkers in the medieval period itself. Any cosmological proof would presumably have to take the form of showing the existential insufficiency and dependence of all finite beings on a transcendent ground of finite existence. And it is none too easy to see how this can be proved in a manner which does not involve an implicit presupposition of the conclusion. Anyway, I have passed over the subject of metaphysics and of the extent, if any, to which it can be said to 'justify' the language of faith. Instead I have confined my attention to some logical points. And this is of course why I find myself in agreement with a number of philosophers who would probably be in sympathy with what I have been saying but who would have no truck with Aquinas's philosophical theology.

It is not however simply a question of whether we prescind or not from the problem of metaphysics. In the medieval cultural situation it was obviously assumed that the language of Christian faith included statements about God which were both meaningful and true. When, for example, Aquinas discussed problems arising out of talk about God, he was not really asking whether the relevant statements were intelligible or meaningful. He assumed that they were and tried to reconcile this assumption with his recognition of real problems in regard to their meaning. It was a question not so much of whether the statements were meaningful but of how they were meaningful. How could the intelligibility and truth of human statements about God be harmonized with insistence on the divine transcendence and incomprehensibility? In our contemporary cultural situation however the assumptions made by the medieval theologians cannot be counted on and are often absent. As we are all aware, there has been a radical criticism of the meaningful character of statements about God, not only by philosophers who make no claim to be Christian but also by some Christian writers who are therefore driven to a revision of Christianity which either eliminates statements about God or re-interprets them as being something else than what they appear to be. It is understandable therefore if some theologians who have no inclination to pursue this policy of revision gladly accept the olive branch provided by the theory of autonomous language-games, as this allows religious language to be itself, so to speak, without interference from outside. And if it is meaningful (of which I have my doubts) to speak of a thirteenth-century theologian being alive and mentally active in the twentieth century, I am obviously not in a position to assert with confidence that in our contemporary cultural situation Aquinas would not side with the theologians to whom I have just referred. For all I know, he might embrace neo-Wittgensteinianism in philosophy and Barthianism in theology. Such a radical change of view would however involve abandonment not only of his metaphysics, or a large part of it at least, but also of general criteria of rationality and of a vision of unity-in-diversity of language, both of which, in my opinion, it is important to preserve.

To conclude. I would not nowadays describe myself as a Thomist. But the unifying vision presented by Aquinas seems to me a valuable and permanent source of stimulus. And I do not think that the fragmentary implications of the theory of autonomous language-games and of seperate forms of life contributes to its preservation. The theory has of course a foundation in fact and relates to elements in our cultural situation. But it seems to me to have been presented in an exaggerated and untenable form by the more extreme neo-Wittgensteinians. And, as I have argued, I think that Aquinas would have to agree, on the assumption, that is to say, that he did not undertake a radical change in his philosophy.

Notes
[1] (London, 1968)
[2] *Lectures and Conversations on Aesthetics, Psychology and Religious Belief,* ed. C. Barrett (Oxford, 1966), p. 59.

CHAPTER 5

MAN, TRANSCENDENCE AND
THE ABSENCE OF GOD[1]

F RANCIS SUAREZ BELIEVED that nobody can be an accomplished
theologian unless he has a firm grasp of metaphysics. He was also
convinced that the existence of God can be proved by metaphysical arguments in such a way that if anyone who understands them fails to
accept the conclusion, this must be due to bad disposition or a bad will.
But then the existence of God was hardly in doubt. Suárez himself was a
member of the intensely Catholic nation, and he lived in any case at a time
when the existence of God was commonly accepted as a premiss. That is
to say, faith preceded rational reflection on the faith and on its presuppositions and implications. Even later, in the eighteenth century, the
Deists, who doubted or rejected essential elements of Christianity,
believed that the existence of God can be proved by what Suárez would
have called, in a somewhat depreciatory sense, 'physical arguments'.
There were, of course, atheists in the eighteenth century; but, apart from
certain circles, the term 'atheist' was still a term of abuse. When in 1745
Hume applied for a professorial chair in the University of Edinburgh, it
was largely his reputation for scepticism and atheism which led to the
failure of the application. Belief in God was commonly looked on as a
necessary pillar of society and as an essential foundation of the moral
life; and many people were not prepared to admit that the professed
atheist could be in good faith. For even among those who took a dim
view of Christianity it was a common enough belief that God has shown
himself in his effects in Nature.

It hardly needs saying that the situation is very different today. On
the side of unbelief we are all familiar with the argument that the
development of the scientific vision of the world, while not actually
disproving the existence of God, has progressively pushed him into the
background to such an extent that he has become a superfluous and
irrelevant hypothesis. It is also maintained not only that morality is in no
way essentially dependent on religious belief but also that the development of a purely autonomous ethic has been rendered absolutely
necessary by the so-called 'death of God'. It is a recognition of common
ends and values, not religious belief, which holds society together. On the
side of belief, already in the first half of the last century we find Søren
Kierkegaard, a profoundly religious thinker, asserting that though we can
find in Nature aspects which are capable of being interpreted as manifestations of God, there is at the same time much that is deeply disturbing
and 'the sum of all this is an objective uncertainty'.[1] Even believers may
feel on occasion, and indeed acutely, that in the universe there reigns a
great silence unbroken by any divine voice, and that if they are to

maintain their faith they have to do so, as Kierkegaard put it, 'over seventy thousand fathoms of water'.[2] In fact they may wonder sometimes whether they really believe. It is not simply a question of agnostic or atheist linguistic philosophers raising difficulties or puzzles about the significance of the statements which we are accustomed to make about God. For even those who do believe in God may ask themselves whether our concepts or representations of the deity are not human, all too human.

Obviously, even in the modern world there are people who have a firm and serene faith in God. But there are people who either doubt because of what seems to be the absence of God, the silence of the transcendent, or believe in spite of it. And to neither class are the arguments advanced by Francis Suárez likely to appear very satisfying. For one thing they will probably receive the impression that Suárez is trying to present as plain and certain what seems to them neither plain nor certain. For another thing they probably think of metaphysical proofs as moving in a void populated only by abstract concepts and as having little or no connexion with human existence and man's hopes and fears. Faith is for them a venture or risk, as it was for Kierkegaard, not an assent to the conclusion of a metaphysical argument. Again, some have the impression that traditional arguments for the existence of God purport to show that in addition to empirical realities there is an additional entity 'out there' which is called God. And they understandably conclude that whatever this additional entity might be, it would not be God.

It is not my intention to suggest that these impressions are all justified. For example, neither Aquinas nor Suárez regarded God as an object among objects, as a being which could legitimately be described as an additional entity. Nor did they look on a living faith in God as identifiable with assent to the conclusion of a philosophical argument. At the same time I think that the impressions are perfectly understandable. For the old arguments for the existence of God formed part of Christian faith's reflection on itself (*fides quaerens intellectum*); and when the whole Christian vision of the world is experienced or felt as problematic, the Christian's reflection of his faith is naturally felt as problematic too. To put the matter in another way, the metaphysical arguments seem to presuppose that the world is intelligible, in the sense that there is one ultimate explanation of the existence of the plurality of finite things. And for many people the main question is whether the world is intelligible in this sort of way. May it not be unintelligible, as far as metaphysical questions are concerned? In other words, it may be said, it is not simply a matter of detecting and correcting logical flaws in this or that argument for the existence of God. Rather it is a matter of basic presuppositions. And the basic presuppositions which were commonly accepted in the time of Suárez are by no means always accepted today.

2

Now, to speak like William James, we can evidently give a cash value to the statement that the situation of contemporary man is very different from that of people for whom Suárez was primarily writing. For we can mention a good many ways, on the intellectual, social-political and economic levels, for example, in which the two situations differ. One hardly needs to labor this point. At the same time is there not a basic and lasting human situation? We may become so hypnotized by differences that we overlook fundamental similarities. It may be said, with Wittgenstein,[3] that it is the differences which are interesting, not the similarities or what things have in common. But this depends on the nature and purpose of one's inquiry. And the idea of a basic human situation is relevant to my theme here.

We are accustomed to being told by modern philosophers that the basic situation of man is that he is a being in the world. And if we take this statement simply by itself, it may seem so obviously true that we are inclined to wonder why any philosopher should trouble to make it. But when a philosopher insists that man is a being in the world, he may be asserting this truth against, for example, any reduction of man to an epistemological ego, a subject which stands outside the world and contemplates it from without or at its limit. Further, the philosopher does not mean that man simply happens to be in space and time when he might very well be outside them. Rather does he mean that man is by his very nature a being in the world, that being in the world is a basic condition of being human. To put the matter in another way, the human spirit is not a spirit which simply happens to find itself in a body: it is by nature 'incarnate' spirit. My body is not simply an instrument which I use, an instrument external to myself. After all, that this is not the case is clearly indicated by the ordinary language which expresses the common experience of mankind. Consider, for example, such a sentence as 'I went for a walk'. Further, it is as a being in the world, as 'incarnate' spirit, that man becomes what he has it in himself to be, through, that is to say, the actualization of his potentialities. It is as a being in the world that he lives and knows and acts.

It must be added, of course, that to be in the world does not mean simply to be in a world in general. Man cannot be in the world without being in a definite historical situation. He may be a Greek in the fifth century B.C. or an American in the twentieth century A.D.; but he must be in some definite historical situation. Even in the case of him whom Christians believe to be the Son of God his earthly life was passed in a definite historical situation.

Though, however, to be in the world is a basic condition of being human, it is clearly not all we mean by being human. A cat or a dog is in the world. At the same time we would hardly speak of a cat or a dog as 'finding itself' in the world or in a definite historical situation. For though I have no wish to dogmatize about feline or canine intelligence, I see no good reason for supposing that cats and dogs have the power of reflecting in this way on their basic situation. Man, however, can objectify his situation; he can reduce it to an object of reflective awareness. True, he does so as a being in the world. He is not reducible to an epistemological ego which can be regarded as an external spectator of all time and existence. But it seems to me absurd to deny that the human person can and does function as subject of consciousness. I do not believe that this function of the human person can be successfully eliminated by an application of the principle of economy or Ockham's razor, as some philosophers have claimed. Hence I am prepared to say that there is a sense in which man transcends the world, though it must be immediately added that he does so as a being in the world. This may be a paradoxical way of talking; but I think that it serves the purpose of drawing attention to a real situation.

At this point I wish to introduce a complication which is also, I hope, a clarification. I have said that man finds himself in a definite historical situation. This means, of course, that he sees the world from a certain angle of vision, according to a certain perspective. We can thus give a cash value to the idea of 'my world'. It means presumably the world precisely as perceived and conceived by me, from my angle of vision. But it by no means follows that each human being is imprisoned, as it were, in a private world of his own in which there are no other persons, no other subjects. The world as I conceive it certainly contains other persons. Further, I am perfectly well aware that these other persons are subjects. Obviously, I cannot be another subject. And there is a trivial sense in which other people are for me always objects, namely, in the sense that I know them as one who is not identical with them. At the same time I think that Sartre has shown that we do encounter other persons precisely as subjects. With a plurality of subjects there must be a plurality of angles of vision. But I am aware that the different visions, including, of course, my own, exist within a common world, within a common historical process. There is indeed a sense in which 'my world' is correlative to me as a subject, namely, in the sense that my perspective is mine and nobody else's. But the different perspectives are perspectives of the world in which we are all situated.

Let me put the matter in this way. If several people are swimming in a certain river, with perhaps several miles between each of them, each of them, if he looks about him, does so from a different point; and what they see is not precisely the same. But it by no means follows that what they see is not there to be seen. Nor does it follow that it is untrue to say that they are immersed in the same river. There is, as it were, a common river which is seen under different perspectives. Each could say 'my river', meaning the river as he sees it. But the phrase 'my river', if properly understood, would not exclude the use of the phrase 'the river'.

Now if I and 'my world' and you and 'your world' exist in a common world, it is not unnatural to think that this common world is the all-comprehensive totality, the One or Absolute. I do not wish to raise the question whether there could conceivably be another world. It is sufficient for my purpose that we find ourselves in a common world, and that this common world presents itself to our minds in the first instance as a totality, an all-inclusive whole. That is to say, this is the way in which we are naturally inclined to conceive the world. It appears that 'in which' we are.

In what sense, however, is the world a totality, an all-inclusive super-entity? We tend to think of it, I suppose, as stretching indefinitely back into the past and forward into the future. But the past no longer exists. And the future does not yet exist. True, the world as it exists now is the result of its past and contains it within itself. And it might even be said to be pregnant with its future, to precontain it. But what we call the present world, the world as it exists, is constantly changing, a process rather than a static entity. And in what sense is it an entity? When we shake off the bewitching influence of the phrase, 'the world', and look about us, we see things, a plurality of finite entities. True, each of them is said to be 'in the world'. Ants are in the world, and stars are in the world. But what is this world in which things are? Is it something over and above the things which are said to be in the world? If so, what is it?

It is not my intention to suggest that no meaning can be given to the phrase, 'in the world'. For things certainly stand to one another in a variety of relations. And I suppose, for instance, that to stand to other things in spatiotemporal relations is to be in the world. But it by no means follows that the world is a superentity over and above the things which stand to one another in various relations. The situation seems to me to be this. When we try to think the concept of the world, to render it articulate or definite, the world tends to break up into the indefinite plurality of finite things and the relations between them. True, this piece of reductive analysis probably appears unsatisfactory to most minds. And we start to talk about a system or a unified process or even, if we are so inclined, about the concrete universal. But the point is that a system is nothing apart from its members. Nor does the concrete universal exist apart from its particulars. It is all very well to say that the world is a totality which is more than the sum of its members, of the things which are said to be 'in the world'. What can this mean except that to think the world we have to think of finite things not as unrelated atoms but as standing to one another in a variety of relations, some of which, like temporal succession, can be described as all-pervasive?

Generally speaking, we take it for granted that we know the meaning of the term, 'the world'. And it is obvious that we can and do employ the term intelligently in ordinary speech. For instance, if someone talks about 'the world', it is usually clear from the context whether he means this planet or the world in the sense in which things are said to be 'in the world' or the world in the Gospel sense of the term. But when we attempt a serious analysis of the concept of the world in the first of these senses, we encounter difficulties. The mind enters into a kind of dialectic in which it tries to find some all-inclusive totality, some super-entity, and yet fails to find anything beyond the plurality of related things.

'Well' you may say, 'what is the point of all this? What has it got to do with transcendence and the absence of God'? The point is this. Man is faced by a plurality of objects. In his effort to understand, to obtain conceptual mastery over them, he unifies them in various ways. In the scientific vision of the world, for example, we obtain conceptual mastery over a plurality through unification, correlation, coordination. In this sphere the unification is primarily descriptive, in terms of general hypotheses and so-called 'laws'. But if we direct our attention to the existential level, to the plurality of things considered precisely as existing, the pursuit of unification takes the form of referring the Many to a One in the existential order, to an Absolute. A natural way of doing this is by thinking of the plurality of things as existing in and through the world, as though the world were itself the One, the Absolute. Reflection, however, suggests that the world is unable to play this role, that on analysis it dissolves into the plurality which we were trying to unify. The mind is therefore driven to transcend the world, to conceive the plurality of empirical things as existentially dependent on and as in some sense manifesting a transcendent One or Absolute.

What I am concerned to argue is this, that the human mind or reason, by its nature, seeks the One. We can, of course, become absorbed in day-by-day practical concerns and use our minds in their service. But if we once make the transition to metaphysical reflection (and nobody can compel us to do this), the immanent direction of the mind or reason to the One asserts itself. But the orientation or immanent finality of the mind is a manifestation of the immanent finality of the human spirit such as. In other words, the movement of the mind in metaphysical reflection is one expression, though only one, of man's orientation to the transcendent Absolute. Man is by nature a being in the world; but he is also by nature the being which transcends the world in the movement toward God. Transcendence, in the active sense of transcending, belongs to man as much as does being in the world. And in my opinion metaphysics can be looked on as man's appropriation in reflection of his own orientation to the transcendent Absolute.

What, however, does man encounter in the movement of transcendence? From one point of view at any rate the answer is 'nothing'. That is to say, one does not see or intuit a thing among things, an object among objects; nor does one encounter a superhuman person in the manner in which one can encounter another human being. In so far as one can be said to encounter the Transcendent in the movement of transcendence, one encounters it precisely as transcendent, as that which lies beyond all limits of the finite. It appears as an all-comprehending presence,[4] but not as the presence of a thing or object of direct intuition. The presence can thus appear as an absence. And in face of the silence of the Transcendent man can easily take refuge in agnosticism or atheism and give himself to the fulfilment of concrete tasks in the world.

At the same time the movement of transcendence in man is not so easily stifled. For example, has not Bertrand Russell clearly shown a hankering after something greater than man? As he thinks that it is slavish to worship the universe because of its size, he cannot find what he is seeking in the physical world. And as he rejects the concept of God, he cannot in fact find anything greater than man. He has said therefore that his intellect goes with the humanists. But he has added that 'my emotions violently rebel'.[5] Lord Russell would add, of course, that his emotions are no guide to the nature of reality. But in his emotive dissatisfaction with scientific humanism and by his admission that he considers some form of personal religion 'highly desirable'[6] he seems to me to recognize, implicitly at least, a religious dimension in man, and thus the movement of transcendence. Similarly Sir Julian Huxley tells us, somewhat surprisingly, that we are confronted with a 'basic and universal mystery . . . the mystery of existence in general'.[7] and that one of the jobs of religion is to keep alive man's sense of wonder at this mystery. The admission is 'surprising' in the sense that recognition of existence in general as a mystery, as a problem, seems to me to imply an indeterminate awareness of an unobjectified and ultimate ground of existence. Again, Sartre, a rather different type of thinker, has spoken of man's need for God on the one hand and of the silence which man encounters on the other.[8] It may be true to say that the more intent Sartre has been on trying to give social and political content to his philosophy by combining it with Marxism, the more has he played down the pessimistic and even tragic aspects of his original existentialism. But it is a paradoxical feature of the atheistic existentialism of Sartre that by the emphasis which it placed on the theme of frustration it drew attention in a forcible manner both to the relevance of God and to the movement of transcendence.

Now I have just spoken of an 'awareness' of the Transcendent. But this way of speaking needs to be taken in conjunction with my earlier statement that man does not encounter the Transcendent as an object among objects or as a thing among things. In the movement of transcendence the transcendent Absolute 'shows itself', if one may use this phrase, as the unobjectified goal of the movement of the human spirit, as a final cause which cannot be grasped as a 'thing' in any ordinary sense. Every attempt to grasp it, to see it, to say that it is here rather than there, to point it out, inevitably fails. And this, I think is one

main reason why it is possible to recognize man's need of God, his movement toward God, and yet to doubt or deny the existence of God. For in
the ordinary sense of 'thing' one finds nothing, that is, no thing.

If the Absolute cannot be a thing among things, a member of a class,
it is no matter of suprise if all language used to describe it betrays its
inadequacy. We may therefore feel that the best policy to follow would
be one of Wittgensteinian silence. But unless it is interpreted as a
tautology the statement that whatever can be said at all can be said
clearly is equivalent to an inhibiting prohibition, which we are free to
reject. And I see no reason why we should not try to talk about the transcendent, provided, of course, that we have some rule or rules governing
our choice of analogies and symbols. For instance, if the transcendent
Absolute cannot be a material thing, we are perfectly justified in
speaking of it as spiritual. At the same time it is important to bear in
mind the inadequacy of our language as applied to God. We make for
ourselves conceptual representations of the Transcendent. And some are
preferable to others. But perfect clarity is not obtainable. And if we
forget the shortcomings of our language, we are soon reminded of them
by the linguistic analysts. Their intentions may indeed be sometimes
destructive. But at any rate they fulfill the useful function of reminding
us that we cannot take photographs of the Transcendent. For the matter
of that, the mystical writers, whose intentions are certainly not
destructive, remind us of the same thing.

True, the Christian believes that in a certain sense there is a photo-
graph. 'He who sees me sees the Father also'.[9] But the Incarnation is God's
revelation of himself in human terms, not the result of a metaphysical
tour de force by the human mind. If the metaphysician is obstinately
determined, as Hegel was, to take the Godhead by storm and to make
plain to view the inner essence of God, the inevitable result is that God
disappears while a conceptual idol takes his place.

3

Now it may seem that the more the divine transcendence is emphasized,
so much the more irrelevant does belief in the Absolute become,
irrelevant, that is to say, to human purposes and tasks within the world.
If it is true that the human spirit is by its nature orientated to the
Transcendent, the thought of the divine reality must indeed be relevant
to man considered as an individual. But does it not then follow that the
ideal for man is what Plotinus described as 'the flight of the alone to the
Alone'?[10] In other words, does not belief in a transcendent Absolute
encourage a turning away from this world? Is it not an expression of the
spirit of escapism, even of an antisocial attitude?

To say that the One is transcendent means, of course, that it is not the
sum total, so to speak, of the Many and that it cannot be identified with
material things or with the finite self. But it by no means follows that

belief in a transcendent Absolute commits us to adopting the view of history as a kind of 'unreal' stage play which finds expression in the *Enneads* of Plotinus. On the contrary, belief that the Many are existentially dependent on a transcendent One commits us to looking on the world as in some sense the manifestation of the Absolute. The transcendent Absolute, however, must be described as spiritual, as, that is to say, infinite Spirit. And Spirit can manifest itself, properly speaking, only in what is like itself, namely, in spirit. We can thus look on the world-process as the progressive manifestation of the Absolute, the physical universe being, as it were, the condition for the appearance of spirit, of the spiritual sphere.

Needless to say, I am well aware that the idea of the physical world as being in any sense 'for man' seems to many people a ridiculous idea, a notion which was finally overthrown by the development of the scientific view of the world from the Renaissance onward. When this planet has been displaced from the central position which was once attributed to it, and when we have come to understand the vast size of the universe, how can we possibly ascribe importance, from a cosmological point of view, to the tiny inhabitants of a very minor heavenly body, namely the earth? To ourselves our concerns are naturally of importance. But in relation to the universe the life of man is surely simply an accidental and passing feature.

This point of view is doubtless understandable. But has size, quantity, really anything to do with the matter? If we once think of the world as the manifestation of infinite Spirit, it is natural to regard the process of evolution as leading up to the appearance of spirit within the world, embodied or 'incarnate' spirit. And the size of the stage and of the scenery does not necessarily diminish the importance of the actor who appears on the stage. Why should it?

The appearance of man on earth, however, is obviously not the end of the matter.[11] The creative activity of infinite Spirit is reflected in the creative activity of man, in the actualization of his potentialities, in his self-objectification in the world, as in the creation of social institutions and a moral order within the physical order. Further, infinite Spirit is one. And though the created expression of infinite Spirit takes the form, in the first instance, of a plurality of finite spirits, they are potentially one, not indeed in the sense that they are capable of ontological coalescence, but in the sense that they are capable of effective union in the bond of love, within an all-embracing society. Such a society, a unity-in-distinction, would reflect the unity of infinite Spirit and can be looked on as the goal of history.

Now Francis Suárez maintained that in a certain context we could look on men as forming 'a single mystical body'.[12] At the same time he thought that the formation of one single political body would be neither possible nor expedient. We, however, live in a situation in which we can see clearly enough the need for some effective visible unification. We can, of course, have different ideas about what form it should take. But the very movement of history, if one may so speak. has brought home to us the imperative necessity of transcending our divisions and enmities, if, that is to say, we wish to avoid the increasing danger of a catastrophe of such magnitude that it might conceivably lead to the destruction of the human race.

It is hardly necessary to say that I regard the creation of some form of effective world organization in the interests of peace and the good of man as a goal which we ought to strive to attain. But this is by no means all that I mean when I speak of the actualization of an all-embracing society as the goal of history. If it were all that I meant, I should obviously lay myself open to the objection that talk about the absolute serves simply to obfuscate a plain practical issue. We are threatened, it could be said, by the possibility of total destruction. Hence, unless we happen to be psychologically maladjusted persons who are fascinated by the prospect of a universal cataclysm and who care nothing for human welfare and the future of man, we all desire that effective practical means should be taken to avert the threatened disaster. And it does not require belief in a transcendent Absolute in order to be able to take this point of view. Atheists and agnostics can perfectly well work for peace in the world. And many in fact do so. Indeed, if one believed that a world society was the goal toward which history inevitably moves, this belief might well encourage passivity, when what is required is effective action by human beings.

When, however, I talk about the goal of history, I am talking about something which has no place in a godless universe. I have, I think, made it clear that I regard man as orientated to the Transcendent, to a participation in the life of the infinite Spirit. But I have also made it clear that I am alive to the social nature of man. And the society which I have in mind as the goal of history is the society of persons united in and through their common participation in the life of infinite Spirit, of God. Further, when I speak of an all-embracing society, I am not thinking of a society which embraces the people who happen to be living at a certain date, to the exclusion of past generations. I am thinking of a society which is capable of embracing all human beings in and through him in whom we live and move and have our being.

Obviously this society of which I am speaking is not realized within history as we know it. It is realized 'eschatologically'. But I see no reason why it should not be realized through the transformation of this world and of history through the clearer self-manifestation of the Transcendent. And in this case we can perfectly well speak of the society in question as 'the goal of history'. Within the world as we know it we have to act in accordance with the values which we recognize. And we have to strive after the creation of a truly human society. The transformation of this society into something greater and permanent will be the work of God himself.

Much of what I have been saying gives rise to difficulties and objections which I have perforce to leave undeveloped and unanswered.[13] Further, I am well aware that I have been sketching a world vision in a thoroughly dogmatic manner. My aim, however, was not that of attempting to prove the truth of a certain world vision but rather to show, even if very inadequately, that belief in a transcendent Absolute can be relevant to our view of the world and of history. It is sometimes said that the believer and the nonbeliever have the same expectations in regard to events in the world, and that consequently it makes no difference whether one believes or not. The first statement obviously contains some truth. After all, two people do not have different expectations about, for example, the coming of spring or of autumn simply because one belives in God while the other does not. Nor do they have different expectations, at least for the reason mentioned, about what would happen if hydrogen bombs were dropped on a large city. At the same time their interpretations of the world are different. And this fact can produce a difference in expectation. If we see in history (the history of the physical world and of man) a progressive manifestation of a transcendent Absolute, we may be lead to expect a further manifestation of God in the future, in a transformed world and a transfigured society. In a godless world one can presumably expect that the comparatively brief episode of human history will be succeeded once more by the silence of the mindless universe.

Notes

[1] *Concluding Unscientific Postscript,*trans. D. F. Swenson & W. Lowrie (Princeton, 1969), p. 182.

[2] *Ibid.*

[3] *The Blue and Brown Books,* (London, 1973), p. 18.

[4] I use the word, 'comprehending', not in the sense of understanding or knowing but in the sense of an all-inclusive grounding.

[5] In *"My Mental Development"*, *The Philosophy of Bertrand Russell,* ed. P. A. Schilpp (New York, 1963), p. 20.

[6] *Ibid.,* p. 726.

[7] *Essays of a Humanist,* (London 1964), p. 107.

[8] *Situations,*Vol I, (Paris, 1947), p. 153.

[9] John 14. 9.

[10] *Enneads,* 6, 9, 11.

[11] I must excuse myself from entering into speculations about Martians and suchlike beings.

[12] *De legibus,* 3, 2, 4.

[13] I do not mean to imply that, given time, I could provide some adequate answers to all questions and objections which might be raised. For example, the relation between divine and human activity has provided a perennial problem for theologians and metaphysicians; and I do not think that I could add anything of value to what others have already said on this subject.

CHAPTER 6

CHRISTIANITY WITHOUT BELIEF IN GOD

THE SUBTITLE of Mr Alistair Kee's *The Way of Transcendence*[1] is 'Christian Faith without Belief in God'. This subtitle expresses the theme of this paper. Christianity is obviously not the only religion in the world. And any reasons which would justify the elimination of belief in God from the Christian religion are likely to be relevant to Judaism and Islam. As however Christianity is the only religion about which I can speak from an internal point of view, I omit consideration of other faiths.

2

On the face of it the idea of Christianity without belief in God is absurd. Jesus of Nazareth may have been, as professor Van Buren put it[2], 'the man for others'. But he was also, and indeed primarily, 'the man for the Father' — to judge at any rate by the Gospels. And I do not see that we have anything else to go by, except some more or less arbitrary reconstruction in terms of one's own preconceived notions. As for St Paul, he obviously expounds a theocentric view of the world. Again, the Creeds express an act of faith in the God who has created the world and revealed himself in Christ, who has done and will do certain things. The world of the Christian, that is to say, is a world which is existentially dependent on God and which moves, in and through human history, to an end foreordained by God. In the words of the Apocalypse, God is Alpha and Omega.

In fine, belief in God seems, to our ordinary way of thinking, to be so basic in the Christian vision of reality that, if it were eliminated, the residue could not be appropriately described as Christianity. This would, I think, be the verdict normally given not only by most Christians but also by most non-Christians, including agnostics and atheists. Indeed, it might perhaps be argued that to eliminate belief in God from the Christian religion and then to continue using the word 'Christianity' to describe the residue would be comparable to the procedure of eliminating from a political system every element of popular control of government and then describing the result as 'democracy' or, more probably, 'true democracy' or 'real democracy'.

3

Those writers however who propose a Christianity without God are perfectly well aware that their proposal is not in accordance with Christian tradition. To put the matter linguistically, they are well aware that the meaning which they propose to give to the word 'Christianity' is not in agreement with ordinary linguistic usage or practice, with the way in which the word is ordinarily understood. What they are proposing is a revision or reform of language. Moreover, they do not attempt to conceal the change. It would thus be unfair to put them on a par with propagandists who try to commend a blatantly authoritarian régime by calling it 'true democracy'.

Ordinary language is not of course sacrosanct or irreformable. But if one proposes a change, one should be prepared to offer a reason or reasons for the change. The proponents of Christianity without God offer such reasons. And it seems to me that they can be summed up in this way. The proposal to eliminate belief in God is based, in part at least, on an empirical judgement, a judgement of fact. The proposal to call the residue 'Christianity' is based mainly on a judgement of value.

Perhaps I ought to amplify somewhat what I have just said; but I do not wish to spend much time on elaborating reasons which may very well be familiar to us all.

<h3 style="text-align:center">4</h3>

First the elimination of belief in God. It is sometimes said that modern man finds himself unable to believe in God, at any rate in a transcendent and personal God. The trouble with this statement is that it can be made true by definition, by so defining 'modern man' that it becomes analytically true that he finds himself unable to believe in God. But this is not of course what is intended. And a better version can be found, for example, in the publisher's blurb for Alistair Kee's *The Way of Transcendence*, where it is stated that 'for more and more people belief in God has become impossible'. The word 'impossible' may create some difficulty. But if it is meant that there is an increasing number of persons who are prepared to claim that they cannot believe in God, this is an empirical statement which can be tested by the use of polls or questionnaires.

For the moment at any rate I am not concerned with the truth of the statement, but simply with pointing out that it is empirically testable. Generally speaking, the contention is, I take it, not that belief in God is logically impossible, but rather that for an increasing number of people belief in the existence of God is becoming impossible in a sense analogous to that in which it has become impossible for most people to believe that there are elves in the woods. It is not a case of one's being able to demonstrate the non-existence of elves in an *a priori* manner. Rather is it a case of one's seeing no good reason for accepting the hypothesis that they do exist. The events which might be explained in terms of the activity of elves can be explained in other ways. Analogously, it is argued, in view of what seems to be the massive silence and the conspicuous inactivity of the alleged divine being, and in view of the fact that events which were once explained in terms of divine activity are now explained in other ways, belief in God has become a superfluous hypothesis.

Some philosophers have indeed maintained that the concept of God is contradictory or so basically incoherent that the question of God's existence is not a meaningful question. This thesis would of course provide an answer to the objection that even if particular events within the world (earthquakes, for example) can be explained without recourse to the idea of God, the existence of finite being as such is not susceptible of an empirical explanation, in terms of natural science. Some philosophers apart however, the main reason why people find it extremely difficult to believe in God is that there seems to be no good reason for doing so. A God who gives no signs of life, so to speak, is in any case irrelevant.

There is indeed another line of thought, namely that belief in God is an expression of man's self-alienation or self-estrangement or, as it would be more commonly put outside Marxist circles, an obstacle to human development, to man's growth, for example, in ethical maturity and to his assumption of responsibility in regard to his future and the moulding of history and society. And it is clear that this line of thought prompts a rather different attitude from that stimulated by the superfluous-hypothesis idea. If belief in God is simply and solely a superfluous hypothesis, like belief in elves, it does not matter much if some people continue to accept it, provided that they are otherwise sane citizens. But if belief in God is also an obstacle to human development, one will naturally desire its disappearance. One will try to ensure, for example, that children are not religiously indoctrinated in schools maintained at the taxpayer's expense. At the same time it is unlikely that many people would think it sensible to adopt an attitude of denial to a God in whose existence they believed, an attitude resembling that of Orestes in Sartre's play *The Flies*. In practice therefore the obstacle line of thought presupposes and constitutes an addition to the superfluous-hypothesis idea. This is clear enough, I think, in the case of Karl Marx, who derived the superfluous-hypothesis idea from French anti-clerical socialism and positivism, while adding to it the alienation idea, derived from Hegel and Feuerbach and interpreted in his own way.

5

What I have just been saying does not do justice to the differences in approach which one can find in the writers who propose the idea of Christianity without God. And I wish to mention two of these approaches. In this way I hope to make clear what I meant by saying that the policy of continuing to use the word 'Christianity' when belief in God has been eliminated rests on or expresses a judgement of value.

In the first place consider the man who finds himself unable to believe any longer in a transcendent and personal God but who remains convinced that there is something of great importance and value in Christianity, namely the vision of a way of life which transcends egoism and the narrow bounds of self and self-interest and tends to unite human beings in the personal relationship of love. As he wishes to remain a Christian, he relegates belief in God to a mythological superstructure which has become outmoded and untenable and represents Christianity as being essentially a way of life without commitment to belief in a supernatural reality. Having reason to suppose that there are other Christians in a similar situation, he writes a book to advocate his interpretation of the Christian religion.[3]

In the second place consider a man who makes the same value-judgement about what is essential and of permanent value in Christianity. He is not however prepared to say that he does not himself believe in a transcendent divine reality. Nor does he aim at turning Christians into atheists. At the same time he is convinced that the Christian religion cannot remain as a living option for modern man if belief in God is required as a prior condition for being a Christian, or indeed as a condition for being a Christian at all. He therefore advocates the idea of Christianity without belief in God; but he leaves open the way for a rediscovery of a transcendent reality from within the experience of the Christian life. This seems to be more or less the approach of Alistair Kee in *The Way of Transcendence,* though I must confess that I am not at all confident that I have understood him correctly.[4]

6

At this point I should perhaps express my own opinion about the propriety of eliminating belief in God from the Christian religion and then describing what is left as Christianity. I am not of course talking about attempts to re-think the concept of God, such as that of Dr John A.T. Robinson. I am talking about the elimination of belief in God, which is a different matter.

It is hardly necessary to say that the advocates of Christianity without belief in God are alive to the need for differentiating between their version or versions of the Christian religion and secular humanism. For if there is no difference at all, it seems preferable to claim frankly that Christianity has fulfilled its mission and that what is of value in it has passed into secular humanism. This would be much more conducive to clarity than attempting to pass off secular humanism as Christianity.

One way of making a distinction is to say that Christians associate certain values and ideals with the thought of Jesus of Nazareth. But is the connexion supposed to be contingent or in some sense necessary? If what is meant is simply that Christians happen to associate certain values and ideals with Jesus of Nazareth as portrayed in the Gospels, whereas other people can maintain the same values and ideals either without associating them with any historical or fictional person or associating them with a figure other than Jesus of Nazareth, I fail to see any adequate reason for continuing to use the words 'Christian' and 'Christianity'. For there seems to be nothing to prevent a secular humanist associating his ideals with Jesus of Nazareth and continuing to call himself a secular humanist. If however it is meant that man *cannot* lead a certain kind of life except through personal self-commitment to Jesus of Nazareth and through his power, I can indeed see a reason for continuing to speak of Christianity. But it seems to me that this position cannot be maintained without the introduction of belief in the risen and operative Christ. And once we arrive at this point, we shall have God back again before we know where we are.

Let me make my position quite clear. I am not talking about attempts to re-think our image or picture of God. I am talking about the total elimination from the Christian religion of any belief in a divine reality which transcends, or cannot be identified with, either our material environment or with man himself. Some people seem to assume that this elimination can be achieved without any essential change in the Christian way of life. But this assumption seems to me highly questionable. Eliminate the indwelling and uniting divine Spirit, and the residue seems to me to be a purely ethical ideal which could be embraced by a secular humanist. In this case it is, I suggest, more conducive to clarity if the phrase 'Christianity without God' is abandoned, and if it is frankly claimed that Christianity has given birth to secular humanism and has found its fulfilment therein.

7

It may be objected, and indeed justifiably, that the real question at issue has not been discussed. After all, an atheist could perfectly well agree with practically all that I have said hitherto. The important question, it may well be urged, is not whether 'Christianity without God' can be appropriately described as Christianity, but whether man can continue to believe in a transcendent and personal God. Let us admit that the Christian religion involves belief in God. If such belief is rapidly becoming impossible, it follows that Christianity is ceasing to be a living option.

The question, as I have put it, really stands in need of analysis. It needs to be made much more precise and perhaps broken up into a number of questions. But I do not wish to spend time on trying to show the complexity of a question which doubtless appears simple enough to a good many people. For this procedure might easily be interpreted as equivalent to evasion of a real issue. I must content myself with making some remarks which seem to me relevant. They are made of course from the point of view of a believer.

8

In the first place I do not think that the policy of producing a ready-made concept of God and then trying to prove that the concept is instantiated is a promising policy. I may once have thought this. But I think so no longer. The existence of God was once a premiss, in the sense that belief in God belonged to the framework of thought and belief which was common to the society of the time.[5] To put the matter in another way, talk about God was part of the common language of a culture; and to participate in the culture involved initiation into talk about God. This is hardly the case today. Talk about God is a realm of discourse which cannot be taken for granted. For some people at any rate, it is, so to speak, a foreign language, an alien tongue. And if the concept of God has once come to be regarded as a superfluous hypothesis or as a projection characteristic of a past culture, the only way in which it can recover reality and relevance is through a man's personal rediscovery of God as a reality, by belief in God issuing from his own experience of his world. He is unlikely to be impressed by ingenious arguments designed to show that in addition to the recognized furniture of the universe there is an additional being called God. At any rate such arguments can have little meaning for him except in so far as they draw attention to what he himself recognizes as validated in his own experience.

In a recent work Dr John A.T. Robinson says that he is 'still convinced that the reality of God, however conceived, is an *implication* of "the way of transcendence" '.[6] Questions might be asked about use of the word 'implication' in this passage. But I find myself in full agreement with what I take to be Dr. Robinson's main contention, namely that it is in the human spirit's movement of transcendence that God becomes a reality or that awareness arises of the reality to which the word 'God' can be applied. For example, awareness of things as grounded in an ultimate reality can arise in confrontation with what Karl Jaspers describes as limit-situations. Again, the human spirit can become reflectively aware of a transcendent goal of its search for ultimate intelligibility, a goal which is not itself a direct object of perception (or of introspection) but which manifests itself in its attracting power, through final causality. Or a man may see in the constraining nature of basic judgments of value or moral convictions, in their overriding claims on his will, the manifestation of an Absolute.

What I am suggesting is this. There can be in the human spirit a movement of transcendence which can take various forms. This movement effects entry into a dimension of experience in which the idea of divine reality makes sense. That is to say, it is the complement of the movement of the finite spirit. I do not claim that this sort of experience necessarily leads a man to use the *word* 'God'. He may not do so. But I doubt whether this is a matter of primary importance. Nor do I claim that these types of experience necessarily lead a man to assert the existence of a transcendent reality, whether he uses the word 'God' or not. All that I claim is that there can be in the human spirit an opening, as it were, to the Transcendent. At this point a man is faced with what is, from the empirical point of view, an option, the option, that is to say, between affirming or denying the reality of the Transcendent.[7]

It may be said that I am begging the whole question, by assuming, that is to say, that what has been described as the religious *a priori* is present in modern man, when this is precisely the point at issue. I can only say in reply that I see no good reason for asserting its absence or disappearance. To be sure, there are plenty of people who feel unable to accept what they regard as the traditional and paradigm concept of God. But that modern man is closed altogether to the Transcendent seems to me a gratuitous assumption. Even in the most unpromising surroundings, in a society, for example, where atheism is officially taught and in which the young are indoctrinated with the view that religion is a thing of the past, not only outmoded but also socially harmful, an interest in religious problems, manifesting what I describe as the movement of transcendence, tends to reassert itself. Even in the modern world there are those for whom secular humanism is inadequate. They may not look to the Churches, but it does not follow that they are not open to God.[8]

9

A good many Christians would probably be inclined to object that I seem to conceive of God as the Absolute or as 'the Comprehensive' of Karl Jaspers, and that this sort of concept is far removed from Christian belief in the loving Father who has revealed himself in Jesus Christ. Do I perhaps advocate substituting the indeterminate concept of 'the Transcendent' for the personal God of the Christian religion?

The answer to this question is 'no'. Perhaps I had better explain that though I am certainly not one of those philosophers who try to exclude metaphysics,[9] I doubt whether metaphysical reflection can do much more than open up the way to the Transcendent as an horizon. I do not indeed agree with those theologians who appear to think that every idea of God which falls short of the determinate Christian concept is an idol. But I am of course aware that Christians think of God in terms of the analogy of a loving Father. And I take it that self-commitment to Christ involves commitment to thinking of God in the way in which Christ taught his disciples to think of God. Further, I think that the analogy of a loving Father is of great importance and value from a pragmatic point of view, namely as stimulating attitudes and conduct.

It by no means follows however that Christianity can be presented as a living option or as meriting serious consideration by taking the Christian concept of God in isolation and starting with it. To put the matter rather crudely, the statement that there is a heavenly Father 'up there' who is lovingly concerned with us all is likely to appear to a good many people as frankly incredible. If a man is dissatisfied with, say, secular humanism or Marxism and is looking for a religious vision of the world, it seems to me that the Christian apologist is best advised to start with the world, with man's situation in it, with his ideals and so on, and to develop what might be described (to borrow a word from Alisair Kee) as an escalating religious vision of the universe which reveals itself as theocentric, in the sense that God is seen as immanent and operative in the world, though not identified with it.[10] This is, I think, the sort of approach pursued by Teilhard de Chardin. He was indeed a deeply religious man, whose personal devotion to God as revealed as Christ gave him the power to put up with the disappointments and restrictions to which he was subjected. But when developing his vision of the universe he started not with God but with the world and man. And while he has little to say about God in himself, he says much of Christ and of the divine presence and operation in the world. It can of course be objected against his thought that it is a mixture of science, impressionistic metaphysics, poetry and theology. It can also be objected that the evil and suffering in the world and the possibility of disaster are passed over far too lightly. The fact remains however that his approach to a religious vision of reality was capable of impressing a humanist such as Sir Julian Huxley, even if Huxley found that he could not follow Teilhard beyond a certain point, and that it has impressed even some Marxists.

In other words, I have considerable sympathy with Mr Alistair Kee's idea of the appropriate procedure, though I would not be prepared to stop where he appears to stop. For what he calls an 'escalating' faith to be Christian faith, it must, in my opinion, become a theocentric faith. On the practical level Christians have to work with non-Christians in the endeavour to realize common ideals in this world. But it does not follow that the Christian should conceal his vision of reality, nor that he should eviscerate it in such a way that it is no different from the vision of a secular humanist who has similar ethical ideals. If a Christian really believes that God is dead, it would be more conducive to clarity, in my opinion, if he ceased describing himself as a Christian.[11]

10

A philosopher such as Professor Antony Flew would probably comment that I persist in evading the real point at issue. This is not the question how the Christian religion can best be commended or made to seem plausible to man today. It is the question whether or not there is any evidence for the claim that there is a God. And before this matter can be profitably discussed, it has to be shown that the idea of God is not self-contradictory or so intrinsically incoherent that we do not know what we are talking about when we ask whether there is a God. For if the idea of God is riddled with contradictions or antinomies, there is no point in discussing God's existence. We might as well ask whether there is a round square.

From one point of view philosophers who argue in this way are in a strong position. Dr Alec Vidler has remarked that 'any definintion of God that purported to be at all adequate would be an idol of the mind'.[12] Some theologians, such as Aquinas, have said roundly that we know of God what he is not rather than what he is.[13] And it is not surprising that an atheist philosopher should have said to me recently that he was unable to obtain from believers nowadays a clear account of what they meant by God. Some of them, for example, reject the concept of God as personal being 'out there', as this seems to be incompatible with the divine infinity and immanence. At the same time they are not disciples of Feuerbach. They do not wish to transform all talk about God into talk about man. Hence we are left wondering what precisely is meant by the word 'God'. What, for instance, can it mean to say that God is not a personal being 'out there' but that the divine reality, 'ultimate reality', is to be conceived as personal and as love?

Though however these philosophers may appear to be adopting an impregnable line of approach, in conformity both with common sense and with the demands of logical reasoning, I do not think that it is the right approach, in relation to the subject-matter, that is to say. I do not think that it can be justifiably demanded of the human mind that it should be able to pin down God like a butterfly in a showcase. As I have already indicated, my own conviction is that, in a general way, God becomes a reality for the human mind in the personal movement of transcendence. In this movement God appears as the unseen goal of the movement. And inasmuch as the Transcendent cannot be grasped in itself and overflows, so to speak, our conceptual web, doubt inevitably tends to arise. But, within the movement of transcendence, doubt is at once counterbalanced by the affirmation involved in the movement itself. It is within the context of this personal movement of the human spirit that God becomes a reality for a man.

Obviously, we cannot remain there, unless we are prepared to prescind from any definite religion. For the Christian the Transcendent is of course determined by means of certain concepts and analogies which belong to the Christian faith. For the Christian Christ himself is, as Bishop Robinson has put it, the 'window' into God. Self-commitment to the Christian religion is self-commitment to Christ as the revelation of God in human terms. Elucidation of the meaning of the terms employed is a task of Christian reflection, of Christian theology that is to say. The statement, for example, that God is a loving Father cannot be treated as an empirical hypothesis in the sense in which Professor Flew tries to take it.[14] It has to be understood in the context of Christian theology. And this process of understanding is, to my mind, an ongoing process. I see no good reason to suppose that the achievement of a perfectly adequate and tidy conceptual synthesis can be achieved by the finite mind. The concept of a loving Father is clearly scriptural, and it is of obvious importance in governing attitudes and conducts. But it needs to be balanced by the equally scriptural concept of God as he in whom we live and move and have our being, and who operates, for example, in man's striving to construct a better society, aspects of or elements in the Christian concept of God which are emphasized by Dr John A.T. Robinson. It is natural enough that the human mind should try to harmonize all the elements involved. But it seems to me to belong to the nature of an analogical knowledge of God that this goal cannot be achieved in such a way that we can say, 'now we know at last precisely what God is and can convey a perfectly clear and distinct idea of his essence'.

Regrettably but inevitably many threads have been left hanging loose. By way of conclusion I wish to try to obviate two possible misunderstandings. In the first place my references to the movement of transcendence may have given the impression that I was thinking simply of a mystical approach, an entry into 'the cloud of unknowing'. Though however I do not exclude this, it is not all that I mean. Suppose that a contemporary Christian writer develops a Christian vision of human life and history, emphasizing the social and political implications of Christian faith. And suppose that with a given reader this vision 'clicks', so that he comes to see the world in a new light, as manifesting in some way the divine creative action. I would regard this as an example of the movement of transcendence, of the opening of the human spirit to the God who is not an object among other objects but who energizes, so to speak, in all objects. If the creative God is eliminated, the resulting interpretation of the world is no longer Christian.

In the second place I may have given the impression that I look on Christianity as a static religious system which must either be transmitted unchanged or disappear altogether. This is not in fact my thesis. If Christianity came into existence as an influx of life (the life of 'the spirit'), the forms of expression of this life are likely to change or develop in the ongoing process of the dialectic between man and his environment and between man and man. What I have been concerned with maintaining is not that Christianity as an objective phenomenon in the world must remain unchanged but that a Christianity from which all belief in and contact with the all-penetrating God has been eliminated would no longer be the Christian religion but something else. In other words, I do not accept the notion of 'Christianity without God', unless perhaps one means by 'God' a certain image or 'deciphering' or God.

In the third and last place I have no doubt that the approach to belief in God to which I alluded above will seem to some a thoroughly 'subjective' approach, a matter of psychology rather than of proof. I do not see however how there can be any approach to God as a reality which is not 'subjective', in the sense of a movement of the human subject towards a goal. For God to be a reality, the approach must be religious. And I happen to think that a religious approach can be exemplified in ways of thought which are sometimes described as metaphysical. Some theologians may disapprove; but their disapproval leaves me unrepentant. I do not believe however that metaphysics can capture God in a conceptual web. I suppose that I have a natural sympathy with Paul Tillich's idea of the movement from 'God' to *God*. But it remains a movement. The Christian believes of course that there is a movement the other way, the movement of what he calls 'revelation'. This movement however must be expressed in human language. Hence the need for being alive to the changing relevance of language.

Notes

[1] (Harmondsworth, 1971)

[2] *The Secular Meaning of the Gospel*, (London, 1963).

[3] This is, I think, the approach of Professor Paul Van Buren in *The Secular Meaning of the Gospel*, a work which shows the influence of logical empiricism or logical positivism on the author's mind at the time of writing.

[4] Alistair Kee insists that he is not trying to reintroduce God by the backdoor. And he finds fault with Bishop John Robinson for trying to change our image of God, while retaining belief in God. At the same time Mr Kee insists that his version of Christianity is not reductionist, and that he conceives an 'escalating' theology which can take in, so to speak, the mystery which used to be conceived as 'God'.

[5] Obviously, I do not mean to imply that belief in God, or profession of belief, was necessarily effective, in the sense of having the social effects which we may think it ought to have.

[6] *The Difference in Being a Christian Today* (London, 1972), p. 47. Dr. Robinson is referring to Alistair Kee's book, *The Way of Transcendence*.

[7] 'From the empirical point of view', because I am prescinding from any theological doctrine about 'divine grace'.

[8] A classic but perhaps by now rather hackneyed illustration of the sort of thing I have in mind is provided by Dumitriu's impressive novel *Incognito* (London, 1964).

[9] I say 'try to exclude', as I do not believe that they are successful, not at any rate unless metaphysics is understood in a very narrow or restricted sense.

[10] In an essay on pantheism (in *Parerga and Paralipomena*) Schopenhauer remarked that to say that the world is God is to say no more than that the world is the world. In other words, one gives a superfluous label to the world.

[11] I am assuming of course that he believes that there is no God. If the death of God is understood as referring simply to lack of human receptivity to the idea of God at a certain stage in cultural development, this is a different matter.

[12] *Objections to Christian Belief* (London, 1963), p.17.

[13] Aquinas also remarks that we could not deny *x* of *y*, unless we had some positive knowledge of *y*. Otherwise we would not know what we were talking about.

[14] In his essay "Theology and Falsification", reprinted in, for example, *New Essays in Philosophical Theology* (London, 1955).

CHAPTER 7

THE LOGICAL EMPIRICISM
OF NICHOLAS OF AUTRECOURT

NICHOLAS OF AUTRECOURT lectured in the University of Paris during the first half of the fourteenth century. In 1346 he had to recant a number of propositions and was dismissed from the teaching staff. Of his later life we know only that he obtained a post at the cathedral of Metz in 1350. In view of the differences in cultural background the label 'logical empiricist' may be judged to be anachronistic. But it serves to draw attention to certain features of his thought as revealed by the regrettably limited evidence available to us.

1

In the case of some leading mediaeval thinkers, such as Aquinas, one may on occasion be left wondering what logical status they intend to attribute to particular arguments. It is not a matter of their being unaware of the distinctions made by Aristotle and his successors. Rather is it a matter of their failing to make it clear whether they regard a particular argument as satisfying the requirements for a demonstrative proof as stated, for example in the *Posterior Analytics*, or whether they regard it as one which would be called, in the terminology of the time, a dialectical or probable argument, as based, that is to say, on premises which are not self-evidently true but which are commonly accepted or accepted by those competent to judge in the relevant field.

In my opinion Aquinas's philosophical argument for the resurrection (*Summa contra Gentiles*, IV, 79) provides an example. I am not concerned here with the question whether or not human beings rise bodily, nor even with the merits or demerits of Aquinas's arguments to show that they do. I am concerned with the logical status which Aquinas ascribes to a certain line of argument. It is described as an *evidens ratio*. Taken by itself this description suggests that the argument is regarded as a strict proof that the resurrection will take place. In this case the presuppositions of the argument (such as the existence of God and the spirituality and immortality of the soul) would presumably be regarded as demonstrated truths. The context however makes it clear that Aquinas is not in fact claiming that philosophy can prove that the resurrection will take place. He seems to be addressing himself to those who accept the doctrine of the resurrection on faith, but who are inclined to think that the belief is contrary to all that one might expect on the basis of what the philosopher is capable of proving. In this case we might be inclined to conclude that the argument is intended as a persuasive support to religious faith or as probable or dialectical reasoning. It seems to me however that the matter is left unclarified.

In the later Middle Ages there was a conspicuous tendency to press the idea of demonstrative argument as expounded in the *Posterior Analytics* and to insist that we can have 'scientific' knowledge only of propositions which are necessarily true and seen to be such and of propositions which can be logically deduced from self-evidently true propositions. Arguments advanced by previous thinkers were subjected to criticism in the light of this model of what constitutes a demonstrative proof. Indeed, the wedge which was driven in the fourteenth century between philosophy and theology was due in large measure to an insistence by the logicians on what was required for a strict proof. This was not of course the only reason. For example Ockham clearly thought that Christian faith had been contaminated by the inroads of Graeco-Islamic philosophy, expecially its necessitarianism. The more however the scope of the philosophically provable was restricted, the less possible did it become to regard philosophy as proving the so-called 'preambles' of faith.

Reference has been made above to propositions which are necessarily true and seen to be such, self-evidently true propositions that is to say. Aquinas held that the proposition 'God exists' is self-evidently or analytically true 'in itself', but not 'for us'. Duns Scotus later objected that a proposition is either analytic or not, and that the number of people who see that a given proposition is analytic is irrelevant from the logical point of view. I suppose that Ockham would have agreed. For in the *Summa totius logicae* (III, part I, ch. 1) he remarks that sometimes we feel as sure about the truth of probable propositions as we do about the truth of propositions which are seen to be necessarily true. Further, in his view there can be propositions which are necessarily true but which appear to many people to be false. (He is referring to certain articles of faith which must be necessarily true if they are true at all.) Ockham rather complicates matters however by defining a probable proposition as one which is in fact true and necessary but is not evidently such and cannot be proved to be such. It would seem to follow that we cannot know that any given proposition is probable. But perhaps this would not bother Ockham. For he states that though we can *believe* that a given syllogism is topical, we cannot *know* that this is the case, not at any rate by natural knowledge. In spite however of complications which were not infrequently introduced for theological reasons, it seems correct to say that the general tendency of the fourteenth-century logicians was to distinguish between the logical and psychological approaches.

2

According to Nicholas of Autrecourt the primary and ultimate logical principle is the principle of non-contradiction. And the only propositions which are certainly true and known to be such are those which are reducible, either immediately or mediately, to the ultimate principle. A proposition is immediately reducible if the predicate is contained in the concept of the subject. A proposition is mediately reducible if the conclusion of an argument is identical with part of the premiss or antecedent, provided of course that the premisses of a syllogism are themselves reducible, either immediately or mediately, to the principle of non-contradiction.

In his second letter to Bernard of Arezzo Nicholas draws the conclusion that certitude (*certitudo*) has no degrees.[1] There is only one kind of certitude. Nicholas does indeed make an exception for the 'certitude of faith', though whether from prudence or out of firm conviction we are hardly in a position to say. Apart however from the assent of faith there is for him only one kind of certitude, that relating to the principle of non-contradiction and to what is reducible to it. This amounts to saying, it seems to me, that the only propositions which give us 'scientific' knowledge are those which are necessarily true and are seen to be such, inasmuch as they cannot be denied without contradiction. In other words, it is only of analytic propositions that we know with certainty that they are true.

Nicholas points out that this applies to the whole of geometry. The mathematician who has deduced a conclusion from premisses which are themselves reducible to the principle of non-contradiction is not less certain of the truth of the conclusion than of that of the premisses. Nicholas does indeed remark that on account of the number of deductive operations the mathematician may not at first be as certain of remote conclusions as he is of the immediate conclusions. But he doubtless means simply that the mathematician may not be immediately sure that he has made no mistake in his process of inference. Once he has assured himself of this, he sees that the truth of the final conclusion is as certain as that of the first.

3

If we can be certain of the truth of a proposition only if it is reducible, immediately or mediately, to the principle of non-contradiction, it naturally follows that we cannot be certain of the truth of any proposition which is irreducible to the principle of non-contradiction. It would not do however to interpret 'be certain' or 'have certitude' as equivalent to 'feel certain'. For we might very well feel certain of the truth of a good many propositions which were irreducible to the principle of non-contradiction. Nicholas is clearly expounding a logical rather than psychological thesis. And in view of his explanation of what he means by reducibility to the principle of non-contradiction it is reasonable to interpret him as saying that it is only analytic propositions which are necessarily true. In this case we can conclude that for him non-analytic propositions are empirical hypotheses.

It would not however be accurate to say that according to Nicholas

we cannot have certain knowledge of the truth of any empirical statement, but only of purely formal propositions. For in his first letter to
Bernard of Arezzo he reminds Bernard that in the course of disputations
at the Sorbonne he has maintained that he was certain 'of the objects of
the five senses' (*Ibid.* p.6). What Nicholas means seems to be this. Suppose
that I see a white patch. The white patch appears to me, and I am aware
that it appears to me. If therefore to say that the white patch exists is
interpreted as meaning that the colour appears to me or is present as a
phenomenon. I am certain of its existence. To assert that I see a white patch
and to assert at the same time that it does not exist would involve me in
a self-contradiction. For it would be equivalent to saying both that the
white patch appears to me and that it does not appear to me.

The context of Nicholas's remarks on this matter seems to me to be
the sort of view defended by Ockham, namely that 'intuitive knowledge'
(*notitia intuitiva*) does not entail the existence of the object. Ockham
bases our knowledge of the world on an immediate apprehension of
individual things, which is naturally expressed in the judgement that x
exists, when x is the object of 'intuitive knowledge'. Ockham believes
however that, as far as possibility is concerned, God can produce directly
any effect which he normally produces through a secondary cause. If
therefore we think of object x as acting on a human sense-organ and
giving rise to the contingent proposition 'x exists', we have to allow that
the same effect could be produced directly by God even if there were no
x. In this case the judgement 'x exists' would be false. Hence 'intuitive
knowledge' does not entail the existence of its object. It can be objected
of course that as Ockham defines intuitive knowledge as knowledge of such
a kind that one can know by means of it whether a thing exists or not, he
has no business to suggest that God could produce in us intuitive knowledge
of a non-existent object. But he explains that in the case of a false existential
judgement, caused by God acting in the manner referred to, the judgement would be the expression of a belief, of a 'creditive act', rather than of
'evident knowledge'. In any case, if we prescind from Ockham's preoccupation with the divine omnipotence, we can say that for him judgements about the existence of the objects of sense-experience are
corrigible or revisible in principle.

Nicholas of Autrecourt however is not prepared to accept this thesis.
In his view there are basic empirical propositions which cannot be false.
This means of course that he has to represent them as reducible to the
principle of non-contradiction. And if my interpretation is correct, he
does so by equating the immediate objects of perception with
phenomena or sense-data. It is all very well for Ockham to claim that God
could cause in me, from the physiological and psychological points of view,
perception of a non-existent star. The fact of the matter is that if to say
that a star exists is to say that a star appears to me, it makes no difference to
the truth of the judgement (that the star exists) whether the appearance is

caused by a natural or a supernatural agent. In either case that which appears exists as a phenomenal object.

Another Paris lecturer, John of Mirecourt, held that there was one empirical judgement which could not be false, namely the judgement by which a man asserts his own existence. Nicholas of Autrecourt extends the number of propositions to which we can give 'evident assent' in the strict sense. Both thinkers however defend their views by arguing that the proposition or propositions in question cannot be denied without self-contradiction. For both men, that is to say, reducibility to the principle of non-contradiction is the test of certainty. I am inclined to think however that Nicholas's inclusion of propositions asserting the existence of the immediate objects of sense-experience in the class of propositions which are reducible to the principle of non-contradiction demands a sense-datum theory. He does not use this language of course. But he insists that if we restrict our judgements to the sphere of appearance, we cannot be mistaken. As far as I am aware, Nicholas does not raise the question to what extent, if any, incorrect use of a descriptive epithet, such as 'white' or 'green', would affect the issue. But I am inclined to think that Nicholas's phenomenal object, that which appears, is equivalent to what in later terminology has been known as a sense-datum. Or, rather, I am inclined to think it ought to be equivalent. As Nicholas professes to be refuting scepticism, it may well be the case that he has in mind physical objects rather than sense-data. But if this is what he has in mind, how does he propose to cope with Ockham's talk about direct action by God? Nicholas does not deny that God could act in the way in which Ockham (or Bernard of Arezzo) says that he could. Instead he argues that even if God causes a non-existent star to appear, the appearance exists.

4

Nicholas is of course taking it that in immediate apprehension of a direct object of sense-experience there is no inference from the existence of one thing to that of another. When he turns his attention to inference, he argues that if A and B are two distinct things, we cannot infer with certainty the existence of A from that of B or *vice versa*. His reason for saying this is, as one might expect, that no contradiction is involved if the existence of one thing is asserted and the existence of another thing denied. In other words, if A and B are distinct things, the existence of one does not entail the existence of the other.

Nicholas applies this thesis to the substance-accident ontology. Bernard of Arezzo argued against Nicholas that if we see, for instance, a colour, we can infer with certainty that there is a substance, inasmuch as colour, being an accident, cannot exist without a substance. Nicholas's reply amounts to saying that this argument is irrelevant. It is indeed true that if we assume that an accident must inhere in a substance and that colour is an accident in the sense defined, the existence of a colour entails the existence of a substance. But this would not show that we can infer with certainty the existence of one thing from that of another, when it is a case of two distinct things. For if an accident is defined as necessarily inhering in a substance, it cannot count as a distinct thing.

Nicholas's position in regard to inferring the existence of the soul from acts of understanding and will is not altogether clear. As in a ninth letter to Bernard of Arezzo he denied the possibility of inferring with certainty the existence of an intellect and a will from acts of understanding and willing, it seems unlikely that he thought that we could infer the existence of a soul. But there is a passage (*Beiträge*, p. 13) which suggests that he did think this. Moreover, he seems to have been so understood by his critics. We are therefore hardly in a position to assert with any real confidence that in regard to knowledge of the existence of the soul he anticipated the position of Hume. At the same time Nicholas certainly argues, in regard to material substance, that from the perceived existence of phenomena we cannot infer with certainty the existence of any noumenal or underlying substance, unless of course we beg the whole question by equating phenomena with accidents defined in such a way as to make it tautological to say that if there is, for instance, a colour there is a substance. It is however worth noting that Nicholas is concerned with delimiting the field of certain knowledge and of the provable rather than with making pronouncements about the nature of reality. It seems pretty clear that he does not intend to assert that *esse est percipi*. For in the treatise commonly known as *Exigit ordo executionis*[2] he suggests that in a perfect universe nothing would perish and adds that if something does not appear, we are not entitled to conclude that it no longer exists.

Nicholas's denial that from the existence of one thing we can infer with certainty the existence of another thing obviously has a bearing on causal inference. From his second letter to Bernard of Arezzo it is clear that Bernard had tried to give examples to show that there are cases in which we know with certainty that the occurrence of A will be followed by the occurrence of B. For instance, if fire is applied to tow and there is no obstacle or hindrance, heat will ensue. In reply Nicholas makes in effect a distinction between our natural expectations and what we know with certainty. If in our experience the occurrence of A has always been followed by the occurrence of B, it is probable that this sequence will be repeated in the future. That is to say, it is natural and reasonable to expect this. If however A and B are distinct things, there is no logical necessity for the occurrence of A to be followed by the occurrence of B. For no contradiction is involved if the existence of A is asserted and that of B denied.

Here again Nicholas is concerned with the limits of our certain knowledge rather than with analysis of the causal relation. If we consider simply what he says about the ground of our expectations and predictions, it is indeed natural to interpret him as implying that the causal relation can be described in terms of regular succession. One of the propositions however which he had to retract was that we do not know with certainty that there is any efficient cause other than God. And it is difficult to suppose that Nicholas thought of the divine causal activity as adequately describable in terms of regular sequence. For he conceived God as able to do anything which did not involve a logical contradiction and as being in no way bound or limited by what he normally does. It is however clear enough that for Nicholas no causal statement is logically necessary. And this would apply to statements about God's causal action.

5

When Nicholas says that we cannot know with certainty that there is any efficient cause other than God, it would be rash to conclude that he regards the existence of God as philosophically demonstrable. In my opinion he has no such conviction. Consider, for example, what he says about Aristotle's knowledge of the existence of metaphenomenal substances. In his second letter to Bernard of Arezzo he does indeed disclaim the view that Aristotle lacked even probable knowledge of the existence of substances, of 'abstract' substances in particular. But he then goes on to draw attention to a problem which he declares himself unable to solve. 'As it was evident to me in the past that when I put my hand to the fire I was warm, it is probable for me that I should be warm if I did the same again' (*Beiträge*, p.13). As however Aristotle never observed a regular sequence or any relation between phenomena and metaphenomenal substances, it is difficult to see how he could have had even probable knowledge of the existence of such substances. This is the problem which Nicholas finds himself unable to solve. And in this case he can hardly have thought that the philosopher was capable of proving the existence of God. On his premisses the Five Ways of Aquinas could certainly not be strict proofs of God's existence, yielding certain knowledge. Indeed, Nicholas seems to have maintained explicitly that we could not have certain knowledge that one thing is better or more perfect (more 'noble') than another, in an absolute sense that is to say. Nor that one thing is the final cause of another. In this case Aquinas's fourth and fifth Ways go overboard. And it seems to me that on Nicholas's premisses the others do too. Indeed, if we press what Nicholas regards as an unsolved problem, it is difficult to see how he can allow the possibility of even probable knowledge of God's existence.

It is true that when Nicholas insists that the only certainty is that of the principle of non-contradiction and of propositions reducible thereto, he makes an exception for 'the certainty of faith'. This is admitted by a certain Giles in a letter to Nicholas in which he comments on the latter's epistles to Bernard of Arezzo (*Beiträge*, p. 15). And it may well be the case that Nicholas shared Ockham's religious faith. From the psychological point of view at any rate a fideist attitude in the religious sphere can quite well co-exist with an extremely critical attitude in regard to the arguments of metaphysicians. While however Ockham's theological preoccupations are plain to any reader, the position of Nicholas of Autrecourt is less clear. The empiricist element in Ockham's thought was intimately related with his insistence on the divine omnipotence and freedom. But though Nicholas made remarks which indicated a similar attitude, he also produced a number of theories which aroused the indignant disapproval of the ecclesiastical authorities; and when he defended himself by saying that they were only probable hypotheses which should be rejected if they clashed with revealed truth, he was accused of making 'foxy excuses'. I dare say that the authorities were unjustified in attributing insincerity to Nicholas. I am inclined to think that they misunderstood his position or were too serious-minded or narrow in outlook to appreciate it. But whereas the sincerity of Ockham's religious faith is in my opinion indubitable, the attitude of Nicholas of Autrecourt is open to different interpretations.

6

At first sight it may seem perplexing that Nicholas should couple trenchant criticism of metaphysical arguments with what appears to be airy speculation about eternal atoms and what not. Though however it may be difficult to assess how seriously he intends his speculative theorizing to be taken, his main concern seems to me to have been what it always was, namely to exhibit the limits of what we can properly be said to know. In the first prologue to his treatise *Exigit ordo executionis* Nicholas refers sarcastically to people who go on studying Aristotle and Averroes up to a decrepit old age and who appear to think that problems can be solved by quoting conclusions drawn by Aristotle and endorsed by his Moslem commentator. He then tries to show that if one starts with assumptions commonly held by philosophers, one can develop equally or more persuasive arguments in support of conclusions which are different from those drawn by the Aristotelians. Suppose that we assume with some of the leading mediaeval worthies that it is better to be than not to be, and also that in the world final causality reigns, geared, as it were, to attaining what is best. On these assumptions it is reasonable to conclude that nothing ceases to be. And a theory of eternal atoms enables us to find a way of reconciling this thesis with the appearances.

What I am suggesting is that there is no need to regard Nicholas as a hopelessly inconsistent writer who first restricts the area of human knowledge in a drastic manner and then proceeds to pass off unverified speculative hypotheses, such as his theory of eternal recurrence, as the truth about reality. It seems to me that what he is doing in the *Exigit* is to argue that the conclusions drawn by the Aristotelians are by no means the only ones which can be drawn from their assumptions, but that quite different conclusions can be drawn equally well or better. In other words, his main concern is a polemical one. Only those premisses of the Aristotelians can be admitted as certainly true which are reducible to the principle of non-contradiction. But even if we pass over this point and are prepared to make questionable assumptions, we can still draw conclusions which are quite different from those drawn by the Aristotelians. Hence their conclusions do not represent even probable knowledge, when this refers to conclusions derived from commonly accepted but undemonstrated premisses.

7

If we understand by 'logical empiricism' neo-positivism, the description of Nicholas of Autrecourt as a logical empiricist is hardly justified. For he is concerned with the nature and extent of our certain knowledge, not with establishing and applying a criterion of meaning. He did not claim, for example, that Aristotle's talk about immaterial susbstances was non-sensical, though he certainly claimed that it did not express knowledge. At the same time Nicholas's use of his test for assessing certain knowledge clearly has implications which have led some writers to refer to him as the mediaeval Hume. And in a wide sense of the term it is not un-reasonable to describe his thought as logical empiricism, as this term serves to draw attention to the fact that the empiricist elements in his thought depend on his logical approach.

It would however be incorrect to represent Nicholas as dividing propositions neatly into two classes, analytic propositions which express 'relations of ideas' and are necessarily true, and synthetic propositions which express 'matters of fact' and are never necessarily true. For, as we have noted, he claims that we can be certain of the existence of the objects of the five senses and of introspection, and that the statements asserting the existence of such objects are reducible to the principle of non-contradiction. He thus claims that there can be incorrigible state-ments of fact. It is understandable that he makes this claim. For we can regard him as asking what it is possible to doubt. And he finds himself unable to doubt, for example, that when he feels pain the pain exists, and that if he sees a colour the colour exists. But if Nicholas asserts that he feels pain or that he sees a colour, the statement can obviously be false. For he may be lying. And in this case the statement that the pain exists or that the colour exists is false. To be sure, if I assert both that a colour appears to me and that it does not appear to me, I contradict my-self. And if to say that the colour exists is assumed to be equivalent to saying that the colour appears to me, I contradict myself if I assert both that the colour appears to me and that it does not exist. But this does not alter the fact that I might be lying when I assert that the colour appears to me, and that in this case the assertion that the colour exists is false.

These remarks may suggest that I am concerned with awarding good marks to Nicholas in so far as he approximates to Hume's distinction between propositions concerned with 'relations of ideas' and those concerned with 'matter of fact', and low marks when he fails to do so. I am not however really concerned with awarding marks. My interest in Nicholas of Autrecourt is primarily historical. I do not believe that there is any simple repetition in history. But the mediaeval mind, if one is permitted to use such a term, was not an exemplification of Lévy-Bruhl's questionable concept of primitive man's prelogical mentality. Nicholas is one of the philosophers who represent most clearly the phase of radical criticism in mediaeval thought, criticism, that is to say, of the claims of other thinkers to extend our knowledge of reality. And when such criticism is developed in a systematic way, it is natural that there should be discernible similarities between the approaches of philosophers living in different cultural situations. If Nicholas is sometimes described as the mediaeval Hume, this need not be a way of suggesting that the eighteenth-century philosopher's ideas were simply a repetition of what had already been said in the Middle Ages. It can be simply a way of drawing attention to a common preoccupation with assessing the limits of our knowledge and to certain similarities between the conclusions reached by the two men. There are of course differences. For example, for Hume the existence of physical objects distinct from our impressions is a matter of natural belief rather than something which can be demonstrated, whereas Nicholas seems to maintain that the existence of physical objects is demonstrable. Again, while Nicholas severely restricts the area of what can be said to be known with certainty by natural means, he allows for the 'certainty of faith', which Hume clearly does not do, not at any rate unless 'certainty' is interpreted in a purely psychological sense, as equivalent to feeling certain, that is to say. At the same time it is arguable that Nicholas can maintain that the existence of physical objects is demonstrable (*i.e.*, reducible to the principle of non-contradiction) only by reducing physical objects to phenomena or sense-data or, in Hume's terminology, impressions. And it is obviously questionable whether what he says about the certainty of faith is compatible with his general idea of what constitutes certain knowledge. He may be sincere; but, if so, is he not logically compelled to adopt a fideist position?

It hardly needs saying that if we restrict the area of certain knowledge to what is reducible to the principle of non-contradiction, we cannot be said to know very much with certainty. Nicholas is perfectly well aware of this and draws the conclusion (*Exigit*, pp. 181-2) that his colleagues should devote their attention to moral matters and to care for the common good rather than to what passes for knowledge but is really nothing of the kind. It can doubtless be objected that a very great part of what we commonly regard and refer to as knowledge is certainly not demonstrable through reduction to the principle of non-contradiction. But Nicholas lived before the development of the empirical sciences; and he lays emphasis on criticism of what he regards as pseudo-knowledge ('sophistry and illusion', to use Hume's phrase) and on delimiting the area of certainty. His attitude is rather inhibiting. It would hardly encourage the visionary aspects of philosophy. But there is doubtless always a place for the provocative questioner of established views. One is left wondering how Nicholas would have developed his ideas, if his academic career had not been cut short by the intervention of ecclesiastical authority. Or had he already said in substance all that he was capable of saying?

Notes

[1] *Beiträge zur Geschichte der Philosophie des Mittelalters,* Band VI, Heft 2, (Münster, 1908), p. 8.
[2] An edition of this treatise, made from the manuscript in the Bodleian, was published by J. R. O'Donnell in *Medieval Studies,* Vol I (1939), pp. 181-280.

CHAPTER 8

SPINOZA AS METAPHYSICIAN

THERE ARE OBVIOUSLY many branches of study which could not be described as metaphysics without contravention of ordinary linguistic usage. Nor is this restriction a matter of arbitrary choice. Reasons for it can be adduced. It is thus an exaggeration to say that there is no agreement at all about use of the word 'metaphysics'. At the same time it is also obvious that different views have been and still are expressed about the nature, method and value of metaphysics. Indeed, William of Ockham asserted that to ask what is *the* subject matter of metaphysics is like asking who is the king of all Christendom.[1] Both questions, that is to say, make a false presupposition. If however a philosopher undertakes to tell us what being 'really' is or to exhibit the nature of reality, we are probably all prepared to describe him as a metaphysician, provided at any rate that he tries to prove the truth of what he says by philosophical argument or reasoning which does not depend on premises which are claimed to have been revealed by God.

Whatever therefore may be our opinion about what metaphysics ought not to be, we can hardly deny that Spinoza counts as a metaphysician. He does not try to do the scientist's work for him. He is concerned with the nature of ultimate reality and with the metaphysical structure of the universe. And he certainly does not take his premises from revelation or theology. In his view Scripture and theology have the aim of promoting piety and obedience. In other words, they are concerned with fostering certain religious attitudes and with conduct. To try to find speculative truths in the Old Testament, as some medieval Jewish philosophers tried to do, is a mistake. It is philosophy which is concerned with the attainment of objective truth; and philosophy is based on self-evidently true premises.[2] Spinoza does not suggest that Scripture contradicts reason, even if he believes that theologians' interpretations of Scripture may do so. What he insists on is that it is not a source of speculative truth. It 'does not teach philosophy, but simply obedience.'[3] Philosophy therefore cannot rely on revelation or theology: it recognises no other criterion than the natural understanding.[4]

It is tempting to depict Spinoza as anticipating the theory of 'stories' proposed by Professor R. B. Braithwaite in his celebrated lecture 'An Empiricist's View of the Nature of Religious Belief'.[5] But Spinoza does not deny, for example, that the scriptural doctrine that there is but one God can be described as true or as possessing truth-value. He insists however that it pertains to philosophy to decide what 'God' means, to exhibit, that is to say, the nature of the divine reality. And in doing this the philosopher does not take Scriptural doctrine as a premiss but works quite independently.

It must be admitted that if we look at the definitions given at the beginning of the *Ethics,* the wording certainly suggests that they express simply the ways in which Spinoza chooses to understand certain terms. For he says explicitly that by cause of itself, substance, attribute, mode, God and eternity 'I understand' this or that. While however it is obviously open to us to claim, if we wish, that the definitions are in fact nothing but stipulative definitions, it by no means follows that Spinoza himself understands them in this way. On the contrary, he regards his definitions as expressing clear and distinct ideas and therefore as true.[6] And he regards the logical deduction of propositions from definitions which express clear and distinct ideas and from self-evident axioms as a method which, considered in itself, cannot lead to erroneous conclusions. Further, as 'the order and connexion of ideas is the same as the order and connexion of things,'[7] logical deduction of conclusions from the appropriate sets of definitions and axioms provides us with knowledge of reality. Spinoza does not claim that the existence of modes, in the sense of particular finite things, can be deduced *a priori* from the concepts of attributes or of infinite modes. On the contrary, he asserts more than once that this cannot be done. His universe is indeed deterministic throughout. And the usual statement that he 'assimilated' the causal relation to that of logical implication is justified. Though however he speaks of things as 'following' from the nature of God, he explicitly denies that the existence of particular finite modes can be deduced *a priori.*[8] At the same time Spinoza is convinced that logical deduction from the appropriate set of premisses leads to conclusions which are valid not only in the order of ideas but also in regard to the order of nature. Even if particular modes cannot be deduced *a priori,* the metaphysical structure of reality can be deduced. We then have certain metaphysical knowledge. And it is this knowledge of reality which philosophy looks for.

2

If one says that for Spinoza philosophy is concerned with demonstrable truths and that the philosopher is seeking for certain knowledge of reality (of *Deus seu Natura*), the statement may be challenged. Surely, it may be said, we have only to look at the opening paragraphs of the treatise on *The Improvement of the Understanding* to see that for Spinoza philosophy is the means of attaining man's true good or the supreme human perfection, which can be found only in love of the eternal and infinite. The quasi-mathematical structure of the *Ethics* gives a very misleading impression of Spinoza's basic motivation. Philosophy is for him a way of life or the framework for a way of life. This is shown by the title of his most famous work. It is primarily an ethical treatise.

It is indeed quite true that Spinoza looks on philosophy as an instrument whereby man can perfect himself and attain blessedness or what St Augustine and the medieval thinkers described as *beatitudo*. We have recalled that in the *Tractatus Theologico-Politicus* Spinoza emphasizes the relation between theology and religious attitudes and moral conduct and contrasts it with philosophy, which is concerned with speculative and demonstrable truth. Though however it is understandable that Spinoza does not wish to cause unnecessary offence either to his Jewish coreligionists or to Christian theologians and that he attributes a positive function to scriptural doctrine, it seems clear that in point of fact he substitutes philosophy for theology as a way of life for those who are capable of what he regards as genuine philosophical reflection. In the Middle Ages people did not ordinarily look to philosophy, in the sense in which it was distinguished from theology, as providing a way of life. They looked to the Christian faith for this purpose or, if they were Jews, to the Old Testament and to Jewish tradition. Some Jewish thinkers had indeed tried to find speculative truths expressed in Scripture in exoteric forms; but Spinoza, as we have noted, rejected this procedure. With him philosophy takes the place of theology as purveyor of a way of life and as enabling man to perfect himself, in the case, that is to say, of those who are capable of grasping adequate ideas. We can say therefore that in his concept of the role of philosophy in human life Spinoza has more affinity with the Greek philosophers than with the medieval theologians who conceived *beatitudo* as a supernatural end or goal, the attainment of which presupposed Christian faith and divine grace.[9]

Recognition however of the facts that Spinoza is motivated by desire for the eternal and infinite and that philosophy is for him a way of life or provides the framework for a way of life is by no means incompatible with the claim that in his view philosophy is concerned with the attainment of truth and that this truth is attained through adequate understanding of the order of nature. He certainly lays great emphasis on ethics and on liberation from the slavery of the passions. But it is obvious that in his view man's highest perfection is to be found at the highest level of knowledge. He speaks indeed of the intellectual love of God; but it is the *intellectual* love of God to which he refers. Man is perfected insofar as he has adequate ideas and insofar as his conduct is ruled by such ideas. We can indeed say that for Spinoza the goal of the human mind is the intuitive vision of all things in God. But of intuitive knowledge he says explicitly that 'this kind of knowing proceeds from an adequate idea of the formal essence of certain attributes of God to the adequate knowledge of the essence of things'[10] Knowledge of God involves an understanding of the divine nature and of God's self-expression in the world. And an adequate understanding of God as immanent cause of all things involves a process of deductive reasoning.

Some writers have regarded Spinoza as a mystic. For example,

Bertrand Russell seems to class Spinoza with the mystics on the ground that his theory of sin as existing only from the human point of view and not in relation to reality as a whole is a mystical doctrine.[11] This way of speaking may pass muster if the term 'mysticism' is used in a wide sense, so as to cover the thought of all those who write in such a way as to imply that God is the one reality.[12] At the same time it seems to the present writer that however un-Aristotelian Spinoza may be in some respects, he has more affinity with Aristotle's intellectualist view of human perfection than with Plotinus's sublime concept of 'the flight of the alone to the Alone.'[13] Even if Spinoza asserts that the mind's intellectual love for God is the love with which God loves himself,[14] knowledge of God does not seem to mean for him a state of ecstatic union in which the subject-object distinction is transcended. His ideal is doubtless that the mind should rise through the second degree or level of knowledge to grasp the whole intelligible system of nature in a comprehensive act of mental vision. But this is not quite the same thing as the exceptional mystical state which Plotinus is said (by Porphyry) to have attained on several occasions. There may be mystical overtones, so to speak, in Spinoza's thought. To describe him as a 'rationalist', given the customary modern use of the term, can be misleading. But it seems to me to be none the less apt. He desires indeed the elevation of the reason to the highest level attainable; but though argument can be adduced in support of a different view, I doubt very much whether he envisages a transcending of rational knowledge in some estatic union with the One. The highest virtue of the mind is to know God.[15] But it does not necessarily follow that 'knowledge' has to be understood in the sense of ecstasy or rapture.

3

Even if, it may be said, Spinoza's philosophy is not geared to the attainment of mystical states such as we find mentioned by writers such as St John of the Cross, it is still a mistake to emphasize his idea of arriving at truth about the universe by a deductive or quasi-mathematical process of reasoning. For the more we emphasize this aspect of Spinoza's thought, the more do we tend to obscure the fact that the whole process of reasoning presupposes a personal vision of the universe. After all, we can hardly imagine that Spinoza reached his general vision of the universe simply as the result of a quasi-mathematical process of deduction. The vision clearly preceded the construction of the system. Indeed, it is presupposed by the very premises of the deductive process. The great metaphysicians have had an intuitive understanding of possible ways of seeing the universe or reality. Such visions are presupposed by the apparatus of argument and proof, the arguments being persuasive devices or instruments to commend the initial visions. Provided that we do not mean by 'visionary' an unbalanced person or one whose ideas are so patently at variance with the facts that they have to be discounted without more ado, we can describe Spinoza as one of the great visionaries in the history of philosophical thought. It is important to bring out and emphasize this basic element of vision. The deductive process of reasoning is of secondary importance, even if it is not an unfortunate excrescence. To lay emphasis on the 'rationalism' of Spinoza and on his employment of a mathematical model of reasoning is to misrepresent him. Indeed, it exhibits a misunderstanding of the real nature of original metaphysics.

We have to proceed carefully here. It can be admitted of course that when Spinoza came to express his philosophy in a systematic manner, he already had certain beliefs about the universe. Indeed, it is worth while emphasizing this point. For example, it helps to dispose of the notion that Spinoza was a Cartesian or that his philosophy was simply a logical development of that of Descartes. It is true that 'the stupid Cartesians', as Spinoza described them in a letter to Oldenburg,[16] would hardly have been so eager to dissociate themselves and their master from Spinozism, had they not believed that there was at any rate a plausible case for arguing that the philosophy of Spinoza was a logical development of certain aspects of Cartesianism. It is an obvious fact, for instance, that Descartes' definition of substance, if taken literally, would apply to God alone.[17] And there are clearly other ideas expounded by Descartes which Spinoza can be represented as having exploited. At the same time it is absurd to suppose that Spinoza arrived at his theory of the one substance simply by taking over a definition from Descartes and interpreting it literally. Even if Spinoza, without ever having been a Cartesian, made some use of Descartes' thought, the vision of the universe expressed in the statement that 'outside God there is nothing at all, and that he is an immanent cause'[18] was certainly not arrived at as the result of a deduction based on Cartesian premises, nor indeed of Spinoza's own deductive reasoning as expressed in the *Ethics*. It preceded the construction of the system.

It by no means follows however that Spinoza's arguments stand in a purely external relation to his basic vision of the Universe. The policy of representing them in this way is doubtless attractive to those who believe that the only way of obtaining what can properly be described as knowledge of the world is through the particular sciences but who at the same time share Friedrich Waismann's conviction that 'to say that metaphysics is nonsense *is* nonsense.'[19] For if a sharp distinction is made between the basic vision on the one hand and the apparatus of argument and proof on the other, one is enabled to discount the arguments or to interpret them as persuasive devices to commend a preexisting vision and yet at the same time to ascribe value to the vision as a possible way of seeing the universe or as having a psychological connexion with a certain way of life or type of conduct.[20] Though however it is understandable

if some admirers of the outstanding metaphysicians insist that it is the
vision which counts and is of primary importance, it must be
remembered that unless the so-called vision is taken to be simply a
matter of feeling or of emotive attitude, it has an intellectual content
which acquires definite shape and features only insofar as it is expressed
and rendered explicit. We can, I suppose, envisage the possibility of a
philosopher taking over a world view ready-made from some source and
then looking around, as it were, for arguments to support its validity and
commend it to others. But in the case of an original philosopher such as
Spinoza it seems clear that the system *is* the vision as given definite form
and as communicated. It is the explicitation of the vision.

It is doubtless true that too much emphasis can be placed on the
quasi-geometrical trappings of the *Ethics*. Attention has often been
drawn to the fact that Spinoza expounded part of Descartes' philosophy
more geometrico when he was not, even at that time, an adherent of
Cartesianism.[21] Moreover, Spinoza's universe is far from being a purely
geometrical universe. Substance is for him essentially active, and so are
finite things. Indeed, the more active something is, the more reality it
possesses and the more perfect it is.[22] At the same time it is questionable
whether the formal structure given by Spinoza to his system can be
explained simply in terms of the influence of a mathematical model or
paradigm of reasoning suggested by the scientific development of the
seventeenth century. It is doubtless true that in forming his ideal of
deductive reasoning Spinoza was in fact influenced by a mathematical
model.[23] But it also seems clear enough that his ideal of reasoning is
dictated by his concept of reason and by his general vision of reality. In a
letter to Oldenburg[24] he criticizes Bacon for thinking that the human
intellect is fallible by nature. In Spinoza's opinion, if the human intellect
starts from definitions which express clear and distinct ideas and axioms
which express self-evident or eternal truths and proceeds deductively, it
cannot err, except of course by making mistakes analogous to those
which the mathematician can make. Further, as he sees the universe as
rational through and through, metaphysical deduction will give us
knowledge of reality and not simply of the implications of ideas understood in a purely subjective sense. As for Spinoza God is the immanent
active cause of all things, he concludes that the proper order of philosophical argument is to start with the concept of the one infinite substance and to deduce the essential properties of God or Nature. It does
not follow that the existence of a finite thing can be deduced from its
definition. As we have seen, Spinoza denies that this can be done. But
the proper order of philosophical reasoning must be deductive. Those
philosophers who have taken the objects of sense perception as their
point of departure and have placed consideration of the divine nature at
the end of their process of reflection 'have not observed the order of
philosophical argument'.[25] In a properly philosophical process of

reasoning we should start with that which is first in the order of nature or reality.

In some respects the situation in regard to Spinoza seems to be analogous to that which obtains in the case of Hegel. It has been remarked often enough that Hegel himself rarely speaks in terms of the triadic concept of thesis, antithesis and synthesis, and that it is a mistake to try to force his thought into this mould or to blame him when this cannot be done. Though however the triadic notion can be overemphasized, the fact remains that Hegel's use of dialectical logic is determined by his general vision of reality as a teleological process. The life of absolute Spirit cannot, he is convinced, be reconstructed for reflection or consciousness in terms of a logic which freezes antithetical concepts in permanent opposition. A logic of movement, dialectical logic, is required. Though therefore Hegel's dialectic should not be forced into a rigid triadic mould, it is by no means a superfluous or dispensable element of his thought.

In Spinoza's case use of formulas such as Q.E.D., as found in the *Ethics,* is obviously an inessential feature of his thought. Choice of a deductive method however seems to be governed or implied by the philosopher's general view of the necessary order of nature and by his idea of the relation between thought and its object. To be sure, the content of the *Ethics* cannot be regarded as a continuous process of deduction simply from the definitions and axioms placed at the beginning of the first part. Nor did Spinoza himself so regard it. He was not ignorant of the fact that at the beginning of other parts he had introduced additional definitions and axioms or postulates, as the subject matter might require. But the overall form of reasoning is deductive. And though Spinoza's philosophy can doubtless be presented in other ways than that in which it is presented in the *Ethics,* he seems to say clearly enough in the treatise on *The Improvement of the Understanding* that it is only through following a deductive procedure that the mind can reflect the order of nature.

To insist at length on the influence exercised by Spinoza's vision of the universe on his choice of method may seem to be a case of labouring the obvious. Perhaps it is. But the point seems to be of some importance. It is natural for us to think that if we start with a set of definitions and a set of axioms and then develop a process of deductive reasoning, there is no guarantee at all that the conclusions which we draw will do anything more than exhibit the implications of the premises. There is no guarantee that they will reveal to us the necessary structure of reality. To use the language which is fashionable among some modern Thomists, our philosophy will be 'essentialist', confined within the realm of essence or ideas or, if preferred, abstract possibility. For anyone however who believes that the structure of the universe is necessary, indeed that the whole series of things and events is necessary and cannot be otherwise than it is, and that 'the order and connexion of ideas is the same as the order and connexion of things,'[26] the situation is different, provided, that is to say, that he can find the right starting point. In the order of things the point of departure is the infinite substance. This must therefore be the point of departure in the order of ideas too. It is therefore essential for Spinoza to hold, however implausibly, that he has as clear an idea of God as he has of a triangle.[27] It is only on this assumption that he can deduce the essential properties (or some of them) of *Deus seu Natura*.

Spinoza's basic vision of the universe finds initial expression, as far as the *Ethics* is concerned, in his premises. And the deductive method is required for its explicitation. Of course, given Spinoza's view of the attributes of substance and of the relation between the order of ideas and the order of things, we may think it misleading to speak of his vision of the universe as determining his choice of method. For the concept of the right method might be said to belong to the vision itself. So it does in a sense. But it can hardly be the right method unless the universe is 'rational'. That this is the case seems to be presupposed. And the presupposition governs the choice of method.

How is this presupposition justified? We may be inclined to think that no other justification is possible except the power of the system to give a coherent explanatory account of the essential structure of reality. In other words, the criterion of truth is coherence. The system or the vision rendered explicit is its own justification, the only one which can possibly be given. It might be objected however that a coherent deductive exhibition of the universe as a rational system would not show that the universe *is* rational but only that it *might* be rational. Perhaps therefore Spinoza was wise to maintain that he started with ideas which were true because they were clear and distinct and with self-evidently true metaphysical propositions. This claim may itself involve presuppositions. But what system does not do so? Some philosophers, including Spinoza, have of course tried to establish a philosophy in which there is no legitimately deniable presupposition.[28] In Spinoza's case however it seems pretty clear that an initial world vision was presupposed, even if he believed that the developed system exhibited its validity.

4

In this essay it has been maintained that Spinoza's vision of the universe is rendered explicit in the deductive system. To put the matter in another way, we are not justified in making a dichotomy between the deductive system and the real mind of Spinoza. The philosopher's mind is expressed in his writings. At the same time we have made another obvious point, that an explicitation must be an explicitation of something. But what is this something? Presumably it is the basic belief in one infinite necessarily existing substance which expresses itself by a necessity of nature in the world of finite things. The system purports to exhibit systematically the nature of the one substance insofar as we can know it,[29] its self-expression in the series of modes or finite things[30] and the way in which the human mind can rise above the point of view of the worm living in the bloodstream to an understanding of its own relation and that of other things to the divine totality.[31] The system, in other words, expresses the vision of *Deus seu Natura.*

'God or nature'. The phrase sounds like an attempt to redefine the word 'God', to change the actual use of language, if, that is to say, we take as our standard the way in which Jews and Christians ordinarily conceive and speak about God. Obviously, a philosopher cannot be prohibited from recommending such changes, though we can demand of him that he should not try to conceal what he is doing and that he should be prepared to offer reasons for his procedure.

It is very natural that this line of thought should occur to the reader of Spinoza's writings. For when Christians and Jews (and Moslems too of course) speak about God, they do not ordinarily regard themselves as referring to nature. It is natural therefore that when they come across a philosopher who uses 'God' and 'nature' as synonymous terms, they should conclude that he does not really believe in God at all but that he attaches some value to religious emotion (a 'cosmic emotion' perhaps) or to some religious attitudes and, by his redefinition of the term 'God', is trying to detach this emotion or attitude from God, as they understand the term and reattach it to nature. Though however this is a natural reaction to Spinoza's identification of God and nature, such readers might ask themselves whether the philosopher means by 'nature' precisely what they mean and what are his reasons for the identification.

Anyone who knows a little about Spinoza is aware that he was brought up in the Jewish religion and tradition, that he found himself unable to accept orthodox Judaism and that he was expelled from the synagogue at the age of twenty-four. He came to the conclusion that the scriptural picture of God as thinking this or that, as deciding this or that, as judging, as intervening miraculously in the natural course of events and so on was thoroughly anthropomorphic and rationally untenable. It by no means follows however that he ceased to believe in God. To what extent he was influenced in the development of his thought about God by the Jewish philosophers of the Middle Ages and by the Cabbalistic writings is a disputed question and one to which no assured answer can be given. In the *Tractatus Theologico-Politicus*[32] he makes it clear that in his view the Cabbalistic writings contain childish ideas rather than divine secrets. And in the same work[33] he refers to the famous philosopher Maimonides only to criticize him, though in a letter[34] he mentions Chasdai Crescas with some approval. Even if however there can be prolonged and inconclusive discussion about particular influences on Spinoza's thought, it seems clear that his idea of

God as the one infinite and necessarily existing substance, the immanent cause of all things, was formed under the influence of his philosophical reading. To say this is not of course to suggest that Spinoza simply took over his idea of God from one of his predecessors. He could at any rate have found in the writings of Jewish philosophers the concept of God as a necessarily existing substance, the idea that the perfections of creatures must somehow preexist in God, the possibility of the series of finite things being infinite and the notion of the compatibility between acting freely and acting by a necessity of nature.[35] But the equation of God and nature was not derived from Jewish philosophy. As for the biblical picture of God, Spinoza did not assert that it was false so much as that it was adapted to promote piety and obedience among people at large, and that it should not be taken as the source of philosophical truth, which must be either self-evident to reason or demonstrated. To picture a God 'out there', a transcendent creator endowed with human or quasi-human qualities, is all very well for the purpose of popular religion. But we cannot speak of God *and* nature, if God is conceived as infinite.

Spinoza has no intention however of asserting that the existence of finite things is illusory. It has sometimes been argued that on his premisses he ought to have held that the phenomenal world was illusion or mere appearance. But in point of fact he does not say this. True, for him there is only one substance. But substance is so defined that to say of something that it is a mode of substance is not to say that it lacks all reality. At the same time Spinoza obviously does not interpret the term 'God' as a class name for the plurality of finite things. 'God' is not the name of a collection or of the members of a class taken collectively. He is therefore faced with the task of combining the concept of God as the one all-inclusive substance with admission of the reality of the series of finite things. Here he has an instrument to hand in a distinction already made by Giordano Bruno, the distinction between *Natura naturans* and *Natura naturata*. So far as the present writer is aware, there is no cogent evidence to show that Spinoza took the distinction from Bruno. But it is unlikely that he had no acquaintance with the Renaissance philosophy of nature in which nature (in the sense of the spatio-temporal world) was represented as the 'explication' or self-manifestation of the infinite in itself. In any case the distinction enables Spinoza to reconcile, to his own satisfaction at least, the statements that God in himself is eternal[36] and immutable[37] with the evident fact of the successive existence of finite things.

What we have been saying is not of course in any way new. In view however of the emphasis placed by some writers on Spinoza's naturalism and in view of certain attempts by Marxists to represent him as a materialist it is perhaps worth drawing attention once again to his endeavour to develop a view of God and of the relation between God and the world which would be, in his opinion, philosophically justified. The working out of this view is found indeed in the system. But behind this system lies Spinoza's rejection of the traditional beliefs instilled into him in childhood, coupled with his lasting conviction that the word 'God' is not devoid of reference. Whatever other people may have done, Spinoza certainly did not regard himself as an atheist. Obviously, if theism is understood as implying an idea of God rejected by Spinoza, he can quite properly be described as an atheist. It is a question of accurate description, not of emotive reaction. Given the ordinary use of language, it is certainly misleading to describe him as a theist. But he was clearly no deist. And there is no good reason for thinking that his talk about 'God' was insincere. He indignantly rejected the accusation that his aim was to 'teach atheism by hidden and disguised arguments'.[38] He regarded himself as explaining the 'real' meaning (reference) of the word 'God'.

5

It can indeed be objected that what really counts is where Spinoza ends, not where he begins. We can argue, if we like, that he sought for a philosophically tenable concept of God. But the search ends in sheer naturalism. What Spinoza actually does is to present a certain view of the world or the universe. To call the world 'God' is an idiosyncracy on his part. It does not alter the plain fact that the world is the world and not at all what is commonly understood by the term 'God'. What Spinoza actually does is to present a philosophical system which has to be interpreted with reference to seventeenth-century science. He is of course primarily a philosopher, not a scientist. His correspondence shows indeed an interest in particular scientific questions, such as Boyle's experiments with nitre. And Spinoza himself conducts some experiments. But he is thoroughly dissatisfied with what he regards as the excessively empirical approach of Francis Bacon and with the way in which a scientist such as Boyle tries to combine experimental science with traditional religious ideas. Spinoza goes behind phenomena to their basic presuppositions, or what he considers to be such, and looks for their ultimate causes. In this sense he is a metaphysical philosopher. But transcendence, as understood in a religious context, disappears. The divine mind appears to be identical with the fundamental laws of nature. And when Spinoza says that the existence of a finite thing cannot be deduced from God considered simply in himself but that the series of modes has to be taken into account, he is really saying that the existence of a finite thing cannot be deduced from any law under which its behaviour can be subsumed but that reference must also be made to empirical causes or antecedent conditions. Talk about 'God' really confuses the issue. For it obscures the fact that Spinoza is thinking in purely naturalistic terms. In ordinary language 'God' signifies a super-natural being. In Spinoza's philosophy the supernatural is conspicuous by its absence. Whatever therefore he himself may have thought, with his religious upbringing and living, as he did, at a time when theological themes were still living issues, his system really demands that the word 'God' should be eliminated from it. The situation would then be clarified instead of obfuscated.

That Spinoza was interested, as far as time allowed, in scientific matters is obvious enough. And he was not such a recluse as to be immune from the influence of the climate of thought of seventeenth-century science. But there seems to be little evidence that he set out to supply a philosophical background for the science of his time, even if he thought that his philosophy did in fact provide such a background. Interpretations of Spinoza which translate his theological language into talk about laws of nature and the general features of the world tend to give the impression of attempts to state what, in the opinion of the writer, Spinoza ought to have said (or what he 'really' meant) rather than what he did say. Such interpretations express no doubt the laudable intention of making Spinoza intelligible and the desire to show that the eminent philosopher who has sometimes been taken as the 'model' metaphysician[39] possessed a better understanding of the presuppositions of seventeenth-century physics than some of the leading scientists themselves. But such interpretations generally have to be qualified by the admission that Spinoza did not think in such terms or that he would not have agreed with the interpretation given. For example, in a recently published work on Spinoza the author connects the philosopher's theory of the unknowable attributes of God with the idea of 'the possibility of alternative scientific accounts of the same phenomena,'[40] remarking that this possibility was a living question for Spinoza and his contemporaries. He then adds however that 'the mature Spinoza would not accept this,'[41] namely a view which would make the unknowable attributes knowable in principle. In other words, there is an element of transcendence (in regard to human thought, not of course in regard to the universe itself) which Spinoza did not eliminate but which ought to be eliminated if the 'real' direction of his line of thought is to be clearly exhibited.

These remarks should not be understood as condemning or rejecting all purely naturalistic accounts of Spinoza's philosophy and all interpretations of his thought in the light of contemporary science. Provided that we allow for what we might describe as recalcitrant elements, it is certainly arguable that his system is best seen in the light of the philosophy of Descartes[42] and of seventeenth-century science. We can see it, if we like, as a stage on the way to a naturalistic philosophy concerned with the broadest presuppositions of science. Criticism is then likely to turn on the rigidity of Spinoza's philosophy and to refer to the fact, which the late A. N. Whitehead liked to insist on, that twentieth-century scientific theory differs in important ways from that of the seventeenth century, with the result that we can hardly be satisfied with a seventeenth-century philosophical system. To be sure, the historic Spinoza would hardly have looked on things in this way. For he believed that he had exhibited *the* truth about reality. But the attempt to interpret his significance in the light of the general development of scientific and philosophical thought is quite legitimate.

Spinoza's *Deus seu Natura* remains however ambiguous. As in the case of the Stoic philosophy, of which Spinozism often reminds us, we may well ask ourselves whether we are dealing with a naturalizing of *Deus* or a divinization of *Natura.* The situation is ambiguous. On the one hand we can emphasize *Natura.* On the other hand we can emphasize *Deus.* And if we adopt the second procedure, it is arguable that we ought to look forward to the philosophy of Hegel who maintained that Spinoza's substance should be redefined as Spirit (*Geist*). To introduce the name of Hegel is indeed most unfashionable. But if von Tschirnhaus and G. H. Schuller were right in suggesting that in Spinoza's philosophy the attribute of thought came to occupy a central position in reality, it becomes easier to see a connexion between Spinozism and absolute idealism.

This line of thought lies open to the objection that Spinoza's philosophy should be considered in itself and in relation to the problems of his time, not as a forerunner of or as looking forward to a later philosophy which was developed in response to other problems. Spinozism, not a stage in the emergence of Hegelianism. It is true that as far as the general task of metaphysics is concerned, both Spinoza and Hegel can be said to have had similar aims, namely the representation in thought of the nature of the ultimate reality. Spinoza exhibits the nature, properties and activity of the one infinite substance; Hegel regards the task of philosophy as the reconstruction for consciousness of the life of the Absolute. Both men call the ultimate reality 'God'. Both men refuse to admit the propriety of speaking of the infinite *and* the finite; but neither is prepared to look on 'God in himself' as identical with the collection or class of finite things. Though however similarities between the two philosophies are visible if we look at them from such a distance that differences become blurred, their problems are different. For example, in the seventeenth century the philosopher had to come to terms with the new scientific developments, not with the romantic movement. Again, insofar as Spinoza's problems were set by another philosopher, they were set by the philosophy of Descartes (possibly in conjunction with the Renaissance philosophy of nature), whereas Hegel was obviously faced with problems arising out of the thought of Kant and his successors. Again, the two men's conceptions of the ultimate reality were different; and the methods which they employed to exhibit its nature were also different. Spinoza may have looked on his system as expressing timeless truth; but Hegel insisted on the close connexion between any system and its historical background. And the plain fact of the matter is that the historical backgrounds of Spinozism and Hegelianism differed in important respects. The philosophy of Spinoza therefore should be seen in his historical context and not treated as a stage in the development of a system of thought belonging to a later and very different age.

True enough. But it is not the intention of the present writer to endorse Hegel's view of the history of philosophy as a necessary dialectical process whereby the universal mind or spirit comes to consciousness of itself. I have no intention of suggesting that the philosophy of Spinoza *must* be transformed into Hegelianism. My contention is rather that Spinoza's philosophy is ambiguous, Janus-faced. If one aspect is emphasized, a naturalistic interpretation becomes reasonable. If another aspect is emphasized, we have a pantheism which can reasonably be seen as demanding the transformation of *Natura* into *Geist*. We can of course try to confine ourselves to exegesis of Spinoza's system as it stands in his writings. But in my opinion such exegesis does not reveal the system as viable. Spinozists would obviously disagree.

It may be said that if there are ambiguities in the system of Spinoza, this is even more true of the philosophy of Hegel. The former has always tended to be a take-it-or-leave-it system, whereas Hegelianism, as we are well aware, gave rise to very different lines of interpretation. But that there should be ambiguities and tensions in any comprehensive metaphysical system is, in my opinion, only to be expected. Nobody swimming in a river can see the whole river. He can indeed enunciate propositions which must be true for it to be proper to speak of there being a river at all. And Spinoza doubtless thought that he was doing something analogous in regard to the world. But the fact remains that the swimmer's perspective and range of vision are limited. And though the impulse to understand reality as a whole is natural enough, the notion that this can be achieved once and for all and with mathematical clarity by the historically conditioned mind is a supposition which most of us nowadays find some difficulty in accepting.

Notes

[1] William of Ockham, *Opera Theologica, I* (St. Bonaventure, N.Y. 1967), p. 259. And see also the prologue to Ockham's commentry on the eight books of Aristotle's *Physics*. Ockham is actually referring to the different views maintained by Avicenna and Averroes about the subject matter of metaphysics.

[2] For Spinoza's view of the relation between philosophy and theology see the *Tractatus Theologico-Politicus*, Chaps. 14 and 15.

[3] *Tractatus Theologico-Politicus*, Chap. 15. By Scripture Spinoza often understands both Testaments. This may seem to be simply a matter of arguing *ad hominem*, as in the correspondence with Van Blyenbergh. But Spinoza obviously writes as one who has broken with orthodox Judaism and for whom all writings which are used as sources for theological thought possess a pragmatic function. If he were writing to a Moslem, he could make similar remarks about the Koran.

[4] This is stated in, for instance, Letter 23 (to Van Blyenbergh).

[5] R.B. Braithwaite, 'An Empiricist's View of the Nature of Religious Belief' (Cambridge 1955).

[6] Spinoza explains this in Letter 4 (to Henry Oldenburg). See also, of course, the treatise on *The Improvement of the Understanding.*

[7] *Ethics,* II, Prop. 7.

[8] For example, in Letter 10 (to Simon de Vries) Spinoza asserts that the existence of a mode cannot be deducted from its definition or essence. Again in Letter 83 (to von Tschirnhaus) he says that it is impossible to prove 'the variety of things' *a priori* from the concept of extension. Similarly, in the treatise on *The Improvement of the Understanding* he makes it clear that it is not the series of particular and mutable things which can be deduced but only the series of 'fixed and eternal things', by which he may mean the infinite modes of substance. Some writers have understood Spinoza as saying simply that *we* cannot deduce the existence of particular things. Though however some remarks suggest this line of interpretation, Spinoza seems to be asserting that such a deduction is impossible in principle. It is at any rate true in principle that it is only in the case of God that existence can be deduced from essence.

[9] What we say about this matter depends to a certain extent of course on the meaning which we give to the word 'philosophy'. For Augustine the Christian religion was the true 'philosophy'. Hence he could look on philosophy as a way of life, the saving wisdom of which had fulfilled and taken the place of true wisdom. When however in the course of the Middle Ages philosophy came to be systematically distinguished from revelation and theology, it could no longer be regarded by Christian theologians in precisely the same way in which Augustine had regarded it. The meaning of the word had undergone a change.

[10] *Ethics,* II, Prop. 40, note 2.

[11] Bertrand Russell, *History of Western Philosophy* (London, 1946), p. 594.

[12] In point of fact Spinoza does not appear to deny the reality of finite things or to regard them as illusory.

[13] *Enneads,* 771b.

[14] *Ethics,* V, Prop. 36.

[15] *Ibid.,* IV, Prop. 28.

[16] Letter 68.

[17] Descartes was of course quite aware of this fact. See *Principles of Philosophy,* I, 51, in *Oeuvres de Descartes,* ed. Charles Adam Paul Tannery (Paris, 1897-1913), VIII, 24.

[18] *Short Treatise,* I, Chap. 2.

[19] Friedrich Waismann, 'How I See Philosophy,' *Contemporary British Philosophy: Personal Statements,* Third Series, ed. H.D.Lewis (London, 1956), p. 489.

[20] In this case the vision will not of course be considered of real value unless the way of life or type of conduct which it is thought of as tending to promote is itself approved and judged desirable.

[21] See, for example, Letter 13 (to Oldenburg).

[22] *Ethics,* V, Prop. 40.

[23] It is obvious in any case that in the *Ethics* Spinoza sometimes abandons or steps outside the quasi-mathematical framework. Further, we may well think that what is supposed to be deduced is by no means always actually deduced. But the deductive ideal remains.

[24] Letter 2.

[25] *Ethics,* II, Prop. 10, note.

[26] *Ethics,* II, Prop. 7.

[27] Letter 56 (to Hugo Boxel).

[28] Sometimes the attempt has been made to reach, by reductive analysis, a starting point for deduction which cannot indeed be demonstrated (for it would not then be an ultimate starting point) but can be vindicated by showing that its denial implies its affirmation.

[29] This proviso is required in view of Spinoza's statement that God consists of in-

finite attributes, coupled with his assertion that we know only two of these attributes, thought and extension.
[30] Spinoza denies that the existence of any given finite mode can be deduced simply from the one substance considered in itself. The existence of the cow in the field cannot be adequately explained without reference to the series of finite modes. In this sense God is not the 'adequate cause' of the cow. But though the series of finite things without temporal beginning, it is none the less ontologically dependent on the one substance. It could not exist unless the one substance existed: and it cannot be understood except in terms of the causal activity of God.
[31] The passage about the parasitic worm occurs in Letter 32 (to Oldenburg). As for the statement above that the mind 'can rise' to adequate ideas, this must be understood in a sense compatible with Spinoza's determinism. Given the antecedent conditions, some minds rise (and therefore can rise) to the highest level of knowledge, while other minds do not so rise (and therefore cannot do so).
[32] Chap. 9.
[33] Chap. 7.
[34] Letter 12 (to Ludovicus Meyer).
[35] Spinoza applied this idea to God, as it is only in the case of God that activity precedes entirely from the essence or nature of the agent, and is dependent on nothing else.
[36] *Ethics*, I, Prop. 19.
[37] *Ibid.*, Prop. 20, Cor. 2.
[38] Letter 43 (to Jacob Ostens).
[39] The word 'model' should not of course be understood as necessarily implying approbation of metaphysics. The reference is to the way in which Spinoza's metaphysics has sometimes been taken as the best and clearest example of the method and aims of metaphysicians. Whether metaphysics is regarded with approval or disapproval is another question.
[40] E.M.Curley, *Spinoza's Metaphysics: An Essay in Interprétation* (Cambridge, Mass., 1969), p. 151. It ought to be added that Mr Curley sees Spinoza's problems as set more by the philosophy of Descartes than by seventeenth-century science in a narrow sense of 'science'.
[41] *Ibid.*
[42] The fact that Spinoza was not a Cartesian obviously does not entail the conclusion that reflection on the philosophy of Descartes was not a powerful instrument in determining the nature of Spinoza's problematics.

CHAPTER 9

HEGEL AND THE
RATIONALIZATION OF MYSTICISM

IN THE PREFACE to his *Philosophy of Right* Hegel maintains that a philosophy is its own time apprehended in thought.[1] It is not the philosopher's business to create an imaginary world of his own. His task is to understand the present and actual as subsuming the past in itself, as the culmination (up to date) of a process of development.

Among the phenomena, the structure and the development of which the philosopher can try to understand, is religion. And from one point of view at any rate religion can be regarded as a particular expression of the human spirit. Thus in the *Phenomenology of Spirit* and in the *Encyclopaedia of the Philosophical Sciences* religion forms the subject-matter of a particular section, while Hegel's lectures on the philosophy of religion form a series alongside other series, the lectures on the philosophy of history, on art and on the history of philosophy.

It would be a mistake, however, to conclude that the philosophy of religion is peripheral to Hegel's main line of thought. He tells us roundly that the subject-matter both of religion and philosophy is 'God and nothing but God and the self-unfolding of God'.[2] Moreover for Hegel the philosophy of religion is not simply reflection about religion from the outside. Obviously the development of religious beliefs and practices constitutes an historical phenomenon about which the philsopher can reflect, even if he does not accept any of the religions which he is considering. And Hegel certainly devotes a good deal of space to reflection about the historical development of religion. But he does so from the point of view of one who believes that Lutheran Christianity is the highest expression of religion, at any rate up to date. For Hegel the philosophy of religion is religion attaining the level of reflective self-awareness and self-understanding. This is why he thinks himself justified in maintaining that he is simply carrying further the programme of St Anselm and other mediaeval theologians, the programme of 'faith seeking understanding'. The instrument of understanding which Hegel employs is, of course, absolute idealism. And it is clearly arguable that what he regards as the process of understanding Christianity is really the process of transforming the Christian religion into idealist metaphysics. But this does not alter the fact that Hegel looks on himself as engaged in solving problems which arise out of a religion of which he is an adherent.

What is it that Hegel wishes to understand, to express in the language of philosophy? I select one basic problem, the relation between the world and God, between finite things and the infinite divine reality.

An obvious question is this. Why, or with what right, does Hegel assume in the first place that there is an infinite, a divine reality? It seems

106

to me that there are two things to be borne in mind. In the first place Hegel enrolled in his youth in the Protestant theological faculty at Tübingen. It is indeed a notorious fact that his initial reaction not only to the theological lectures delivered at Tübingen but also to the Christian religion itself, as developed by the Apostles and their successors, was far from favourable. The point is however that Hegel came to philosophy from theology. This meant in effect that he assumed that Christian belief was in fact true, in some sense at any rate of the word 'true'; and that he then tried, by means of philosophical reflection, to exhibit what we may call the 'inner truth' in religious belief.[3] In the second place Hegel was convinced that from the philosophical point of view the finite is not intelligible except in the light of its relationship to an infinite whole, which is the ultimate reality. His philosophy is therefore concerned with exhibiting the nature of the ultimate reality rather than with trying to prove its existence .

The problem which I have selected for consideration can be expressed in this way. In the religious consciousness, as it manifests itself in both Judaism and Christianity, we find God objectified. God is set over against nature and the finite subject. In other words, an opposition is asserted between God and the world, God and man. For Hegel, this opposition cannot be anything but repugnant to speculative philosophy. On the one hand God is declared to be infinite. On the other hand, if the alleged infinite is set over against the finite, so as to exclude it, how can it properly be described as infinite? Again, if the finite is set over against the infinite, is it not absolutized, with the result that the infinite becomes a superfluous hypothesis? In fine, pictorial theism, with its God 'out there' or 'up there', cannot satisfy the reflective mind.

Yet how can we overcome in thought the opposition between the finite and the infinite, between the world and God, between man and God? In Christianity there is indeed a synthesis, an overcoming of the estrangement of the finite subject from God. But this synthesis is lived rather than thought. The difficulty lies in thinking it, in constructing a genuinely philosophical theism. If on the other hand we use the term 'God' as a label for the Many in their given empirical existence this is tantamount to embracing atheism. For the word 'God' would then refer simply to the class of finite things, the existence of which is not denied by the atheist. If on the other hand we declare the Many to be illusion, this is equivalent to embracing what Hegel describes as 'acosmism'.[4] In neither case can we be said to have solved the problem at issue. What we have done is to eliminate one of the factors (in the first case God, in the second case the world) which need to be brought together in a unity which at the same time preserves a distinction.

Hegel's problem, as actually raised and treated by him, has obviously to be seen in the light of the presuppositions involved in his adherence to the post-Kantian idealist movement. And, in my opinion, the spirit and demands of the romantic movement are also relevant factors. At the same time there is a real sense in which the problem to which I have been referring is a contemporary problem. We have only to think, for example of the Bishop of Woolwich's famous book *Honest to God* and of its author's attack on pictorial theism, with its God 'out there'. There are, of course, contextual differences. For instance, one of Dr Robinson's themes is the apparent growing irrelevance of the concept of God when seen in the light of such factors as the growth of the scientific outlook and of depth psychology. But the differences can, I think be exaggerated. It would be an obvious anachronism to attribute to Hegel a knowledge of depth of psychology and of psychological explanations of the felt need for religion. But Hegel was by no means unaware of the way in which God 'out there' can appear as a superfluous addition to the world. 'Science', he remarks 'thus forms a universe of knowledge which has no need of God, lies outside religion and has, directly nothing to do with it'.[5] In any case Dr Robinson's basic problem seems to me to be similar to that of Hegel. How are we to think of God if we are not to think of him as a super-person over against the world? In the language of Paul Tillich we can speak of both Hegel and the Bishop of Woolwich as trying to make the transition from 'God' to *God*.

2

In the notes which form the so-called *Fragment of a System* of 1800 Hegel expresses a serious doubt whether philosophy is capable of thinking, of conceptualizing that is to say, the unity-in-difference between the divine spirit and the human spirit which is lived, but not clearly thought on the level of Christian love. Philosophy is a process of thinking; and thought posits an object over against itself, an object about which we think. Further, discursive thought, working with the categories of traditional logic, asserts antitheses, such as that between the infinite and the finite, which it is unable to overcome. 'Infinite' means 'not finite'; and there is an end of the matter. The same idea seems to be re-echoed in a recent book by the Bishop of Woolwich when he asserts that to express the overcoming of dualism (between Creator and creature) 'within the logic of non-contradiction is of course finally impossible'.[6] Hegel's conclusion is that 'philosophy therefore has to stop short of religion because it is a process of thinking'.[7]

Every student of Hegel is aware that the philosopher very soon looked to dialectical thinking to accomplish what was impossible for a 'static' logic which posited antitheses and then was unable to overcome them. It is not so obvious, however, that Hegel was concerned, in part, with thinking through, with raising to the level of pure conceptual thought, a relationship between the finite spirit and God which he regarded as having found expression in the paradoxical utterances of religious mystics. I am not indeed prepared to follow Richard Kroner in describing Hegel as a 'Christian mystic, seeking adequate speculative expression'.[8] For it seems to me extravagant to speak of Hegel himself as a mystic, whether Christian or otherwise. But when Professor W. T. Stace maintains that Hegel endeavoured to turn the mystical idea of identity-in-distinction into a logical concept,[9] and when Mr G. R. G. Mure writes of Hegel's 'strenuous and uncompromising effort which has no serious parallel, to rationalize and to bring to light the mystic union of God and man proclaimed by men such as Meister Eckhart and Jacob Böhme, to reveal it as a union through distinction for which the whole world is evidence',[10] they are saying, I think, what is quite true. Hegel was doubtless hostile to the taking of short cuts in philosophy by substituting appeals to intuition or to mystical insights in place of the patient effort to understand and to express the truth in a systematic way. Moreover, his sarcastic references in the preface to the *Phenomenology* to Schelling's insistence on approaching the Absolute by the 'negative way' are well known. But it by no means follows that Hegel did not regard mystical writers as having given expression, even if in paradoxical form, to valid insights which the philosopher should try to conceptualize, exhibiting their universal significance.[11] In point of fact he quotes Meister Eckhart to the effect that 'the eye with which God sees me is the eye with which I see him; my eye and his eye are one ... If God were not, I should not be; if I were not he would not be either'.[12] Hegel further remarks that the older theologians among whom he numbers Eckhart had, as he puts it, a better grasp of 'this depth'[13] than their modern successors. So I do not think that it is at all far-fetched to represent Hegel as trying to give philosophical expression to a mystical insight.

3

Now perhaps I have given the impression that in my opinion Hegel regards the sphere of religion as concerned only with feeling and with emotive language. This impression would however be erroneous. In his phenomenological analysis of the religious consciousness Hegel does indeed allow for the basic importance of immediacy, of feeling, the feeling of dependence for example. In his view thought and knowledge are essential to the development of the religious consciousness. He tells us for example, that 'knowledge is an essential element of the Christian religion itself',[14] and he insists on the truth of the Christian dogmas. It is indeed true that for Hegel the mode of thinking characteristic of the religious consciousness is pictorial thought. And inasmuch as philosophy, in his view, converts pictorial thought into pure conceptual thought, we can say that for Hegel philosophy demythologizes the context of religious belief. At the same time it must be added that he regards this process of demythologization as starting within the religious sphere; in, that is to say, the course of the historical development of the religious consciousness and its self-expression. In other words, even though Hegel asserts a distinction between the modes of conception characteristic of the religious consciousness and of speculative philosophy, he also asserts a continuity. This is why he feels entitled to make the claim, to which I have already referred, that he is continuing the task of theologians such as St Anselm, and why he thinks himself justified in making such statements as that philosophy 'only unfolds itself when it unfolds religion, and when it unfolds itself it unfolds religion'.[15]

This point, namely that there is continuity as well as distinction between the modes of conception characteristic of the religious consciousness and of speculative philosophy, has, I think, a certain importance for the understanding of Hegel. We are told, for example, that if we ask 'what is God?' or what does the term *God* signify?', we are trying to grasp the nature of God in thought, and that 'the nature of God as grasped in thought'[16] is what is called in philosophy the Absolute. Hegel thus translates talk about God into talk about the Absolute. And we may thus draw the conclusion that according to Hegel the religious consciousness projects the ulitmate reality into the celestial sphere in the form of a personal transcendent being out there, over against the world and the human spirit, whereas philosophy rejects this externalization of God and conceives the ultimate reality as the all-comprehensive Life, the self-actualizing Absolute. Though, however, there is certainly some truth in this account of the matter, the account is defective or inadequate. For it neglects the fact that, according to Hegel, the truth of the fundamental unity between the finite spirit and the divine spirit finds expression in the Christian religion in such doctrines as those of the historic Incarnation, the indwelling of the Holy Spirit in the Church, the Eucharist and the communion of saints. In other words, what philosophy does is not to supply a truth of which religion has no inkling but rather to present the truth as following from the nature of the Absolute instead of presenting it in the form of contingent propositions, depending for their truth on historic events which might or might not have occurred.

To put the matter in another way, at the time of the Enlightenment it was generally agreed, both by opponents and defenders of Christianity, that the Christian religion stood or fell according as it was able or unable to make good certain historic claims. Hegel however, is trying to show that Christian beliefs are true independently of these historic claims. This means, of course, that Christianity is presented, to use McTaggart's phrase, as exoteric Hegelianism, while absolute idealism is presented as esoteric Christianity. And the natural conclusion is that the fall of absolute idealism would entail the fall of Christianity. For absolute idealism, according to Hegel, is Christianity, in its cognitive aspect at any rate, when in possession of full self-understanding. This is indeed an idea which most Christian theologians would hardly receive with enthusiasm. And understandably so. But the point which I am trying to make here is simply that Hegel does not separate the concept of truth from religious statements and attach it only to philosophical statements. Religious statements can be true. And when the philosopher expresses their truth in a different form, it is the same truth which he is presenting. That is to say, in Hegel's opinion the truth remains the same.

Now if we consider the sort of statements to which Hegel refers in the writings of mystics such as Eckhart, it is clear that they assert a unity between God and man, between the finite spirit and the divine spirit. At the same time it is clear that they do not assert the reducibility of the concept of God to the concept of man. Whatever may seem to be the literal meaning of some of Eckhart's utterances, the general line of his thought makes it quite clear that he had no intention of asserting that 'God' and 'man' are convertible terms. It is also clear, I think, that mystics such as Eckhart did not assume that a realization of the unity between man and God is something given from the start. Rather is it something to which the human spirit can attain, though it does not necessarily do so. In other words, there is a unity-in-distinction which the human mind can grasp or apprehend, though it does not always or necessarily do so.

These, it seems to me, are some of the ideas to which Hegel thinks that he has given expression in terms of absolute idealism. In the first place the Hegelian Absolute is clearly not reducible without residue to the human mind. For it is the One which, though not temporally prior to the Many, manifests itself or expresses itself in the world. In Hegel's opinion, the national State, considered as an organic whole enduring in time, is irreducible to any given set of citizens, to those for example who are living here and now. In an analogous manner the Absolute is irreducible to any given set of finite things, including finite minds. The Absolute or God is, in St Paul's words, he in whom 'we live and move and have our being'.[17]

In the second place, just as the national State does not exist apart from its citizens but in and through them, though at the same time it is more than the sum of them, so does the Absolute exist in and through the Many, immanent in them while compromising them within its own life.

In the third place, though the Absolute must be defined as self-thinking thought (for this is what it is in essence, as Aristotle saw), it must also be conceived as a dynamic process of self-actualization. When Hegel asserts that 'of the Absolute it must be said that it is essentially [a] result, that only at the end is it what it is in very truth',[18] and that the Absolute is 'the essence which completes (or actualizes) itself throught its own development',[19] I think that he means precisely what he says. That is to say, the Absolute comes to know itself in actuality in and through the human mind as its vehicle. But when Hegel says that 'God knows himself in the finite Spirit',[20] it is not any and every sort of knowledge to which he is referring. He is referring above all to the knowledge of God in religion and philosophy. It is this knowledge which from another point of view is God's knowledge of himself. 'Finite consciousness knows God only in so far as God knows himself in it'.[21] That is to say, at the level at which the finite spirit becomes the vehicle of the divine self-knowledge it rises above its particularity and becomes in actuality a moment in the divine life. The divine self-knowledge is not reducible to any individual's knowledge of God; but the individual's knowledge of God is a moment in the process of the Absolute's return to itself in self-reflection.

Awareness of the identity-in-distinction which obtains between the human spirit and the infinite Spirit is not something given from the start. Just as we cannot come to know the true nature of the universal in general except by first objectifying it as a reality apart from particulars (as in the traditional interpretation of Platonism), so the human mind cannot come to know the true nature of God except by first objectifying him as a personal transcendent being 'out there', over against the world of man. This is a dialectically necessary stage in the process by which the universal Spirit comes to see itself, in and through the human mind, as the one reality, the Alpha and Omega. As we have noted, Hegel believes that the true view of God is expressed in the Christian dogmas in the form appropriate to the religious consciousness. What philosophy does is to exhibit the unity between the human spirit and God, not as a privilege gratuitously bestowed upon some men but rather as a truth which follows from the nature of reality itself. It exhibits Spirit, manifesting itself in the religious and philosophical development of mankind, as 'the living process by which the implicit unity of divine nature becomes actual and attains concrete existence'.[32]

4

From what I have been saying it should be clear that I accept neither the right-wing interpretation of Hegel, according to which God in himself is to be conceived as enjoying self-knowledge independently of all creation, nor the interpretation which pretty well identifies the position of Hegel with that of Feuerbach. As for the right-wing interpretation, I am of course aware that in his very favourable review in the *Jahrbuch für wissenschaftliche Kritik*[23] of K.F. Göschel's book of aphorisms Hegel refers with approval to Göschel's statement that God in himself is self-knowledge in itself, while as knowing himself in creatures God is self-knowledge outside himself. But though I may be wrong, I do not think that Hegel really commits himself to saying more than that the divine essence must be defined as self-thinking thought. As for the identification of Hegel's position with that of Feuerbach, Hegel is not concerned, as Feuerbach was, with transforming theology into anthropology, with reducing God to man. He is concerned with bringing God and man together by employing the concept of identity-in-distinction. This was, I think, seen by Kierkegaard. The Danish thinker's picture of Hegel as producing a *tertium quid*, a fantastic metaphysical abstraction, absolute thought, in which both God and man disappear, may be a caricature, but it at any rate expresses Kierkegaard's recognition of the fact that Hegel does not aim at a reduction without residue either of God to man or of man to God.

Hegel might perhaps be described as a panentheist by intention. Needless to say, he is not concerned with overcoming theism in the sense of imaginative representations of God as an old man on a throne beyond the clouds. The theism to which he tries to give consistent philosophical expression already recognises God as infinite Spirit. And what Hegel endeavours to accomplish is to think the relation between the infinite and the finite in such a way as to allow the infinite to fill, as it were, all reality while at the same time a distinction is preserved. If we take pantheism as representing the concept of identity and theism that of distinction, Hegel's aim is to show how the two concepts, which appear antithetical, can be reconciled at a higher level. All things are 'in God', moments in the divine life; but God, as the One, is not simply reducible to 'all things', to the Many. To give, however, a clear statement of this idea is no easy task. And it is arguable that the result of Hegel's reflections is so ambiguous that it is questionable whether it can be properly described as theism of any kind, unless the meaning of the term is extended well beyond what seems to be permitted by ordinary usage. This is why I suggest that Hegel might be best described as a panentheist 'by intention'.

5

The ambiguity of the results of Hegel's philosophizing is a point which merits a little amplification. As we have noted, he regards the philosopher as concerned primarily with the problems which arise out of his contemporary world. And in the sphere of religion he mentions this problem. "There was a time when all knowledge was knowledge of God.'[24] That is to say, there was a time when knowledge of God himself was considered the highest form of knowledge and when knowledge of the world was thought to be in some sense knowledge of God, that is of God's handiwork. In the modern world, however, scientific knowledge of finite things has increased to such an extent that the sphere of the knowledge of God has been progressively contracted. Indeed, 'it is a matter of no concern to our age that it knows nothing of God. On the contrary, the belief that this knowledge is not even possible passes for the highest degree of insight'.[26] Hegel, however, believing that the real is the rational and the rational the real, that God is the supreme reality and hence the supremely rational (or, rather absolute reason itself), and that the rational must be penetrable by reason, insists that the essence of God can be known by the human reason. In fact it is not altogether unreasonable to say that the task which Hegel proposes to the philosopher is that of attaining by philosophical reflection to what the mediaeval theologians called the beatific vision of God and which they reserved for heaven. This idea, however, would be clearly absurd if God were represented as a transcendent reality of such a kind that we know of him, as Aquinas put it, what he is not rather than what he is. Given therefore Hegel's conviction of the power and scope of the human mind, he has so to speak to bring God down from his state of transcendence and at the same time to elevate man. And this means in effect two things. First, what traditional Christian doctrine represents as the free creation of a world by a transcendent creator must be represented, from the philosophical point of view, as a divine self-exteriorization which is essential to the divine life. Secondly, man's knowledge of God and God's knowledge of himself must be depicted as two aspects of one reality. Hence Hegel can say that 'without the world God is not God'.[26] That is to say, the essence of the Absolute as self-thinking thought is not actualized in concrete reality except in the sphere of spirit which requires the sphere of Nature as its necessary presupposition. And in the sphere of spirit man's knowledge of God is God's knowledge of himself.

Now Hegel himself did not think of this doctrine as equivalent to the elimination of God. Individual human beings perish, but the One remains. The individual's knowledge of God, considered precisely as knowledge possessed by this individual, is transitory; but the development of the religious consciousness in general continues. The universal mind lives in and through particular minds; but while particulars are transitory, the universal abides. At the same time there is no great difficulty in seeing the force of the contention that Hegel's theory is well on its way to becoming a recommendation to look on the world in a special way, namely as one organic and developing whole which, with the emergence of man and the subsequent growth of scientific knowledge, can be represented as coming to know itself in and through the human mind.

In other words, a plausible case can be made for representing Hegel's philosophy of religion as a stage in a process in which the concept of God is progressively eliminated. Hegel, it may be said, undertakes a demythologization of Christian doctrine. But the result of his own philosophizing is a cloud of metaphysical mystification which is subsequently dissipated by naturalism and positivism. Hegel saw the problems arising out of traditional theism. But he was unable to solve them, not because he lacked ability, but because they are insoluble. If therefore religion is to be preserved, it has to be separated from talk about God. Or, if the word 'God' is retained, it must be given a meaning which involves no reference to an alleged transcendent being of any kind. We can thus see in the contemporary death-of-God theology the spiritual heir of Hegelianism, even if Hegel himself would not have been prepared to recognize it as such.

6

If this point of view is adopted, it follows that the statements about God which were made by men such as Meister Eckhart and which evidently impressed Hegel were not about God at all, about God, that is to say, as an existent reality. Suppose, however, that we believe that the claim of religious mystics to have enjoyed knowledge by acquaintance of a reality which is identifiable neither with Nature nor with the finite spirit and which is in some sense the only 'true' reality cannot be simply dismissed. Or suppose that we believe that God is inescapable in the sense that a One reveals itself as the attracting goal of the human spirit's movement towards an ultimate unity or as the hidden ground of the demands which impose themselves upon us in the recognition of ideal values in relation to the successive situations which call for action in the world. If we have beliefs of this kind, we could, I suppose, pursue a policy of Wittgensteinian silence and refrain from trying to state their content. But if we choose to speak, we shall need the word 'God' or some equivalent term.

Once, however, we begin to speak, we encounter the sort of problems which Hegel encountered, such as the problem of stating the relation between the world and God. As this relation is presumably unique, we might designate it by the symbol x. But though the construction of a purely artificial language might conceivably be of some use in academic discussion, provided that we could state some rules for the manipulation of the selected symbols, it would be useless for general communication and for exhibiting the relevance of our beliefs to human life and society. Hence in practice we are inevitably thrown back on ordinary language. And this means in effect that we have to use counterbalancing analogies and 'projections', by means of which we try to grasp and state that which cannot be adequately grasped and stated. To anyone who believes that all that can be said can be said clearly, this is not a satisfactory state of affairs. But is is an essential characteristic of this particular language-game, talk about God. And if we try to eliminate it by translating talk about God into the language of the absolute idealism of Hegel or into that of logical positivism, we shall soon find ourselves talking about something else, about the world when looked at in a special way, or about man, no longer about God. In fine, Hegel attempted, in my opinion, to do what cannot be done, namely to make plain to view what can only be simply apprehended through the use of analogies and symbols.

A final point. The analogies and projections which we use tend to get a grip on the mind, holding it captive and leading it to imagine that it understands more than it does. The mystical writers, however, such as St John of the Cross, remind us of the inadequacy of our conceptual representations of God, of the shortcomings of our language in this region of thought. To employ once again a phrase of Paul Tillich, it is the religious mystics who most strikingly exemplify the movement of the human spirit from 'God' to *God*. But this, I think, is a feature of mysticism of which Hegel failed to appreciate the significance.

Notes

[1] *Werke* (Glockner, 1928), vii, p. 35. This edition will be referred to in footnote references as *W*.

[2] *W*, xv, p. 37.

[3] With Leibniz we can already find a tendency to find an 'inner truth' in Christian beliefs. With Lessing, in his mature thought, this tendency is much more marked. But whereas Lessing did not think of himself as a Christian, Hegel came to think of himself as a champion of Christianity, even if it is pretty obvious that in his developed system Christianity is transformed into exoteric Hegelianism, as McTaggart puts it.

[4] This is what Hegel understands by pantheism when he denies that he is a pantheist.

[5] *W*, xv, p. 32.

[6] *Exploration into God* (London, 1967), p. 141.

[7] *Hegel's Early Theological Writings* (Chicago, 1948), p. 313.

[8] Ibid., p. 8.

[9] *Mysticism and Philosphy* (London, 1961).

[10] *The Philosophy of Hegel* (London, 1965), p. 103.

[11] For example, if a religious mystic writes simply of an exceptional state of union between the soul and God, Hegel would see in what the mystic says a general metaphysical truth about the relation between the finite and the infinite.

[12] *W*, xv, p. 228.

[13] Ibid.

[14] *W*, xv, p. 35.

[15] Ibid, p. 37.

[16] *W*, xv, p. 42.

[17] Acts 17:28.

[18] *W*, ii, p. 24.

[19] Ibid.

[20] *W*, xvi, p. 192.

[21] Ibid., p. 191.

[22] *W*, xvi, p. 210.

[23] *W*, pp. 276-313.

[24] *W*, xv, p. 52.

[25] *W*, xv, p. 53.

[26] *W*, xv, p. 210.

CHAPTER 10

FOREGROUND AND BACKGROUND
IN NIETZSCHE

IT HAS OFTEN BEEN STATED that Nietzsche's predominantly aphoristic style of writing militated against the construction of any system analogous to those of Spinoza and Hegel. The statement is doubtless true. But it is essential to add that Nietzsche had no wish to construct such a system. Spinoza was convinced that the order and connexion of ideas is the same as the order and connexion of things; and Hegel believed that the rational is the real and the real the rational. Nietzsche, however, had no such conviction or belief. Hence it would be rather misleading to say that he 'failed' to construct a system comparable to those of Spinoza or Hegel.

At the same time it would need an incredibly careless reader not to notice the emergence of certain basic ideas which serve to unify Nietzsche's thought. Further, though the philosopher's writings can certainly be used to support different positions (for example, by means of a careful selection of texts one can represent him either as a devotee of war or as pretty well a pacifist), no great amount of reflection is required in order to see that some at least of the sets of, at first sight, incompatible statements become compatible when they are interpreted in the light of their contexts, and of the writer's purpose in making them. In other words, the outlines of a building, of a positive philosophy, are undoubtedly discernible. And the writers about Nietzsche who insist that the philosopher is not simply a destroyer, but expounds a positive philosophy which is intended as an antidote to nihilism, are certainly justified. As Mr. R. J. Hollingdale puts it, 'the recognition that all values had been disvalued, and that reality no longer had any intelligibility was the *beginning* of his [Nietzsche's] philosophy, its *pre*supposition',[1] while the theories of the will to power, of superman and of the eternal recurrence constituted an attempt to 'establish a new meaning for man and reality in a world become meaningless'.[2]

Though, however, the outlines of a building are undoubtedly discernible, it is unfinished; and any presentation is both an interpretation and, to some extent, a construction by the historian. Hollingdale tells us that by the end of 1889, Nietzsche's philosophy was 'available to anyone who could read and reach a bookshop'.[3] True, he is concerned partly with insisting that we ought not to prefer a philosopher's unpublished jottings to the works which he either actually published or prepared for publication,[4] and partly with dissociating Nietzsche's real ideas from their misuse and exploitation by, for example, the Nazis. But to the extent to which the statement suggests that the nature and structure of Nietzsche's positive philosophy are plain for all to see, it is open to criticism. In his outstanding work on Nietzsche, Karl Jaspers claims that no system which we find in the philosopher's writings will reveal itself as a 'complete, single and unambiguous whole.'[5] And Mr Danto says of his own account of Nietzsche's philosophy that 'the system which I offer must be appriciated as a reconstruction, to be understood as one must understand any theory; that is, as an instrument for unifying and explaining a domain of phenomena — in this case the domain of an individual's writing.'[6] Certainly, it is clear that Nietzsche proposed the theories of the will to power, of superman and of the eternal recurrence. It is also clear that every account of a past philosopher's thought can be described as a reconstruction, involving personal interpretation. But Nietzsche's thought seems to lend itself to a greater variety of interpretation than does the thought of, say, David Hume or Auguste Comte.

One of the differences between the interpretations of Nietzsche given by Hollingdale and Danto lies in their respective attitudes to the description of Nietzsche's philosophy as 'metaphysical'. Hollingdale tells us that Nietzsche's mature philosophy, unlike Schopenhauer's, 'is not metaphysical but materialistic'[7] and that 'not until he [Nietzsche] had put metaphysics of any kind behind him did he enter into his own proper field.[8] Danto, however, speaks of the philosopher as 'a metaphysician [who] sought to provide a picture of the world as it actually is'.[9] and he describes the idea of the will to power as 'a metaphysical or, better, an ontological concept'.[10]

To a certain extent of course this difference can be eliminated by the use of an appropriate distinction. When Nietzsche rejects metaphysics, he is thinking primarily of the contention that there is a reality other than this world, a reality in comparison with which this world is not truly real. In other words, he is thinking of the metaphysician as a man who depreciates this world in favour of another and imaginary world, and who tries in this way to comfort and reassure the weak who are unable to accept the world as they find it, or who find life too much for them. Or, to put the matter in a slightly different way, Nietzsche regards the metaphysician as a man who contructs an imaginary reality to confer order, intelligibility and purpose on a phenomenal world which lacks these characteristics. Metaphysics in this sense is rejected by Nietzsche. And Danto does not deny this obvious fact. On the contrary, he explicitly admits that when Nietzsche uses the term 'metaphysics', 'he often has in mind only a philosophy that speaks of a reality which is higher and purer than the one we are seemingly acquainted with through the senses'.[11]

As for Hollingdale's description of Nietzsche's philosophy as materialistic, which at first sight may seem to conflict with Danto's justified observation that Nietzsche rejects the concept of substance, whether material or immaterial, it need not be understood as implying that Nietzsche accepted a theory of material substance. For it may mean that for Nietzsche there is no reality other than the phenomenal world, and that, in man, there is no spiritual and immortal soul.

At the same time, if one goes simply by what is written in the two books in question. I doubt whether the difference between Danto and Hollingdale can be completely eliminated in this way. For Danto admits two senses of metaphysics and is willing to describe Nietzsche as being, in one of these senses, a metaphysician, whereas Hollingdale depicts Nietzsche as putting metaphysics 'of any kind' behind him. And this second position I find rather hard to understand. For if we refuse to admit that Nietzsche is in any sense a metaphysician, we must claim, I suppose, that he is engaged in putting forward empirical or scientific hypotheses. After all, we can hardly claim that Nietzsche of all people is engaged in mapping out the field of current linguistic usage. To claim, however, that the theories of the will to power and of the eternal recurrence, as put forward by Nietzsche, are simply scientific hypotheses, does not seem to me a reasonable procedure. I do not wish to assert that Hollingdale makes this claim. But if he seriously thinks that in his mature philosophy Nietzsche has put metaphysics 'of any kind' behind him, what else can he say?

Hollingdale tells us that Nietzsche's theory of the will to power is 'an induction from observed data, not a metaphysical postulate like Schopenhauer's will to live'.[12] Well, Nietzsche certainly appeals to empirical data. So for that matter did Schopenhauer, who was assiduous in finding empirical conformation of his thesis in history and in scientific writings. The retort can indeed be made that Schopenhauer first postulates a metaphysical theory and then looks round for empirical confirmation, whereas Nietzsche's approach to his theory of the will to power is more inductive. At the same time, even if Nietzsche's approach is inductive, he extends the concept of the will to power to the totality, to all reality. And the theory of the eternal recurrence is precisely about the totality, the totality of all phenomena. It is all very well to add, as Hollingdale does, that it is not a theory about 'ultimate reality'.[13] It is clearly not a theory about an ultimate reality beyond this world. But, equally clearly I should have thought, it is a theory about the whole of the reality which is, for Nietzsche, ultimate. Hollingdale says that the theory of the eternal recurrence 'provided Nietzsche with a new picture of a non-metaphysical reality'.[14] This is doubtless true, if 'metaphysical' is understood in the sense which seems to be intended. But Hollingdale goes on immediately to add that the theory provided Nietzsche with 'a reconciliation of 'becoming' with 'being'. And I do not think that to put 'becoming' and 'being' in inverted commas is sufficient to stop them from being metaphysical themes.

It is indeed true that Nietzsche offered scientific arguments in support of the theory of the eternal recurrence. Further, I admit that I lay myself open to the objection that some theoretical scientists are given to constructing hypotheses about 'the whole'. Is the theory of the eternal recurrence, it may be asked, of an altogether different type than the theory of a successively expanding and contracting universe? Where do I propose to draw the line between metaphysical and non-metaphysical theories?

Sometimes it is rather difficult to draw the line. But let us assume that we are prepared to adopt Karl Popper's criterion of falsifiability as a means of marking off non-metaphysical theories. Is the theory of the eternal recurrence empirically falsifiable? I find difficulty in seeing how it could be. The supporting arguments offered by Nietzsche may be refutable. But this is a different matter. There is such a thing as inductive metaphysics. And the theory of the will to power seems to me of this nature. It may be a generalization based on, for example, interpretations of psychological phenomena. But it is none the less a universal generalization. And it is very difficult to see how it could be falsified. For phenomena which at first sight seem to count against it will be interpreted in such a way that they are converted into confirmations. We can of course put forward another theory and claim that, for certain reasons, it is a superior theory. But this is not quite the same thing as showing that the generalized theory of the will to power is empirically falsifiable.

In general, I agree with Jaspers that though Nietzsche warns us against talking about the world as a whole as this is inaccessible to us, he then goes on to offer 'his own exegesis of the world in its entirety'.[15] And it seems to me that this exegesis can properly be described as metaphysical. It is, I suppose, an example of what Mr P.F.Strawson has called revisionary metaphysics.

2

Now all scientific theories are for Nietzsche 'fictions', conceptual constructions which we impose, as it were, on the world. And if we interpret the theories of the will to power and of the eternal recurrence as scientific hypotheses, we must obviously conclude that they too are fictions, unless we are prepared to declare Nietzsche guilty of an obvious inconsistency. If, however, we describe the theory of the will to power, in its generalized form, and the doctrine of the eternal recurrence as metaphysical theories, the question arises whether or not this description is intended to imply that Nietzsche, in his capacity as a metaphysician, intends to provide us with *the* truth about the world, truth in an absolute sense.

It can of course be admitted at once that Nietzsche sometimes speaks as though, in his positive philosophy, he is revealing the truth about the world. It would be very difficult for him to recommend his theories strongly, even passionately, without speaking in this way. Moreover, it is clear from what the philosopher himself says that in 1881 the idea of the eternal recurrence came to him as a kind of revelation. To be sure, it was not the first time that the idea had occurred to his mind. But it was in

1881 that the significance of the idea impressed itself vividly on his mind for the first time. He then tried to support it with empirical evidence. But the idea itself was of importance to him both for its metaphysical significance, inasmuch as it set the seal on a purely this-worldly philosophy, and for its 'existential' significance, as a test of strength of character and of vigorous life.

All students of Nietzsche are aware, however, that when the philosopher describes scientific theories as fictions, he is simply giving an example. That is to say, it is not simply our scientific hypotheses which are fictions. As Danto rightly notes, in the sense in which, for Nietzsche, science is not true 'neither is anything else'.[16] In this respect scientific hypotheses, logical and mathematical principles and axioms, and the theories of the will to power and of the eternal recurrence are all in the same boat. Hence we can hardly suppose that Nietzsche really imagines that the theories which he expounds provide us with the absolute truth about the world. He may on occasion use language which implies that he does think this. But it seems to me clear that, if pressed, Nietzsche would admit that his theories too are fictions. Indeed he sometimes almost says as much. As already suggested, the language which seems to imply the contrary can be explained as the language of passionate recommendation of a particular persepective.

Hollingdale, while indeed recognizing that Nietzsche is faced with a problem in regard to truth,[17] seems to me to skate rather lightly over it. Danto, however, considers the matter at some length. He distinguishes two senses of truth. First there is the correspondence theory of truth, the idea that 'truth consists in the satisfaction of a relationship between a sentence and a fact'.[18] This idea of truth is rejected by Nietzsche. There are no facts but only interpretations, perspectives. Secondly there is a pragmatic view of truth. And the criterion which Nietzsche accepts is in fact pragmatic. Some interpretations 'serve life'. others do not. Nietzsche expounds his own theories as 'true', not in the sense that they express *the* truth about the world, but in the sense that they serve or promote ascending life.

This view of the matter certainly accords with Nietzsche's famous definition of truth as 'that sort of error without which a particular type of living being could not live'.[19] But while recognition of the fact that Nietzsche's theories of the will to power and of the eternal recurrence are no less 'fictions' than are scientific hypotheses certainly eliminates the inconsistency which would be present in his thought if he claimed that the theories in question provided us with the absolute and final truth about the world, it by no means solves all the problems in regard to truth which arise out of his position. For example, Nietzsche tells us that the world in itself is without order, intelligibility and purpose. But if this view is itself a fiction, Nietzsche obviously cannot claim to *know* that the world in itself is of this nature, while if he does claim to know it he cannot at the same time reject the correspondence theory of truth. For the statement that the world in itself is without order, intelligibility and purpose would be absolutely true because it corresponds with, or 'pictures', an actual state of affairs.

To a certain extent at least this difficulty can be diminished by considering what Nietzsche has to say about language. For the present reviewer at any rate, the most interesting feature of Danto's book is his examination of Nietzsche as a philosopher of language. And one of Danto's remarks is obviously relevant in the present context. 'The claim that the world is valueless *(wertlos)* is not to say that it has some low value in the scheme of values, as when we say, of something, that it is of little worth or none, but rather, it is not the kind of thing of which it logically makes sense to say either that it is worth little, or that it has such and such a higher value. Values have no more application to the world than weights do to numbers'.[20] In other words, when Nietzsche says that the world is in itself without value, he need not be claiming either to have had an intuitive vision of the world in itself, apart from our interpretations of it, or to have deduced this truth from *a priori* principles. He may be saying simply that 'value' is a relational word. To assert that *x* has value is either to express one's own act of evaluation or to assert that human beings value *x*. To speak of *x* having value 'in itself', apart from all evaluation, is to talk nonsense.

At the same time Danto goes on to say that 'it follows that the world has no value from the fact that there is nothing in it which might sensibly be supposed to have value. There is neither order nor purpose, things nor facts'.[21] How does Nietzsche know this? Can we argue from language alone that it makes no sense to speak of there being order or facts in the world? If we can, are we driven to the paradoxical conclusion that it is a fact that there are no facts?

The retort can be made that Nietzsche rejects the Kantian thing-in-itself, and that for him there is no world in itself. There are only interpretations, perspectives, fictions. To suppose that there is a world in itself is to be misled by language, by the natural tendency to suppose that interpretation implies the existence of something to be interpreted.

Nietzsche does indeed propose the doctrine that if we substract the perspectival, there is nothing left about which we can say anything intelligible. Presumably, therefore, the theory of the eternal recurrence, for example, must be understood simply as a possible way of conceiving the world (or, perhaps better, of projecting or creating a world) and not as a revelation of what the world is like in itself. To be sure, one of the reasons why the theory commends itself to Nietzsche is that it effectually gets rid of all metaphysical substitutes for God, gets rid of, that is to say, any teleological interpretation of the world such as we find in Hegel. And it is thus natural to think that for Nietzsche the theory tells us something about the world in itself which is absolutely true, namely that the world in itself is without meaning or end *(telos)*. If, however, we wish to make Nietzsche self-consistent, we are forced to regard the theory as simply a perspective, an interpretation of something about which nothing 'neutral,' that is to say, nonperspectival, can be said. (For that matter are we entitled to speak of 'something'?) Certainly, Nietzsche recommends this particular way of seeing the world, as against other possible ways, because of its value for life. But the distinction between ascending and decending life, and the whole interpretation of life in terms of the theory of the will to power, must also be perspectival, fictional.

In other words, on Nietzsche's premises there can be no neutral criterion for deciding between the view of the world which he recommends and any other view. Everything seems to hang in the air. And to alter the situation one would have to have recourse at some point to an, at least tacit, acceptance of a non-Nietzschean theory of truth. Indeed it is arguable, as Jaspers argues, that it is only on the basis of a distinction between truth and error which is sharper than that allowed by Nietzsche that we are able to speak meaningfully of truth at all; that it is only on the basis of a sharper distinction that 'we can make the paradoxical attempt to remove the antithesis by maintaining that truth and error differ merely in degree of illusoriness but do not differ in kind'.[22]

3

Critical discussion of this type probably seems tiresome to a good many people. Why? Partly, no doubt, because the game of finding inconsistencies in Nietzsche is by no means a novelty. But also, I think, because it is felt that the criticism, however valid it may be, fails to do justice to Nietzsche. It is felt, for example, that the critic who suggests that Nietzsche contradicts himself by asserting the truth of the statement that there are only degrees of error, reveals his failure to appreciate the significance of the philosopher's thought.

This feeling is, in my opinon, justified. But a condition for its being justified is that there should be an aspect of Nietzsche's thought which possesses a significance more or less independently of his 'positive philosophy', of the doctrinal results of his philosophizing. After all, if we focus our attention simply on his positive doctrines, we are inevitably faced with a choice. Either we interpret Nietzsche's theories as claiming to provide *the* truth about the world; and then we make the philosopher guilty of an obvious self-contradiction. Or we interpret the theories as constituting a highly personal fiction or myth which we can accept or dismiss as we choose.

Perhaps a remark which Hollingdale makes at the end of his book hits the nail on the head. 'His [Nietzsche's] life and thought were both in a sense experiments'.[23] Nietzsche is in fact a great questioner and experimenter. He challenges our most cherished assumptions, such as the sharp distinction between truth and error. He calls in question the values which we tend to take for granted. He turns a critical eye on what many philosophers have regarded as self-evident principles or truths. He subjects to critical examination the most pervasive concepts, such as the concept of "thing." He tries to expose the bewitching influence which language tends to exercise on our ways of seeing the world. He develops experimentally a new way of seeing the world. And though his mental and physical collapse, the onset of what was probably general paralysis of the insane, left his thought frozen, as it were, in the set of doctrines which constitute his positive philosophy, it is clear that in moments of self-criticism he saw that, on his own premises, these doctrines were themselves 'fictions.'

If one emphasizes this aspect of Nietzsche's thought, it may appear that one is representing him simply as a nihilist, a destroyer. But this is not necessarily the case. It is indeed arguable that in spite of Nietzsche's desire to overcome nihilism, it is in fact nihilism which has the last word. But, quite apart from this question, it seems clear to me that philosophy has always had a radically critical aspect, an aspect which is of course more clearly revealed in certain periods than in others, with some philosophers more than with others, but which pertains to philosophy as such. Nietzsche distinguishes himself by the radical and extended nature of his criticism. He does not content himself with questioning the arguments and assumptions of the thinkers of whom he happens to disapprove most strongly. He subjects to critical examination the presuppositions of all our ordinary thought and language. As Danto well puts it, Nietzsche's 'purpose was in part to crack the habitual grip on thought in which language holds us, to make us aware of how much our minds are dominated by concepts from which we can hardly escape, given the rules our language follows . . . The concepts he attacked had to be the most basic ones, the piers, so to speak, which supported the entire ramified network of human ideas, piers sunk so deep in the human psychology as scarcely to be acknowledged'.[24] Nietzsche was not concerned, however, simply with undermining an old building. He hoped in this way to render possible new buildings. And he himself tried to construct one.

It seems to me that in a real sense Nietzsche's constructive effort was a failure. I do not mean to deny of course that he developed some doctrines which together form his positive philosophy, a philosophy which is greatly admired by ardent Nietzscheans and which has also been misused by some Nazi theorists. But if one is expecting the entirely new, the hitherto unheard-of, many people feel a sense of disappointment when they come to reflect on this philosopher's theories. It is a common enough remark, for example, that Nietzsche's new values look suspiciously like old values. And when one considers the development of the theory of the will to power, one can notice that tacit employment of concepts which have been subjected to criticism and found wanting. Moreover, this is really inevitable. For Nietzsche does not invent an entirely new language. He uses existing language. And if he is trying to express in existing language what cannot, *ex hypothesi*, be so expressed, failure is bound to result. If Nietzsche is in fact reaching out after the hitherto unthought, he cannot tell us what it is. Indeed, we might ask whether he can think it.

At the same time, if we are prepared to admit that an examination of basic presuppositions is part of philosophy's job, I do not see how the questioning and critical movement of Nietzsche's thought can be adequately described as nihilistic. If profound questioning is converted into dogmatic denial, we may then have nihilism. But I am talking about the movement of thought rather than about the dogmatic pronouncements. Further, if we fix our attention on the questioning and critical movement of Nietzsche's thought, the inconsistencies and contradictions which may show themselves lose the 'scandalous' aspect which they assume if we concentrate simply on the results of his philosophizing. If we call in question the concept of truth, and if in the end it is found that the questioning presupposes what is called in question, this in no way destroys the value of the experimentation. On the contrary, we have learned something. If, however, we state dogmatically that it is true that there is no truth, we have contradicted ourselves.

4

According to Jaspers, Nietzsche's thought never finds a resting-place but undermines, denies and transcends every fixed or determinate position. And at first sight this view seems open to serious objection. For it may appear to lay such an exclusive emphasis on the critical and destructive elements in Nietzsche's philosophizing as to involve the unverifiable hypothesis that if the philosopher had retained sanity and mental vigour, he would have denied the theories of the will to power and of the eternal recurrence and the idea of superman as the meaning or goal of human existence, indeed of the whole earth.

What Jaspers says, however, cannot be dismissed quite so easily. In developing the concept of superman, for example, it is quite obvious that Nietzsche is constantly tending to transcend the actual. The 'higher men' of history are weighed in the balance and found wanting, and the concept of superman emerges as that which lies beyond man. Nietzsche does indeed attempt to give some content to the concept. But when he does so, he inevitably paints a picture in terms of the characteristics of the higher men who have already been found human-all-too-human. Even if he sometimes refers to the doctrine of evolution, he does not appear to believe in the automatic production, as it were, of superman. For he calls upon men to set themselves a goal, namely superman. This goal transcends the actual and, for this very reason, becomes vague and nebulous. When referring to the term 'overman,' which some commentators or translators have preferred to 'superman,' Danto remarks that 'if it is over — it is so in the sense of "over the hills and far away"',[25] It seems to me to be a plain fact that Nietzsche is never satisfied with actual man. This is, of course, one main reason why the notion that the philosopher would have seen examples of superman in Adolf Hitler and his associates is simply laughable. Indeed, to speak paradoxically, one may well have the impression that if a superman had ever appeared to the philosopher, Nietzsche would very soon have dismissed him as human-all-too-human.

Any general assertion that Nietzsche is never satisfied with the actual, shows a singular degree of misunderstanding. For who is more insistent than Nietzsche on affirming life and the world as they are? Yes, but did Nietzsche really affirm life and the world 'as they are'? There is a good deal to be said in favor of Crane Brinton's observation that the great 'yea-sayer' spent most of his life saying 'No'.[26] It seems to me that if the doctrine of the eternal recurrence tells us how we ought to see the godless world, namely as without goal or end, without any metaphysical significance or purpose, then the demand that we should will that super-man be the meaning of the earth is equivalent to an act of defiance, a no-saying, to the meaningless world.

Some writers on Nietzsche tend to link up the theory of superman with the empirical hypothesis of evolution. But if I understand Jaspers correctly, he maintains that, to the extent to which Nietzsche himself makes such a link, his thought degenerates into 'unphilosophy', just as it degenerates into 'unphilosophy' when Nietzsche attempts to represent the doctrine of the eternal recurrence as a scientific hypothesis. In other words, according to Jaspers, when Nietzsche's thought tries to find a determinate resting-place, it tends to become something other than genu-inely philosophical. Obviously, Jaspers' idea of what constitutes genuine philosophizing is open to discussion. But I do not think that his view of Nietzsche's thought is absurd. It does not seem to me unreasonable to argue that when Nietzsche is not engaged in anticipating the psychology of Adler, or in hazarding empirical hypotheses about the origins of moral distinctions, he is engaged in a flight from actual man and from what we take to be reality.

Jaspers is not, however, concerned simply with drawing attention to what one might call the passing-on character of Nietzsche's thought. He conceives this thought as directed to a goal. And this goal is 'authentic being rather than nothingness . . . It is authentic being toward which the passionate will to truth, in the form of an ineradicable scepticism, strives with ever renewed insistence.'[27] To be sure, in certain contexts Nietzsche denounces the will to truth. But Jaspers' contention is that underlying the scepticism of Nietzsche, his constant critical attacks, is a persistent will to truth which never attains its object. If we look at the matter from the point of view of Jaspers' own philosophy, it is obvious that Nietzsche's 'will to pure this-worldliness'[28] means that he cannot possibly attain the goal of 'authentic being.' But, for Jaspers, the construction of substitutes reveals the inner direction of Nietzsche's thought, a direction of which the philosopher himself is unaware.

To anyone acquainted with the philosophy of Jaspers this sounds as though he is claiming that Nietzsche is engaged in searching for God. And this is of course, in a sense, what Jaspers believes. Nietzsche's 'godliness is the increasing agitation of a search for God that perhaps no longer understands itself'.[29] Needless to say, Jaspers does not deny Nietzsche's godlessness. He does not try to make out that Nietzsche is 'really' a Christian. Nor does he suggest that in his opposition to Christianity Nietzsche is 'in reaction against his aunts'.[30] He is perfectly well aware that Nietzsche regards the concept of God, not simply as a harmless myth or fairy tale, but as an extremely dangerous enemy of human life and creative freedom, and that he therefore both proclaims and wills the 'death of God'.[31] He is also obviously well aware that Nietzsche rejects not simply the Christian idea of God, as he understands it (or misunderstands it), but also any concept of an ultimate reality, or Unconditioned, or Absolute which could reasonably be described as 'God'. With Nietzsche there is indeed 'a radical negation of all belief in God.'[32] At the same time Jaspers argues that though Nietzsche's reflections are directed to showing man how he can attain the highest level of self-development in a godless world, his radical denial of God leads to the construction of substitutes.

When listing Jaspers' book in his bibliography, Hollingdale remarks that it is 'to be read in the light of the author's own philosophy'.[33] This is obviously true. What Jaspers gives is an interpretation of Nietzsche as *Existenz;* and what one thinks of it depends to some extent on one's sympathy, or lack of it, with Jaspers' philosophy of existence. Further, it is hardly necessary to add that the interpretation will not commend itself to anyone who rejects the idea of God altogether, including 'the hidden God, the indemonstrable God' of Jaspers.[34] We must remember, however, that Jaspers would not claim that his interpretation of Nietzsche is the only possible one, or that its validity can be proved by logical argument. Moreover, he emphasizes the ambiguity of Nietzsche's philosophizing. And if I may venture to suggest an example, the doctrine of the eternal recurrence may serve for this purpose. From one point of view it can be seen as a physical hypothesis. From another point of view it is a metaphysical theory. From another point of view it is an existential challenge. If we leave out of account the first point of view, can the eternal recurrence be reasonably regarded as a substitute or surrogate for God? One might argue that it cannot. For it is intended by Nietzsche as the decisive alternative to God and to all metaphysical substitutes for

God. But one might also argue that Nietzsche's desire to confer on the
flux of becoming the semblance of being betrays the hidden orientation
of his thought to what Jaspers calls 'authentic being', in spite of the fact
that Nietzsche's aim is to exclude any transcendent being and to depict
the world in such a way that it could not be looked on as the expression
of mind or reason.[35] To many people it doubtless seems absurd to argue
that Nietzsche's thought is 'really' orientated to God, in any sense of the
term. After all, we know very well what the philosopher said. And
this is, what he thought. Does it make any sense to look for anything
more? Well, in depth psychology this is a common enough procedure.
And I suppose that Jaspers is engaged in what might be described as
existential psychology. But I do not see how the issue can be decided to
everyone's satisfaction. In any case Jaspers is not trying to turn his interpretation of Nietzsche into an unquestionable conclusion. What he
invites people to do is to 'philosophize with Nietzsche', when philosophizing with Nietzsche does not mean learning his doctrines, but
following the path of questing, wiht a view to becoming aware of one's
own being, of *Existenz*, which by its very nature is orientated to unobjectifiable 'authentic being'.

5

After reading *Beyond Good and Evil,* Erwin Rohde remarked that
Nietzsche was always promising 'hair-raising audacities of thought,
which then, to the bored disappointment of the reader, never come'.[36]
However this may be, I suppose that there must be a good many readers
who are at first excited by Nietzsche's ideas, by his doctrines, and then in
the course of time find that they either become tiresome, sometimes
even banal, or show themselves unable to survive the difficulties which
arise out of the philosopher's own premises. Exasperating though it may
be, we can understand and pardon Nietzsche's shouting, as expressing a
desperate effort, in the midst of almost total contemporary indifference,
to draw attention to what he considered to be of great importance. The
trouble is, however, that 'Nietzscheanism', when separated from the
philosopher's exaggerated language and reduced to a set of theses or
doctrines, hardly has the power to cause us very much excitement. Some
readers who were thrilled (and perhaps repelled or even horrified) by
Nietzsche when they first became acquainted with his writings, find it
difficult at a later date to read him again without boredom.

Nietzsche is, however, much more than a set of theses or doctrines.
He has a lasting historical importance, as anticipating, with remarkable
insight, the upheavals and convulsions of the twentieth century, and as
representing in himself the spiritual crisis of modern man.[37] Again, some
at least would agree with Jaspers about the significance of Nietzsche as
representing an 'exception', one of the extreme possibilities of human
Existenz.[38] We can also recognize the importance of Nietzsche, in the

philosophical sphere, as a radical questioner of presuppositions. We are all accustomed (if we are philosophers, that is) to questioning other people's presuppositions and assumptions. But Nietzsche calls in question the presuppositions which underlie the language which we all use. By calling them in question he may have deprived himself, logically speaking, of the means of saying anything at all. But at any rate he makes us conscious of our presuppositions and stimulates experimentation. And this is no mean feat. Having remarked, as already mentioned, that Nietzsche attacks the most basic concepts, those which support the whole network of human ideas, Danto adds: 'it is for this that he is entitled to be called a philosopher'.[39] It is not, I think, the only reason.[40] But it is a reason, and one of the main ones, one which can be admitted even by those whose judgment about Nietzsche's positive philosophy is extremely reserved.

Notes

[1] R.J. Hollingdale, *Nietzsche: The Man and His Philosophy* (Baton Rouge, 1965), pp. 310-311. This work will be referred to in footnotes as *H*.
[2] *H*, p. 173.
[3] *H*, p. 302.
[4] This point was insisted on by Mr. Walter A. Kaufmann in his notable work *Nietzsche: Philosopher, Psychologist, Antichrist* (Princeton, N.J., 1950).
[5] Karl Jaspers, *Nietzsche: An Introduction to the Understanding of His Philosophical Activity*, trans. Charles F. Wallraff & Fredrick J. Schmitz (Tucson, 1965). This work will be referred to in footnotes as *J*. (In spite of what the translators say on p. vii, it seems to me regrettable that they have omitted references locating quotations from Nietzsche's writings. The references need not have been to the edition of the writings used by Jaspers in the 1936 original.)
[6] Arthur C. Danto, *Nietzsche as Philosopher* (New York & London, 1965), pp. 25-6. This work will be referred to in footnotes as *D*.
[7] *H*, p. 84.
[8] *H*, p. 96.
[9] *D*, p. 195.
[10] *D*, p. 215.
[11] *D*, p. 81.
[12] *H*, p. 84.
[13] *H*, p. 87.
[14] *H*, p. 177.
[15] *J*, p. 293.
[16] *D*, p. 31.
[17] *H*, p. 217.
[18] *D*, p. 72.
[19] *Werke (Schlechta)* III, p. 844.
[20] *D*, pp. 32-33.
[21] *D*, p. 33.
[22] *J*, p. 187.
[23] *H*, p. 305.
[24] *D*, p. 12.
[25] *D*, p. 197.
[26] Crane Brinton, *Nietzsche* (Cambridge, Mass., & London, 1941), p. 17.
[27] *J*, p. 211.
[28] *J*, p. 429.

[29] J, p. 435.

[30] J.J.Figgis, *The Will to Freedom, Or the Gospel of Nietzsche and the Gospel of Christ* (London, 1917), p. 51.

[31] Nietzsche did of course regard the concept of God as mythical. He did not believe, as Mr Altizer appears to believe, that there was once a transcendent God who has since died. But Nietzsche's hostility to belief in God is based on other grounds. And, on these grounds, he positively willed the disappearence of belief in God, at least for all those capable of living without such belief.

[32] J, p. 434.

[33] H, p. 318.

[34] Karl Jaspers, *Way to Wisdom: An Introduction to Philosophy*, trans. Ralph Manheim (London, 1951), p. 50.

[35] In a sense, of course, the world is for Nietzsche the expression of mind. For what I call the world is an interpretation. But the mind in question is not a divine mind or a creative cosmic reason.

[36] Quoted in H, p. 208.

[37] Nietzsche also prided himself on his insight as a psychologist. This claim can of course be admitted. But it is not perhaps a strictly philosophical matter, even if what Nietzsche has to say in this sphere has philosophical relevance.

[38] This way of looking at Nietzsche does not necessarily entail acceptance of Jaspers' interpretation of the hidden goal of the philosopher's thought.

[39] D, p. 12.

[40] For that matter Danto himself goes on immediately to say that Nietzsche was 'more than a critic of concepts and a word-tormenting anarchist,' *Ibid.*

CHAPTER 11

BERGSON ON MORALITY

HENRI BERGSON, who died at an advanced age in 1941, was at one time an influential and fashionable philosopher. William James hailed the appearance of *Creative Evolution* as marking the beginning of a new era in the history of philosophy. But today Bergson is no longer fashionable. In his own country the philosophy of life was succeeded by existentialism, while the style of his thought and his mode of expression are so alien to the spirit of the dominant philosophical movement in this country that it is in no way surprising if his writings are neglected here. However, his theory of morality is not without interest; and when the Council of the British Academy did me the great honour of inviting me to give the first lecture under the new Dawes Hicks Foundation I decided to take as my subject Bergson's reflections on ethics as set forth in his *Two Sources of Morality and Religion*.[1] It may be an irrelevant remark, but on reading the obituary notice of Professor Dawes Hicks in the *Proceedings of the British Academy* I learned that after the publication of his work on Berkeley he received an appreciative letter from Bergson.

Perhaps I should make it clear at once that I wish to devote this chapter to a discussion of certain features of Bergson's moral theory and not to an examination of the historical antecedents of this theory. It is sufficient to recall that his philosophy was the culmination of the so-called spiritualist movement in French thought, and that he was indebted for a number of his characteristic ideas to the inspiration of men such as Maine de Biran, Guyau, Fouillée, and Ravaisson. In the *Two Sources* he relied for a good deal of his information about the empirical data relating to morals on the writings of sociologists such as Lévy-Bruhl and Durkheim. In developing his theory of what he calls 'closed morality' he seems to have been influenced by what he had read years before in the writings of Fouillée, to name but one philosopher, and his interpretation of mysticism, as this is expressed in his theory of 'open morality' and, of course, in the theory of 'dynamic religion', was at least encouraged by his reading of Henri Delacroix and Evelyn Underhill. But Bergson never claimed to be particularly original. And in any case discussion of the writings which contributed to the formation of his ideas is not really relevant to discussion of the ideas themselves.

2

As the title of his work *The Two Sources of Morality and Religion* indicates, Bergson was concerned primarily with the sources or origins of morality. But if one asks what is the source or what are the sources of morality, it is not at all clear precisely what the question means. And

Bergson does not begin his discussion of morality by formulating explicitly a problem or problems for solution. Nevertheless, inspection of
his actual procedure reveals the questions which he has in mind. He starts
with two sets of empirical data. The first set consists of facts relating to
the connexion between codes of conduct and particular societies. The
second set consists of facts relating to moral insight and especially to the
part played in this progress by outstanding individuals. And he asks himself, what are the causes of these two sets of data. That is to say, he
develops an hypothesis designed to provide a causal explanation of the
data, the phrase 'causal explanation' including explanation in terms of
final causality. Another way of putting Bergson's question is, what part
does reason play in the moral life of mankind, as revealed in these two
sets of data?

Bergson's discussion of morality thus conforms to his general pattern
of procedure. In earlier works he had taken, for example, psychological
and biological data and had endeavoured to interpret them. Here he
takes ethically relevant data and proceeds to interpret them. At the
same time he tries to link up his immediate interpretation of the data
with the wider metaphysical hypothesis to which his earlier reflections
had led him. I do not mean that Bergson simply tried to force ethical
data into the framework of a hard-and-fast preconceived metaphysical
system. For he never possessed any hard-and-fast system. Rather was it
a question of developing further a general hypothesis in the fresh light
shed by reflection on morality and religion. Yet there can be little
doubt, I think, that the conclusions to which his earlier reflections on
psychological and biological data had led him influenced his interpretation of morality and religion in the *Two Sources*. It is possible that
this influence was not always beneficial.

3

Now, if we wish to develop a moral philosophy by reflecting on empirical
data, as Bergson did, it is clear that one of the chief data which we have
to take into account is the sense of obligation. And it is indeed with this
topic that Bergson begins. We might expect, therefore, that he would try
first of all to give a phenomenological description and analysis of the
sense of obligation, before proceeding to inquire what are the cause or
causes of the sense of obligation and what part it plays in the general
scheme of things. But in point of fact he does not do this. And when we
find a description of the sense of obligation we also find that controversial
interpretative elements have been introduced. In the course of his long
chapter on morality he does indeed say that he presupposes the ordinary
consciousness of obligation as something which is so well known that it
needs no description. But though it is doubtless true that anyone who
has a sense or consciousness of obligation knows, in some sense of the
word 'know', what it is, I think that Bergson's failure to give a prelimi-

nary careful description of it, or, if preferred, to say clearly what is meant by the term, has unfortunate consequences. I shall return later to this point. Meanwhile I wish to approach the subject of obligation more or less as Bergson himself approached it.

Bergson was struck by the obvious connexion between codes of conduct and ideas of duties on the one hand and human societies on the other. That there is a *de facto* connexion can easily be seen by considering how each one of us receives his or her preliminary moral notions and by recalling historical data. In the course of his upbringing the individual is gradually initiated into the way of life of the society to which he belongs, a way of life in which certain standards, certain values, are accepted, and which is governed by certain rules. Society, through the mediation of parents, teachers, religious guides, transmits its moral code to the individual. In history different societies, the Greek city-state, for instance, or the Jewish theocracy, had their own codes of conduct and ways of life. Actions which have been disapproved of in one society have been tolerated or even approved of in another society. There is no need, I think, to labour this point. More important is Bergson's conclusion that it is the pressure of society on the individual to conform himself to the standards of action operative in the community which is felt as obligation, as an impersonal imperative bearing upon him. It is felt as an imperative because he is free. Though Bergson strongly disagreed with Kant about the part played by reason in morality, he agreed with him that obligation presupposes freedom. 'A human being feels an obligation only if he is free, and each obligation, considered separately, implies liberty' (p. 19). Social pressure, then, is felt by the individual in the form of the sense of obligation, and society exercises this pressure with a view to its own cohesion and preservation. We have, therefore, an efficient cause of the sense of obligation, namely social pressure, and a final cause, namely the cohesion and preservation of society.

This theory, whether true or false, may seem at first to be perfectly clear. But some elucidation seems to be needed. In the first place, what is meant by the word 'society' when it is said that society exercises pressure on the individual? Happily, Bergson is quite explicit on this point. He is referring to what he calls the 'closed society' and not to some ideal society of all men. A particular society, whether it is a primitive tribe or a modern State, is conscious of itself as *this* society, as distinct from another society or from other societies. And the primary function of the morality of obligation is to preserve the cohesion and life of a closed society in this sense.

Now, if society is understood in this sense, we can obviously give an empirical content to the term 'social pressure'. If we take a macroscopic society such as our own, we can mention ways in which society exerts a pressure on the individual with a view to the performance or non-performance of certain actions. The whole legal, judicial, and penal apparatus of the State exercises a constant pressure on the citizen to refrain from those actions which are prohibited by law and for the infringement of which certain penalties are inflicted. Similarly, in the case of a microscopic society such as a public school, empirical content can be given to the statement that the individual boy is subject to the constant pressure of society, directed towards the performance of certain actions and the non-performance of others. At the same time, whatever our views on human freedom may be, we all have some idea of what is meant by saying that social pressure can be resisted. After all, some people do disobey the law of the State, consciously risking the penalties attached to such behaviour; and some boys do infringe the code of conduct obtaining at their school. Again, empirical content can be given to the statement that a closed society exercises pressure with a view to its own cohesion and preservation. Thus we read in a book by a missionary among the Eskimos that 'the penal code of the Eskimo people is intended to protect the general welfare and is not concerned with personal crimes such as murder. The only crime is an action that weakens the social body itself' (*Inuk*, p. 66). Actions such as suppressing baby daughters and committing suicide in old age were approved of, because they rid the community of useless mouths and so contributed to the survival and preservation of the tribe in its very hard conditions of life.

Now, Bergson maintained, as we have seen, that social pressure is felt by the individual in the form of the sense of obligation. But this statement is ambiguous. On the one hand it might mean that social pressure is an empirical, non-ethical factor which causes in us the peculiar (that is, specifically ethical) feeling of obligation, without our adverting to this social pressure. We should then have an answer, though in my opinion a thoroughly inadequate answer, to the question, what is the cause or source or origin of the sense of obligation. The case would be analogous to that of a man who had feelings of, say, great happiness and peace under the influence of a drug. The feelings would be caused by the drug, but they would be specific feelings of happiness and peace. On the other hand the statement that social pressure is felt by the individual in the form of the sense of obligation might mean that when we feel obliged to perform or not to perform action *x* this feeling is a feeling of social pressure directed to the performance or non-performance of an action, in the sense that consciousness of the obligation is consciousness of the social pressure. In this case social pressure would be obligation. We should then have an answer to the question, what is obligation.

It seems to me that Bergson is none too clear in his own mind which meaning he intends to attach to the statement that social pressure is felt by the individual in the form of the sense of obligation. That is to say, he does not seem to make it altogether clear whether he is making a psychological statement about the origin of the sense of obligation or an ethical statement about the nature of obligation. But inasmuch as he tends to speak of social pressure as though it were itself obligation, to this extent he appears to understand his statement in the second sense.

The sense of moral obligation must, I think, be a sense of being morally obliged to do or not to do this or that. I am not morally obliged in a purely general and vacuous sense: moral obligation has reference to some definite performance. And social pressure must, of course, take the form of particular social pressures. But Bergson attempts to find the essence or core of obligation, that which is common to all obligations and to which obligation can be finally reduced even in its most complex manifestations. And if obligation is to be defined in terms of social pressure, to discover the essence of obligation will be to discover the essence of social pressure, that which lies at the root of all particular social pressures. This essence of obligation is called by Bergson 'the totality of obligation'. And he defines it as 'the concentrated extract, the quintessence of innumerable specific habits of obedience to the countless particular requirements of social life' (p. 13).

Now, I do not wish to quarrel with the attempt to find that which is common to all obligations. But I wish to make some comments about the meaning of this definition. For its meaning is far from obvious. At first sight it may seem that the concept of the totality of obligation is the general and comprehensive concept of all particular obligations. It would then be logically posterior to the latter. But the totality of obligation is said to be the primitive essence or core of obligation. In this case it would seem to be logically prior to particular obligations. For the latter constitute the manifold concrete manifestations of the former. This interpretation may appear to clash with the reference in the definition to 'innumerable specific habits of obedience', which suggests that the concept of the totality of obligation is the general and comprehensive concept of these specific habits of obedience. But Bergson's meaning seems to be that the totality of obligation is the primitive force or 'habit', as he puts it, which is manifested in these specific habits. And this primitive force or habit is what he calls 'the habit of contracting habits' (p. 17) or the necessity of forming habits. Even if he does sometimes speak as though the totality of obligation were simply an accumulation of specific habits of obedience to social rules, what he means is, I think, that there is a fundamental natural impulse to form social rules relating to the cohesion and preservation of society and to contract habits of obedience to these rules. This fundamental impulse, which he describes sometimes as 'habit' and sometimes as 'necessity', informs all particular manifestations of social pressure and unifies them in itself as in a kind of common essence. Presumably it is for this reason that Bergson speaks of 'each obligation dragging behind it the accumulated mass of the others' (p. 15).

It seems to me, therefore, that Bergson uses the term 'obligation' in different senses. Sometimes it means a particular obligation, as when he speaks of particular duties and obligations. Sometimes it seems to mean the pressure actually exerted by a particular closed society. At other times it appears to mean the natural necessity of forming habits of conduct in obedience to social requirements, the so-called 'habit of contracting habits'. It can hardly be denied that his use of terms is somewhat confusing and perplexing. Starting from the sense of obligation he tries to discover its cause. He then proceeds to call this cause obligation. To complicate matters still further, he seems to speak of the sense of obligation as obligation. He tells us, for instance, that 'the sense of this necessity, together with the consciousness of being able to evade it, is none the less what he (the individual) calls an obligation' (p. 5). The use of the phrase 'this necessity', referring to the necessity of contracting habits, seems to me to introduce a controversial interpretative element into the description of the sense of obligation. And in any case it is questionable whether as a matter of fact the individual does call the sense of obligation an obligation.

However, let us suppose that the ultimate root of obligation is a natural impulse. It must be found, of course, in individuals; for society is not an entity apart from its members. Within the human being, according to Bergson, we can distinguish between the social ego and the individual self; and the morality of obligation is grounded in the social ego.[2] This is one reason why society and its pressure do not normally appear to the individual as an alien force. For through his social ego he partakes in social solidarity and is himself to some extent the cause of the social rules which he obeys. 'Generally the verdict of conscience is the verdict which would be given by the social self' (p. 8).

This natural impulse is obviously not the product of intelligence. The impulse to contract habits of obedience to social rules is no more the product of intelligence than is the natural impulse to procure food for one's preservation. And if obligation is rooted in a natural social impulse, it follows that the origins of obligation are infra-intellectual. This was in fact one of Bergson's main points. He entirely disagreed with the Kantian derivation of obligation from the practical reason. This does not mean, of course, that reason has no part to play in the development of the morality of obligation. Nature has no more provided ready-made social rules than she has provided the vocabularies and syntactical forms of different languages. And though obligation itself is of infra-intellectual origin, particular rules are subject, to some extent at least, to the regulation of reason. I think that Bergson would say that even in the quasi-instinctive feeling that certain lines of action are destructive of the preservation and cohesion of society, mental activity, even if of a rudimentary type, is involved. Further, though we can point to all sorts of 'irrationalities' in the codes of conduct of primitive societies, a rule which may appear irrational to us may well appear rational to the primitive. A quotation from a book to which I have already alluded will show the sort of thing which Bergson has in mind. 'The only impediment to Eskimo marriage is kinship — by blood, by alliance, or even by name. Homonyms, to the Eskimos, signify kinship of soul, and people bearing the same name never marry' (*Inuk*, p. 153). Here we have a rule of real utility coupled with a rule which we might call irrational because we do not share the belief on which it is based. But to those who shared the belief the rule doubtless appeared to be 'rational'. In any case reason tends in the course of time to sift and discriminate and to introduce some consistency into a complex of rules, some of which may once have been useful but are so no longer, while others may have been occasioned by chance association or by beliefs which are no longer operative. And this positive activity of reason with regard to moral rules is greatly stimulated by the critical activity of intelligence. It is possible for individuals to question the validity of the whole set of values and standards of the society to which they belong; and this questioning is felt as a threat to the stability of that society. Hence intelligence itself must supply a remedy. When, for example, the values and standards of the Greek city-state were questioned at the time of the Greek Enlightenment, Socrates and Plato attempted to provide a rational foundation for these values and standards. And philosophy can indeed reconstruct morality, in the sense that by choosing one of the ends at which man aims, or can be interpreted as aiming, in society and by interpreting morality in function of it the philosopher can construct a system of rules which sufficiently resembles what Bergson calls 'current morality' to give the impression that reason is the fount of morality, including obligation. Yet in reality obligation is always presupposed by reason when it attempts to reconstruct morality, and its origin is infra-intellectual.

4

At this point I wish to make some comments on Bergson's theory of closed morality, though one important comment must be deferred until I have said something about his theory of open morality. And the first comment, perhaps a rather obvious one, which I wish to make is that historical content can undoubtedly be given to the terms 'closed morality'. If a member of a tribe regards as reprehensible a refusal to help a fellow tribesman who is in danger of drowning but sees nothing wrong in refusing assistance to the member of another tribe who is in a like situation, this is an example of what Bergson called the closed mentality. And he is justified in drawing attention, as he does, to the persistence, sometimes in disguised forms, of this mentality. For at times when a modern society feels that its cohesion and survival are threatened and still more when it is actually at war, the closed mentality may be very much in evidence, even though appeal is made to the principles and values of what Bergson calls open morality.

But though the terms 'closed morality' and 'closed mentality' undoubtedly refer to observable facts or to historical data, it does not necessarily follow that Bergson's interpretation of the facts is justifiable. And, in particular, I think that his theory of obligation is open to serious objections. In the first place Bergson seems to confuse x with 'cause of x'. And this is an obvious blunder. We can determine, for instance, the physical causes of our perception of colours, but it does not follow that these causes can appropriately be called colours. Nor, even if Bergson's account of the origin of the sense of obligation were correct, does it follow that the cause of the sense of obligation can appropriately be called obligation, when the assigned cause is a non-ethical empirical fact. It may be said that this is merely a question of words, and that Bergson is free to settle the meaning of his terms as he wishes. But it is not merely a question of words in the ordinary sense of the phrase. If Bergson had given the name obligation to the cause of what is generally called obligation and had then inverted a new term for the latter, his language might have been confusing, but it would have had some consistency and it would have been possible to learn it and talk it. But the point is that he uses the name obligation both for obligation as given to consciousness and for the cause, or supposed cause, of the consciousness of obligation. And this practice is misleading because it conceals important differences. Hence the matter is more than 'a mere question of words' in the depreciatory sense of this term. If we wish to say that the State developed out of the tribe, it is none the less misleading to speak of the State as a tribe or of a tribe as a State. If it could be shown, for example, that the affection of friendship was a sublimation of sexual desire, it would none the less be misleading to call friendship sexual desire; for it would conceal important differences. And whether we understand by Bergson's 'pure obligation' social pressure or the habit of contracting habits, it is misleading to call it obligation in the context of an ethical inquiry. Perhaps I may develop this point a little further.

Let us assume that pure obligation or the essence of obligation is social pressure or the habit (or 'necessity') of contracting habits of obedience to social requirements and demands. And let us assume that the sense of obligation is the feeling of this pressure. It seems to follow that all the lines of action to the performance of which social pressure is directed are obligatory and that all the actions the performance of which is opposed to the direction of social pressure are morally wrong. Now, social pressure is directed against the performance of acts of robbery with violence, acts which we would doubtless all call morally wrong. But society can also be said to exercise a pressure on the individual not to make loud smacking noises with his lips when eating something he likes. And though one might be prepared to say that this way of behaving would be wrong if it were done to show one's contempt for one's table-companions, most of us, I imagine, would be disinclined to say that it is morally wrong in itself. Similarly, as anyone who has been at a public school is well aware, social pressure is brought to bear to secure the observance of certain traditional conventions which we would not normally be disposed to call moral laws. Further, infringement of such conventions may meet with stronger and more effective disapproval than the infringement of some at least of those rules which many or perhaps all of us would regard as moral rules. My point is, therefore, that, given Bergson's theory of obligation, the distinction between moral rules and social conventions disappears, and that the theory thus conceals important differences and is incompatible with at least our own moral consciousness.

In drawing the above-mentioned conclusion from Bergson's theory of obligation I have not been treating him unfairly. For he draws the same conclusion himself. Thus he gives as one of the reasons why it is a mistake to define obligation with reference to resistance to self the fact that we are constantly observing social conventions without effort. For example, he says that it is impossible to do one's shopping or to go for a stroll 'without obeying rules and submitting to obligations' (p. 10). Bergson was, of course, perfectly well aware that we do in fact distinguish between moral rules and social conventions. But he would ascribe this distinction partly to the work of reason, which has come to distinguish between actions which are necessary to the cohesion and preservation of society and those which are not, and partly to the penetration of the closed morality by the open morality. As far as pure obligation is concerned, it is social pressure which determines duties. In primitive societies,[3] where obligation comes nearest to the ideal limit, namely to 'pure obligation', and is least modified by elements deriving from other sources, do we not find, for instance, cases where an action such as murder and an action such as carving meat in an unconventional manner are regarded as reprehensible actions of the same type from a moral point of view?

It is, of course, undoubtedly true that in ancient codes of conduct we come across the most curious juxtapositions of what we would call moral rules with what we would call social conventions or pure superstitions. But I doubt whether these historical data are as relevant to the point at issue as they are sometimes supposed to be. Let us imagine that in a given society social pressure is directed equally against stealing a man's cow and against eating beans. And let us suppose, for the sake of argument, that this pressure leads a member of the society to say that both actions are morally wrong. The statement that they are morally wrong is still different from the statement that social pressure is directed against the performance of these actions. Or let me put the matter this way. When the ordinary man says that he ought to do something, meaning that he is morally obliged to do it, it is often the case that what he believes he ought to do is also something to the doing of which social pressure is directed. And it might be because of this social pressure that he has come to believe that the performance of the action is a duty. Similarly, when the ordinary man says that he ought not to perform an action, it is often the case that the action in question is disapproved of or even prohibited by the society to which he belongs. And it might be that he has come to believe the action to be morally wrong because he has been told that it is morally wrong, that is, because the pressure of society has been brought to bear upon him. But it does not follow that to say that one ought to perform action *x*, which is a moral statement, is the same as to say that one is under social pressure to perform action *x*, which is a non-moral factual statement. The two statements are distinct, and no amount of reference to historical data will make them identical. And in so far as Bergson's theory of obligation tends to make them identical, it expalins morality by explaining it away. Indeed, Bergson almost admits this. For he writes: 'From this point of view obligation loses its specific character. It ranks among the most general phenomena of life' (p. 18). But though I have every sympathy with Bergson's attempt to link up morality with a general interpretation of human experience and of the world, I think that if obligation is stripped of its specific moral character and reduced to a non-moral element, this residue should no longer be called obligation. To do so is misleading because it conceals important differences. And this is the point which I have been trying to make.

5

Hitherto we have been concerned with what Bergson calls closed morality, which is relative to the closed society. But it is obvious that this concept will not cover the whole moral life of mankind. When Sophocles depicts Antigone as appealing from the commands of the king to the unwritten laws of heaven, he depicts her as rising above the morality of social pressure. And to turn from the theatre to the Gospel, the ideal expounded in the Sermon on the Mount cannot be brought under the heading of closed morality as Bergson understands this term. Further, whatever one may think of the validity of Kant's moral theory, it has little to do with the cohesion of the closed society to which he happened to belong. For it proposes universal ideals and enunciates the principle that every human being should be treated as an end and never as a mere means.

Bergson was, of course, aware of all this. But instead of revising his conception of the morality of obligation to fit the case of the great moral idealists of mankind he postulated another and radically different type of morality. If he recognized on the one hand a static morality of pressure and obligation, relative to the closed society, he recognized on the other hand a dynamic morality of appeal and aspiration, relative to the open society, to all men or to man. He speaks as though the great moral idealists and innovators of mankind, through their contact with the source of life (that is, with God) were animated by an ideal which they embodied in their own persons and lives and words and which, as so embodied, was capable of acting on others as an appeal and as a liberating influence, setting them free from the shackles of the mentality of the closed group. This open morality has its source in mysticism, in contact with God, and its source is thus supra-intellectual. In the morality of obligation there is obedience to the rules issuing ultimately from an infra-intellectual source. In the open morality there is free response to an invitation represented by the ideal embodied in the person and life of an individual. The open morality, therefore, transcends obligation.

We are thus presented with two fundamental types of morality, the closed and the open. And in view of the fact that the origin of the one is infra-intellectual, while the origin of the other is supra-intellectual, there is no possibility of passing from the one to the other by a gradual and continuous process of transition. Thus according to Bergson attachment to the fellow members of a closed society is different in kind, and not simply in degree, from love of all humanity or of man as man. For attachment to the members of a closed society is attachment in view of 'the other', that is to say in view of another closed society, actually or potentially hostile, whereas love of man as man has no intrinsic reference to mutual solidarity in view of a common enemy.[4] Similarly, there is a radical difference between closed and open ideas of justice, liberty, and so on. And such distinctions obviously underline the dichotomy between the two types of morality. The question arises, therefore, whether Bergson attempted any unification.

Bergson brings together the two moralities in this way. Each morality, regarded purely in its essence, represents an ideal limit. Social pressure is always embodied in concrete social pressures, and the influx of life and love from above, which is involved in mystical experience, is expressed from the moral point of view in the ideals formulated by the mystic, western or oriental as the case may be. Both the infra-intellectual drive and the supra-intellectual appeal are projected on to the plane of reason; and reason tends to introduce universality into the closed morality and obligation into the open morality. The ideals of supra-intellectual origin become operative in human society only in so far as they are received and interpreted by reason and rendered consistent with the morality of obligation, while the latter receives a fresh influx of life from the former. Morality as we know it includes both 'a system of *orders* dictated by *impersonal* social requirements and a series of appeals made to the conscience of each of us by persons who represent the best there is in humanity' (p. 68).

There is, therefore, a factual intermingling of the two moralities. At the same time there is a certain tension between them. While the open morality strives to inspire the closed morality with a new moral vision, the latter tends to crystallize into a code what is essentially appeal and personal response. We can, however, envisage an ideal product of human moral development. Technical progress has rendered possible the broadening out of particular closed societies into a world society, and if this world or human society were informed by the moral vision and impulse which comes from above, the evils attending a mere quantitative extension of a closed society might be avoided. Instead of some world-imperialism, animated by the closed mentality writ large, we would have a truly human society in which obligation would not be absent but in which obligation would be transformed in the light of man's free response to those ideals which are the expression of an influx of divine life. Thus in the last chaper of the *Two Sources* Bergson suggests that there is within the reach of man the goal of a world-society in which free response to the highest ideals rather than the tyrannical force of a world-imperialism would be the uniting factor.

6

Now, if we are willing to speak of moral progress at all, we can hardly refuse to admit that outstanding individuals have played an important part in this progress either by opening people's eyes to higher ideals or by revealing to them implications and applications of principles which they had previously admitted but the reach of which they had failed to recognize. We can certainly point to moral idealists who have transcended what Bergson calls the closed mentality and whose example and teaching acted as an appeal to others to do likewise. It does not necessarily follow, of course, that progress in moral insight is due to mystical experience. It can be explained in other ways. But even if we prescind from Bergson's metaphysical and theological interpretations of the data, we can give empirical content to the term 'open morality' just as we can to the term 'closed morality'. In both cases he drew attention to important facts.

Further, there is, in my opinion, ground for a distinction in the moral life between obligation and free response to a personal invitation. Possibly a distinction of this kind would be unacceptable to those moral philosophers who make obligation the cardinal feature of the moral life. I mean, the distinction may presuppose an ethical theory in which the concept of the good is paramount and in which 'right action' and 'obligatory action' are not synonymous terms. However, even those who reject ethical theories of this type would presumably admit that there is at least a psychological difference between obedience to an impersonal imperative and response to an ideal embodied in a person. But though Bergson's notion of open morality was founded on reflection about historical and psychological data, a fact which probably leads many readers of the *Two Sources* to think, as I myself think, that 'there is something in it', I wish to argue that by restricting obligation to what he calls closed morality Bergson places himself in a very difficult position.

On Bergson's theory of obligation particular obligations will have reference to the particular rules and customs of particular societies. And from this a relativistic conclusion seems to follow. It would seem to follow, for example, that it was a moral duty for an Aztec priest to offer human sacrifice because as a result of the religious beliefs of the Aztec people there was strong social pressure on him to act in this way. I do not mean merely that if the priest sincerely thought that he ought to offer human sacrifice, he was bound in conscience to do so. I mean that it would seem to follow from Bergson's theory of closed morality that he was objectively obliged to act in this way, and not simply subjectively by reason of an erroneous conscience. On the other hand Bergson did not assert a purely relativistic ethic. For he believed in moral progress. And he speaks of the advance towards the open morality as an advance towards the 'complete' or 'absolute' morality (cf. p. 23). Yet according to him obligation is a characteristic of the closed and not of the open morality; as must indeed be the case if obligation is defined in terms of social pressure while open morality is said to transcend social pressure. If, therefore, one of Bergson's moral heroes had arisen in the Aztec society, he could not have condemned contemporary practices, supported by social pressure, in the name of obligation, though he could have appealed to his fellow citizens in the name of a higher ideal. Furthermore, if one cares to press the point, the moral hero would appeal to his fellow citizens, not only to rise above the obligatory, in the sense of doing more than was obligatory, but also to act in a manner that was opposed to what was obligatory. And from this the paradoxical conclusion would seem to follow that his appeal would be an appeal to do what was morally wrong in the name of a higher ideal. This is what I meant by saying that Bergson appears to place himself in a very difficult position.

It may be said that I have surreptitiously given to certain terms a meaning which they do not possess in Bergson's theory, and that the force of my criticism depends entirely on this substitution of meanings. For, given Bergson's analysis of obligation, the moral hero would be doing no more than to appeal to his fellow citizens, in the name of a higher ideal, to rise above the prevailing social pressure and by changing their convictions and beliefs to change the direction of social pressure. And there is nothing paradoxical in such an appeal. True, but this answer seems to imply that Bergson is using the term 'obligation' in a non-ethical sense, even when speaking of particular obligations. And it was not his intention to do so. In so far as he does use the word in this way, he does not explain what he set out to explain except, as I remarked earlier, by explaining away. He lays himself open to the line of criticism to which I referred at an earlier stage. If, however, the term is used in an ethical sense, he seems to me to place himself in the difficult position of which I have just spoken.

But how did Bergson come to propound this theory of two moralities, the closed morality of obligation and the open morality of appeal and response? I have already indicated one influential factor, namely reflection on two sets of data, as presented respectively in the writings of ethnologists and sociologists on the one hand and of writers on mysticism on the other. But it seems reasonable to say that in his interpretation of these data he was influenced by another factor, namely his own conception of intelligence and its function, which had already found expression in *Creative Evolution*. Intelligence is there described as the faculty of manufacturing artificial objects, especially tools to make tools. Besides its primary practical function it can, of course, exercise a theoretical function. But in its theoretical activity, carried on by means of concepts, it arrests the flow of life, taking a series of snapshots, as it were, of what is essentially moving, changing, developing, creative. Now, if we consider the purely practical function of intelligence, it obviously cannot be the source of morality. For if it is directed towards the manufacture of artificial objects, it is not concerned with the ideals and standards of human conduct. It is represented much more by the activity of the technician than by that of Socrates. Nor can we say that intelligence, when considered under its theoretical aspect, is the source of morality. For morality, according to Bergson, is a vital or biological phenomenon (he uses the word 'biological', as he himself notes, in a very wide sense) which intelligence views from without. The latter can systematize and introduce logical consistency into what is already there; but it cannot be the original source of morality. The source must be either infra-intellectual or supra-intellectual. But if it is said that the source must be exclusively infra-intellectual or exclusively supra-intellectual, the statement does not seem to be compatible with the empirical data. We must postulate, therefore, an infra-intellectual source, which is a prolongation of instinct, and a supra-intellectual source, mysticism, which is a development of the concept of intuition in *Creative Evolution*. And it will then be necessary to postulate two types of morality, the pressure and aspiration of the *Two Sources* corresponding in some way to the instinct and intuition of *Creative Evolution*. Reason or intelligence will have only a mediating and not an originating role.

But Bergson's concept of intelligence and its function is bound up with his general metaphysics. And I think that we can also discern the influence of his general theory of creative evolution on his interpretation of morality. Thus he tends to speak of nature as having designs or plans. He speaks as though nature guided the members of an insect-society by means of the necessitating pressure of instinct towards the accomplishment of its purpose. In human society, the members of which are intelligent and free, nature accomplishes its end by means of the feeling of obligation, which is the result of that social pressure that takes the place in human life of the neccessitating pressure of instinct in the societies of bees and ants. The instinctive life of the infra-human animal world is a manifestation of creative life at one level; the social life of man is a manifestation of creative life at another level. But social life is but one manifestation of the creative impulse on the human plane. According to Bergson, 'we can easily conceive that life, which has had to set down the human species at a certain point of its evolution, imparts a new impetus to exceptional individual who have immersed themselves anew in it, so that they can help society further along its way' (p. 82).

This language is obviously borrowed from the theory of creative evolution as set forth in the work of this name. But we can very well ask why nature or life, supposing that it can will or intend anything, intends that there should be closed societies and that these societies should be preserved yet at the same time permeated with a fresh impulse of life communicated through exceptional individuals, the moral heroes and idealists of mankind. A hint at least of an answer is provided in the *Two Sources*. There we are told that 'creative energy is to be defined as love' (p. 220) and that this creative energy is God. God intended to create beings, that is, men, 'who were destined to love and be loved' (*Ibid*). But in order that the chief actor, so to speak, should appear, the whole scene had first to be set. And in order that the goal of human history should be reached, the creation of a truly open society, the matter had to be present which was to be progressively informed by the influx of divine life. The appearance of man presupposed the evolution of the infra-human world, and the formation of a truly open society presupposed the existence of closed societies. In the whole process of creative evolution there is emergence of the new but there is also continuity, the later stages requiring the previous existence of the earlier. Taking it, therefore, that mystical union with God is the highest realization in this life of man's potentialities, Bergson speaks of the universe as 'a machine for the making of gods' (p.275). As I said at the beginning of the chapter, it seems to me that though the general theories of *Creative Evolution* influenced Bergson in his interpretation of morality, his reflections on morality and religion, as expressed in the *Two Sources*, led to a development of his earlier metaphysical hypotheses. The conception of God is made somewhat clearer, and the teleological interpretation of the evolutionary process is given a moral and religious setting.

It seems to me to be obvious that Bergson's language is allusive, pictorial, vague. He is much better at providing general impressions and vague, if brilliant, hypotheses, than a formulating in a clear and precise way his questions and answers. He tries to do far too much in a small space; and though he draws attention to important aspects of the moral life, analysis is sacrificed to over-hasty synthesis. He is, in ethics, as elsewhere, an impressionistic philosopher. In particular, his theory of two moralities appears to me to be an impressionistic hypothesis which is unduly influenced by theories previously formed through reflection on non-ethical data and which is too little influenced by careful analysis of ethical terms and concepts. At the same time I feel considerable sympathy with the teleological element in his thought, and I think that he might have developed it to advantage. His awareness of the *de facto* connexion between particular codes of conduct and particular societies doubtless stimulated his marked propensity to emphasize the analogy between human societies on the one hand and the societies of ants and bees on the other. And these two factors together led him to give a teleological interpretation of obligation with reference to the cohesion and preservation of a particular society. But he was far from suggesting that man is nothing but an intelligent ant or bee. His theory of open morality and his theory of dynamic or mystical religion make this perfectly clear. It seems to me, therefore, that he could quite easily have assigned to man as a natural end the development and perfecting of the whole man rather than the development of the social ego (as far as obligation is concerned). Indeed, this would have fitted much better what he has to say about open morality and dynamic religion. I am quite well aware, of course, that some philosophers would maintain that a teleological interpretation of morality is always exposed to the criticism which I myself have brought against Bergson, namely that he tends to deprive ethical terms of their specifically ethical character and to explain morality by explaining it away. I do not think that this is true of all forms of teleological ethics; but I cannot discuss the question in the concluding sentences of this lecture. My point is that by rethinking his interpretation of ethics in the light of a more careful consideration of the teleological element in it Bergson might have avoided the unfortunate association of moral obligation with social pressure and its restriction to the so-called closed morality. He could thus have avoided the dichotomy between two different types of morality. This dichotomy is doubtless linked with Bergson's view of the two sources of moral convictions. But even if there are two (or more) ways in which people can come to have moral convictions, this does not prove that there is not one human morality which can be known in different ways and into which different individuals and different societies can have varying degrees of insight. The suggestion that there is one moral law may seem to be incompatible with the empirical data of which Bergson had such an acute awareness, and it may even seem to imply that there are subsistent values or a subsistent moral law, a theory which I at least would reject. But it is possible, I think, to develop a teleological interpretation of morality which is compatible with the data that Bergson stressed but which at the same time is more consonant than is his own theory of two moralities with the datum to which he paid insufficient attention, namely the ordinary moral consciousness.

The fact that I have devoted a good deal of this chapter to criticism of Bergson's theory of morality may possibly suggest that I do not esteem him as a philosopher. But though I think that his theory, when considered under one aspect, provides an object-lesson of what one ought not to do, namely to neglect the indispensable analysis of ethical terms and concepts in the light of common usage, I also think that he draws attention to a variety of important data relevant to ethics and that he provides valuable material for a possible reassessment of the teleological interpretation of morality. In any case the fact that one criticizes a philosopher does not necessarily mean that one does not esteem him. If it did, Plato and Kant would presumably be among the most despised thinkers of humanity.

Notes

[1] All quotations from Bergson are taken, with kind permission of Messrs. Macmillan & Co. Ltd., from the English translation (1935) of this work by R. Ashley Audra and Cloudesley Brereton with the assistance of W. Horsfall Carter. I am also indebted to the same publishers for permission to quote from *Inuk* (1953) by Roger P. Buliard.

[2] Bergson did not accept the theory that there is a social consciousness which somehow subsists as an entity distinct from individual consciousnesses. Perhaps there is some affinity between his idea of the social ego and the existentialist conception of 'the one'.

[3] It is worth while remarking that Bergson shows himself too apt to assume that the beliefs and behaviour of modern primitive societies, to speak paradoxically, are necessarily a sure guide to the beliefs and behaviour of primitive societies in the strict sense, of which we obviously know little.

[4] One may note in passing that the first type of attachment is for M. Sartre the only possible form of human solidarity, whereas for Bergson this was not the case.

CHAPTER 12

JEAN-PAUL SARTRE

AS FAR AS my experience extends, everyone agrees that Sartre is an extremely intelligent man. This is a difficult concept to define. But at any rate it does not entail the judgment that Sartre is an original philosopher. For after having paid tribute to his intelligence some people go on to claim that his philosophical ideas are all derived from Husserl and Heidegger or, in the case of his second major philosophical work, from Marx. For these critics presumably Sartre's intelligence is manifested primarily in his skill as dramatist and novelist and in his ability to use ideas derived from other thinkers for his own purposes.

Differences in judgment about Sartre are not however confined to the question of his originality. On the one hand I have heard it maintained that Sartre is one of those writers who simply state and do not argue. It is also sometimes suggested that his thought is unsystematic and disconnected. On the other hand I have heard a Polish logician putting forward the view that Sartre is an extremely systematic philosopher, who deduces his conclusions from a few basic concepts.

Such differences in judgment are understandable. If we consider the existentialism of Sartre, as represented by *Being and Nothingness*,[1] it seems to me a perfectly tenable view that it is derived systematically from the basic concept of being-in-itself *(l'en-soi)* or at any rate from the two concepts of being-in-itself and being-for-itself *(le pour-soi)*. At the same time, after having been presented with atheist existentialism in *Being and Nothingness* it is admittedly somewhat disconcerting to be told in the *Critique of the Dialectical Reason*[2] that Marxism is the one living philosophy of our time, and that anyone who tries to go beyond it inevitably falls back into a pre-Marxist position. Sartre tries of course to fuse these points of view and to clarify the relation between existentialism and Marxism. But it is understandable that some critics refuse to admit that the two points of view can be harmonized.

The first topic however about which I wish to make some remarks is this question of argumentation. Is it true to say that Sartre simply states what he believes to be the case, without providing any real arguments to show that it is the case?

2

It would be quite wrong to suggest that Sartre gives no argument at all. Consider his view of consciousness, being-for-itself. If being-in-itself is as Sartre describes it, opaque, massive, undifferentiated, without distinction, it seems indeed to follow that the emergence of consciousness must take place through the introduction of a gap or fissure in being. It follows, that is to say, if consciousness is regarded as intentional in structure, as being essentially consciousness *of*. For in this case the subject-object distinction is essential to consciousness. Whether we regard the object as phenomenal or transphenomenal seems irrelevant to this issue. For a distinction is present in any case, a distantiation of the subject from the object. Of course, if we ask what separates subject from object, the answer is 'nothing'. This is the answer which Sartre gives. And he draws the conclusion that nothingness lies at the heart of consciousness, of being-for-itself.

Sartre goes on to deduce atheism. It is not true to say that he simply assumes an atheist position, or that he simply states it. He argues that the concept of God, in theism that is to say, is the concept of a being which is being-in-itself and being-for-itself in one. That is to say, it is the concept of a personal Absolute. This concept, he argues, is self-contradictory. For being-in-itself excludes differentiation and distinction, whereas being-for-itself involves distinction. In other words, consciousness is essentially derived, dependent, fugitive, temporal. A self-conscious Absolute is impossible. There can no more be a God than there can be a round square.

Or consider Sartre's use of Dostoevsky's statement that if God did not exist, everything would be permitted. It may seem that Sartre is denying without more ado the autonomy of ethics and stating without argument that acceptance of moral values depends logically on belief in God. Whether this view is right or wrong, it needs to be supported by argument, not simply asserted.

It seems to me however that what Sartre is saying is that if there is no God, he cannot impose moral obligations, and that values cannot be divinely constituted. And this is, I think, a conclusion which follows pretty obviously from an atheist premiss. As for Sartre's positive view, this might be summed up by saying that for him values are constituted by man, in the sense that they depend on the act of valuation. He is of course perfectly well aware that we are all born into societies in which there are at any rate some commonly accepted values. But he would insist that if I accept the values of the society to which I belong, my acceptance is my act. It may be true that I accept them unthinkingly, so to speak, taking the line of least resistance. But I *could* refuse to accept them. And if I do accept them, it is my choice, whether the choice is made deliberately or in a spirit of social conformism. If I conform, I choose to conform.

It can still be objected of course that Sartre simply assumes that human beings are free in a psychological sense. But this is not the case. For he tries to deduce freedom from the structure of being-for-itself. He does indeed try to answer objections to the theory of human freedom. But we often advance a theory and then try to meet objections to the theory on the assumption that it is true. To be sure, we may simply be

taking the theory as a working hypothesis which we accept until forced
to recognize that there are fatal objections to it, whereas Sartre argues
not that man may be free but that he *must* be free. The point is however
that he does argue, his argument being deductive, based on the intrinsic
structure of being-for-itself.

3

Now it is not my intention to suggest that all Sartre's arguments are good
ones or that all his conclusions are tenable. Consider, for example, his
way of speaking about consciousness in terms of the negation of being,
as though consciousness was non-being. In spite of his rather portentous
terminology, there is no great difficulty in following his line of thought.
If I am conscious or aware of a table, I differentiate myself from the
table and, in a sense, negate the table. While however Sartre does not
deny the occurrence of consciousness, he cannot put all the weight, all
the positivity, on the side of being-in-itself *(l'en-soi)*, unless he eliminates
any substantial conscious subject. He is not of course alone in doing this.
But the more positive activity he attributes to consciousness, such as the
conferring of meaning, distinguishing one thing from another, and so on,
so much the less plausible becomes his description of the for-itself in
negative terms. And the less plausible it becomes, the weaker becomes
the particular argument for atheism to which I have referred.

Though however one may think that Sartre does not in fact prove the
truth of certain theses, this does not alter the fact that he argues his
position. If someone thinks, for instance, that the Five Ways of St
Thomas Aquinas are invalid or that, while formally valid, they involve
premises or presuppositions which beg the question, this does not alter
the fact that the Five Ways are arguments. And we can make analogous
remarks about Sartre.

4

Most of what I have been saying is so obvious that one wonders on what
ground or grounds it has been suggested that Sartre simply states and
does not argue. It may be however that one main reason is the use which
he makes of phenomenological analyses. That is to say, the impression
may perhaps be formed that when he wishes to make a point or prove a
thesis Sartre often presents us with a picture, an imagined scene, which
takes the place of argumentation and from which general conclusions are
drawn without more ado. The question which I wish to raise however is
whether the presentation of a picture or of an example cannot itself
constitute a form of argument, and indeed one which is quite commonly
employed.

Let me take a concrete instance. Sartre wishes to show that it is
incorrect to say that for a given person every other person is always
object, never subject. He presents the picture of a man squatting down in

a hotel corridor and looking through the keyhole of one of the rooms. The man believes that he is unobserved. His attention is focussed on what is going on inside the room. He is subject, and the people inside the room are for him objects. Someone however comes quietly along the corridor and stands silently observing the inquisitive fellow. The latter suddenly adverts to the fact that he is being watched, that he is object for a subject other than himself.

Suppose that someone says 'for me the other person is always object, never subject'. Sartre might reply on these lines. 'In one sense what you say is quite true. For I can be aware of another person only by constituting him 'or her as my intentional object of consciousness. To put the matter more plainly, I cannot be aware of someone without being aware of him or her. If however you mean to imply that I cannot be aware of the other person as a subject for whom I am object, this is not true. And to show that it is not true I give an example or two of situations in which I am clearly aware of myself as object for another person'.

This seems to me a perfectly respectable way of arguing. Suppose that someone says that the Sahara consists entirely of sand dunes, with an occasional oasis. Another person points out that in considerable parts of the territory covered by the name 'Sahara' there are rocks and earth but not sand dunes. He is not indeed deducing conclusions *a priori* from a concept of the essential nature of a desert. But he is giving a perfectly reasonable argument to show that the original statement stands in need of qualification.

5

Some people may perhaps feel inclined to comment that though Sartre's use of portentous and mystifying terminology tends to give the impression that he is concerned with matters of profound, if obscure, significance, it not infrequently turns out that he is really labouring the obvious.

For example, Sartre talks about nothingness being introduced into the world by the for-itself. And according to taste or inclination one may conclude either that he is concerned with profound metaphysics or that he is representing nothingness as a special kind of something and thus falling victim to the bewitching influence of language. But then Sartre gives an example to show what he means. I go to a café where I have an appointment to meet my friend Peter. I am extremely anxious to talk with him. He does not turn up. The café is full of people, but Peter is not among them. For me the café is 'haunted' by his absence. This absence is not of course a physical object in the sense in which the other people, the chairs, the tables, the bottles and so on are physical objects. None the less the absence of Peter is for me, for my consciousness, a real privation, as the Scholastic philosophers would put it. A café haunted by the absence of Peter is relative to and dependent on my desires and expectations. And in this sense not-being enters the world through the agency of the for-itself.

This sort of situation is familar enough. Most of us, if not all of us, have had at some time or other the experience of a room being pervaded, as it were, by the absence of someone whom we hoped to see but who was not there. This experience of 'non-being' (or, better, of a privation) is certainly not the result of thinking that because we use words such as 'nothing' or 'absence', there must be realities corresponding to them. From the phenomenological point of view it is an experience which certainly occurs, and once we have seen from the example the sort of thing which Sartre has in mind, we may well be inclined to conclude that he is labouring the obvious but dressing it up in a cloak of terminological mystification, by talk, that is to say, about being and non-being.

A partial answer is that Sartre is concerned with the views of Hegel and Heidegger about nothingness. For instance, Sartre takes it that for Hegel concrete being is a union of being and non-being, and that non-being is therefore a constituent element of cóncrete being. To this theory Sartre opposes the view that non-being is not *in* things but is dependent on the for-itself, that is to say on consciousness. In other words, the illustration of Peter's absence from the café is designed to cast doubts on the views of other philosophers.

To be sure, Sartre's view of the matter exposes him to obvious objections. For instance, if non-being enters the world through consciousness, it follows that the non-being which, according to Sartre, is to be found at the heart of the for-itself, of consciousness, must be due to the agency of the for-itself. And this is indeed what Sartre says, namely that the for-itself secretes its own nothingness. I must admit that this theory baffles me. I can see that if being-in-itself is as Sartre says it is, it cannot be the origin of negation. But I would think it preferable to revise the concept of being-in-itself than to propose the very odd idea of consciousness secreting its own nothingness. However this may be, my main point is that Sartre is certainly engaged in argumentation, though to see against whom he is arguing we have to examine his relations to philosophers such as Hegel and Heidegger.

6

Now though I think it incorrect to represent Sartre as simply stating his views without producing supporting arguments, I do not intend to imply that his views are always the results of the arguments which he employs. Consider a philosopher who tries to prove the existence of God. Most probably he believes in God already, and on grounds which may well be different from the grounds which he presents as formal arguments. Or consider Spinoza. It would be absurd, in my opinion, to represent him as coming to believe in one infinite Substance as the result of a quasi-geometrical demonstration. The general view of reality doubtless preceded the formal argumentation. Similarly, it may very well be true that Sartre is a man for whom, in Niezsche's phrase 'God is dead', who starts, as it were, with a godless world and for whom atheism is, from the psychological point of view, a premise.

If however the theistic philosopher offers arguments to prove the truth of an antecedent belief, this does not alter the fact that the arguments are arguments and can be treated as such. Again, Spinoza's proofs in the *Ethics* can be treated on their own merits. And even if, as is probable, Sartre presupposes the truth of atheism, this does not alter the fact that he offers arguments in support of it. Sometimes indeed his line of thought is an hypothetical account of how the idea of God might have arisen. This is the case when he presents this idea as an hypostatization of 'the look' *(le regard)*, as though the idea of the all-seeing God were an hyposatization of our being-for-others, potential objects of a look which is not confined to any given human observer. But the argument to which I have referred above, namely that the concept of God is self-contradictory, is quite clearly an argument purporting to demonstrate the truth of atheism.

Let me put the matter in another way. Psychological and sociological approaches to philosophers and philosophies are often of interest, and they can illustrate connexions between philosophical reflection and other factors, both personal and in the cultural milieu. But such approaches should not be pushed to the point at which arguments presented by philosophers are dismissed as irrelevant. It is not altogether unreasonable, for example, to see in logical positivism an attempt at a theoretical justification of a fairly widespread outlook or mentality in modern society. But it would not do to dismiss unexamined the arguments advanced by logical positivists in support of their positions simply because one disapproved of the outlook or mentality which found expression in this philosophical current.

This would apply of course to Sartre's arguments in favour of atheism. But in making these remarks it is another aspect of his philosophy which I have in mind. Some critics have seen in Sartrian existentialism the last convulsive kick of the dying bourgeoisie. In other words, they have seen in its emphasis on the total freedom of the individual a final and exaggerated expression of a liberal humanism linked to a moribund form of society. Even if however Sartrain existentialism were a frantic expression of the death throes of the bourgeoisie, Sartre's arguments to support his theory of liberty might still be valid. I do not claim that they are. My point is rather that their validity is not dependent on historical transitions in society. An obvious point indeed. But it is perhaps worth making all the same.

7

Though some critics have seen in Sartrian existentialism a bourgeois neo-liberalism or neo-radicalism or what not, Sartre himself has maintained that the only living philosophy of our time is Marxism. He has never joined the Communist Party. He condemned unequivocally the Soviet suppression of the Hungarian revolution in 1956 and wrote in strong terms about the way in which the French Communist Party tried to excuse the Soviet action. He also condemned the way in which the Soviet Union choked to death Mr. Dubcek's attempt to humanize the régime in Czechoslovakia. But this does not alter the fact that he still regards Marxism as the philosophy of our time. And the question arises, how does this point of view fit in with his existentialism? Or does it not fit in? Has Sartre abandoned existentialism for Marxism?

It is of course in regard to Marxism as a philosophy that this question arises. If Sartre chooses to commit himself to supporting social and political causes and if, in so doing, he finds himself, allied with the Communists, this does not seem to me to be in any way incompatible with his existentialism. For he has constantly maintained that it is through action and self-commitment in an historical situation that freedom is expressed and that man makes himself. Nor is he involved in inconsistency with his existentialist philosophy if he speaks out and writes with vehemence in support of the causes which he embraces. For though he has maintained that it is the individual who chooses or creates his own values, he has also maintained that in choosing a scale of values the individual chooses ideally for all. In other words, he has maintained that the value-judgment, though made by the individual, has a universal element. Hence he can quite consistently call upon other people to rally to a given cause and condemn his opponents or the indifferent. Or so it seems to me. But to claim that Marxism is the one living philosophy of our time and that anyone who tries to go beyond it inevitably falls back into a pre-Marxist position is presumably to claim that the Marxist doctrines are true, at any rate for our time. If therefore we think that there is some difference, to put it mildly, between the existentialism of *Being and Nothingness* on the one hand and dialectical materialism on the other, the question naturally arises whether Sartre has abandoned existentialism for Marxism.

Sartre's own view of the matter seems to be more or less this. Marxism began as a philosophy of revolution; and it had a marked humanistic aspect. For it aimed at the overcoming of all forms of human alienation. It aimed at liberating man. Marx started with the idea of man in a dialectical relationship with his environment, a relationship in which man is not only acted upon by his environment but also acts upon it, transforming it through action and labour. Further, though Marx certainly emphasized the concept of class-war and the victory of the proletariat, his vision of history did not stop with the dictatorship of the proletariat. He envisaged the development of a human society transcending the antagonism of classes. Marx produced a revolutionary myth, spurring man on to the overcoming of oppression, exploitation and alienation in general. And this myth remains the only genuinely revolutionary philosophy of our times. It has however become fossilized, an arid ideology. It has been converted into the instrument of an authoritarian régime and of an entrenched and self-perpetuating bureaucracy. Further, human freedom has been forgotten. To be sure, lip-service is paid to it; but in practice the philosophy of human liberation is used to stifle original thought, and in the name of Marxism-Leninism man is enslaved. Marxism thus stands in need of rejuvenation and renewal. It needs to have at its centre the idea of the free self-transcending human being, transcending, that is to say, the present social order towards a society which does not yet exist. This rejuvenation could be achieved by an injection of existentialism or, rather, through the incorporation of the existentialist view of man into Marxism. If this were done, existentialism would no longer have any reason for continuing to exist as a separate philosophy or line of thought. It would have been absorbed in Marxism.

Fulfilment of this programme of incorporating existentialism into Marxism seems to me somewhat difficult. For example, Sartre has maintained that the we-consciousness is created only in the presence of a third party, the exploiting class for example. In this case the human race could rise to the we-consciousness only in the face of a non-human subject. And as for Sartre there is no God, it is difficult to see how this can come about in an effective and lasting manner. The Marxist however would presumably wish to hold that in a classless human society there could be, and would be, genuine unity, a genuine we-consciousness. Again, for Sartre Marxism seems to be a myth, the myth of our time to be sure, but none the less a myth, whereas Marxist philosophers, of the 'orthodox' type at any rate, present it as expressing scientific knowledge. Again, Sartrian existentialism represents all intelligibility and meaning as conferred by man, whereas dialectical materialism presumably claims to present the objective intelligible structure of reality as mirrored in and through the human mind. To be sure, we can find some passages in Marx which might be given a Sartrian sense. But Engels at any rate thought that nature was an objectively dialectical process, and Lenin had little use for any form of theoretical idealism or phenomenalism. Indeed, some Thomists have claimed that realism is precisely what they have in common with the Marxists.

Drawing attention to differences between existentialism, as presented in *Being and Nothingness*, and Marxism-Leninism is a somewhat tiresome procedure. And it may seem to be unprofitable in the present context. For it is clear that Sartre is attempting a fusion between existentialism and Marxism which involves some revision of both elements rather than a simple incorporation of one philosophy into another. On the one hand he tries to develop existentialism in such a way that it comprises a view of history which can serve as a theoretical background for self-commitment to the cause of social revolution. And he goes so far as to try to give an *a priori* foundation to the Marxist dialectic in man himself, considered as existing in the basic situation of his relationship with his environment. On the other hand he is determined to eliminate from Marxism any idea of history as being governed by laws which operate independently of human freedom. Thus while he is perfectly perpared to admit that human activity is limited by the concrete historical situation, by the mode of production for example, he rejects any theory of economic determinism and insists that it is man himself who freely creates the situation. Or consider alienation. The possibility of alienation, according to Sartre, is grounded *a priori* in man himself. At the same time alienation arises through man's free activity.

Obviously, as a philosophy of revolution Marxism has had to find room for human initiative and activity. Marx was concerned not only with understanding human society but also with changing it. A purely mechanistic view of historical development would not fit in with the call to revolutionary activity. And Sartre can of course appeal to a number of statements by Marx, for instance that it is man who makes history. At the same time, the more the Marxists represent the triumph of socialism as assured, as something on which man can rely, the more they are pushed in the direction of the idea of historical development as a law-governed process, moving inevitably towards a certain goal. Marxists have tried to combine this idea of a law-governed teleological process with a recognition of man's power to accelerate or retard it. But unless they are prepared to relinquish belief in the inevitable triumph of socialism and regard dialectical materialism as an hypothesis which may or may not be verified, Engels' concept of philosophy as the science of the laws of development in nature, society and thought can hardly fail to occupy a prominent position. It is not however a concept which Sartre is prepared to accept. In his view the philosopher cannot take the place of God and foresee the future. Nor indeed is the future determined in such a way that it could be foreseen with certainty. It depends on man, on human choice. The possibilities are grounded *a priori* in man's basic situation, as existing in a dialectical relationship with his environment. But Sartre is determined to make the realization of these possibilities dependent on human freedom and not on any law or laws operating independently of man, first in nature and then in history. In other words, he makes the dialectic dependent on man. And though he admits that man often seems to be the victim or instrument of forces outside his control, he tries to retain his existentialist view that obstacles and limitations to human freedom are obstacles or limitations because man makes them such.

It is clear that Sartre rejects the dogmatism which has been a conspicuous feature of Marxism-Lenism when presented as an official ideology. He sees Marxism as a philosophy of revolution, a call to action, a powerful myth, rather than as a metaphysical revelation of the nature of reality. To be sure, he claims that it is the unsurpassable philosophy of our time. But if social revolution were achieved and the historical situation were surpassed, presumably Marxism would then itself be surpassed, just as the bourgeois philosophy of the preceding epoch was surpassed. And though it is conceivable that Marx himself might not be unduly perturbed by this prospect, I very much doubt whether it would be acceptable to the party dogmatists. It is hardly surprising if orthodox Marxists are disinclined to applaud Sartre's revisionism.

In attempting a fusion between existentialism and Marxism Sartre shows, as one would expect, a great deal of ingenuity, even though he uses what is to my mind an unnecessarily obscure jargon, which makes the *Critique of Dialectical Reason* an even more difficult book to read than *Being and Nothingness*. As far as I know however, the *Critique* has not been completed. And though this may be due in large measure to Sartre's activities outside the field of theoretical philosophy, it seems reasonable to venture the hypothesis that the intrinsic difficulty in effecting a real fusion is a major factor in holding up completion of the work. After all, it is no easy task to combine a philosophy which claims to present the objective dialectical structure of reality with one which regards all intelligibility as conferred by the self-conscious agent, man. One of the two has to yield to the other. Or both have to be revised in such a way that something new is created.

In any case is the enterprise really worth while? There can obviously be more than one opinion. If someone believes with Sartre that Marxism is the living philosophy of our time but one which has unfortunately become the victim of anaemia or hardening of the arteries or what not, he will doubtless also believe that some rejuvenation would be appropriate, if, that is to say, we need a philosophy at all. If however someone believes that Marxism, if left to itself, would have suffered the fate of other nineteenth-century systems and that the process which has kept it alive is the very process which has led to its transformation into a fossilized dogmatism, he is likely to think that the mental energy expended by Sartre in trying to rejuvenate it is so much wasted effort.

It may be said that sarcastic remarks of this kind completely miss the point. When Sartre says that Marxism is the one living philosophy of our time, he obviously does not mean that in the second half of the twentieth century Marxism is the only line of philosophical thought which is being actively pursued and to which philosophers are making original contributions. For this would be patently false; and Sartre is neither blind nor stupid. What he means is that however much Marxism may have been devitalized and scholasticized by the theoreticians of the

Kremlin, it still remains the one genuinely revolutionary philosophy of our time. Phenomenology and linguistic or conceptual analysis are certainly living currents of thought, in the sense that they are actively pursued. But neither is a philosophy of revolution. Neither expresses the self-consciousness of the ascending class as it transcends the present social order towards a future which is not determined but the realization of which depends on human activity and struggle. Marxism does, as far as its essential nature is concerned. And it is the only philosophy which does so. If therefore it has been transformed into an instrument for maintaining the position of an authoritarian régime and of an entrenched bureaucracy, it needs to be liberated from this captivity and revitalized through a recall to its humanistic origins. It can then become the instrument of social revolution, the myth which spurs man on to transcend the present social order.

This is, I think, more or less Sartre's line of thought. But to mention it is, in a sense, to give the game away. Sartre is a socially committed man, who is acutely aware of injustices, exploitation and so on. He does not approve of bourgeois democracy. And he looks for a philosophy of revolution. Can he find it in his own existentialist philosophy as presented in *Being and Nothingness?* Hardly. For Sartrian existentialism tends to give the impression of being an atomic individualism. In any case it would need revision and development before it could perform the required function. Sartre therefore has to look elsewhere. Though he has never actually joined the Communist party, he believes that it is the only genuinely revolutionary party, and that its myth, Marxism, is the only available vision for a revolutionary movement. Unfortunately, it has been converted into a dogmatic system and into an instrument for the protection of vested interests, ceasing to express man's movement of transcendence. It needs to be recalled to a vision of man as constantly reaching out towards a future which he alone can actualize through his initiative and free action. This vision can be contributed by existentialism. Hence the attempted fusion or marriage.

It seems to me that there is a certain continuity between the existentialism of Sartre's previous writings and the revised Marxism of the *Critique of the Dialectical Reason.* Sartrian existentialism can indeed be regarded as an analysis of the basic concepts of being-in-itself and being-for-itself. But it can also be regarded, I suppose, as illuminating the possibilities of choice and the nature of self-commitment. If we then add the value-judgment that social revolution is desirable, we can understand Sartre's effort, by means of a revised Marxism, to direct man's self-commitment in this direction. If we are prepared to regard provision of a revolutionary myth as a proper function of philosophy, we shall at any rate sympathize with Sartre's project, whether or not we believe that Marxism is the myth best adopted for the purpose. If however we do not regard the provision of revolutionary myths as a proper function of

philosophy we may be inclined to think that Sartre has abandoned
philosophy for social and political action, and that his original
contribution to philosophical thought lies in the phenomenological
analyses of his earlier writings.

Notes
[1] London, 1969
[2] Paris, 1960

CHAPTER 13

THE EXISTENTIALIST CONCEPT OF MAN

WE CAN SEE THINGS in a variety of ways. Ordinarily, I suppose, we see chairs as chairs, as things to sit on that is to say. But if we were fumbling for the electric light switch in a dark room we might experience them as obstacles. In certain circumstances we might see chairs as potential weapons, while in other circumstances we might see them as firewood, provided of course that they were made of wood. Again, some chairs might be seen as antiques, possessing a certain value in the market, while others might be seen in the light of some historical or personal association. That is the chair on which Queen Victoria sat to write up her diary: this is the chair in which my grandmother.died.

So too with human beings. In what are sometimes described as personal relationships attention is focussed on an individual, who stands out, as it were, from mankind in general. A child's relationship to its mother is an obvious case. And we might possibly include the relationship between a psychiatrist and his patient. Or human beings can be seen globally, as it were, individuals being considered as members of a class or as instantiations of a type or as exemplifying or failing to exemplify a universal concept. In the light of certain theological beliefs human beings can be seen globally as children of God. Or they can be looked at from the point of view of the physiologist or from that of the psychologist or from that of the sociologist. And so on.

Some of the possible ways of regarding human beings may be mutually exclusive. I do not think that we could sincerely regard human beings as children of God and at the same time regard them as suitable material for forced scientific experimentation in a Nazi concentration camp. But to look on people as citizens and voters does not necessarily exclude looking on them as moral agents. And though it is unlikely that Tom, who is in love with Jane, will regard her at one and the same time from the standpoint of a lover and from that of a scientist, he can take these points of view or attitudes successively without involving himself in contradiction. For Jane *is* both this unique individual and, say, a member of society.

2

Let us consider for a moment the scientific study of man. It seems true to say that in the sciences relating to man, no less than in other sciences, the scientist is concerned with generalization and that he tries to formulate testable hypotheses or laws of some kind which enable him to predict. Of course, it has been said of Freud, Adler and Jung that their theories are rarely testable hypotheses, and that when they are not subject to empirical falisification in principle, they cannot count as scientific hypotheses.[1] And as for social science, Professor A.J.Ayer remarks that 'all in all, the stock of generally accredited and well tested theories that the social sciences can muster is comparatively small'.[2] Hence the question arises whether we ought to say that depth pyschology, considered as a science, is still in its infancy, and that the social sciences have not made such rapid progress as Auguste Comte seems to have expected, or whether we should say that the subject-matter of such disciplines makes it inappropriate to take physical science as a model. But I am not in a position to make any useful contribution to this discussion. In any case it seems to remain true that in anything which can be properly described as an empirical science we have to look at any rate for testable hypotheses and coordinating laws of some kind, at least statistical laws.

In regard to human behaviour, this procedure seems to involve what might be described as a methodological determinism. I do not mean that the scientist is committed to rejecting belief in human freedom and embracing a theoretical determinism. I mean that the scientist, concerned as he is with generalization, naturally looks for hypotheses which will enable him to predict human behaviour. He need not claim that infallible prediction of all human actions is in principle possible. But part of what is involved in his obtaining conceptual mastery over his material or data is surely the ability to make useful predictions. Hence even if he does not assert a philosophical theory of determinism (whatever this may be), his procedure seems to presuppose that prediction is at any rate possible to some extent.[3]

Let me put the matter in another way. The physical scientist obviously looks at molecules and atoms from outside, as a spectator.[4] So of course does the entomologist examine, say, butterflies and moths in a an objective manner, as a scientific observer. And the same is true, up to a point, of the sciences which treat of man. Man can objectify himself and regard himself as an object 'out there', in a manner analogous to that in which the astronomer considers the heavenly bodies. And when he does this, he naturally tries to fit human actions into causal patterns. We can perhaps see this tendency at work when we look back at our past actions, constituting ourselves spectators of ourselves. But the tendency becomes much more obvious, when we are concerned with the understanding of societies and their development.

3

If, however, man turns himself into an object of scientific study, it is man himself who does this. In other words, though man can objectify himself, he remains subject, the subject of consciousness or awareness. True, some philosophers have tried to eliminate the subject. But I do not think that this attempt has been, or can be, successful. Perhaps one reason why some philosophers have tried to eliminate the subject is that they have imagined that to acknowledge the existence of the subject is tantamount to admitting the existence of an occult entity, hidden away inside, which is called the 'pure subject' or the 'transcendental ego' or something of the sort and which is thought to be the real man or the real self. But there need not be any question of an occult entity in this sense. The plain fact of the matter is that the human person can function as subject. When David Hume looked inside himself, it was David Hume who did the looking.

Though, however, it makes sense, as it seems to me, to speak of a man as spectator of himself, the human subject is clearly not simply an epistemological subject. I should not care to go so far as to say with Wittgenstein that 'the thinking subject is surely mere illusion. But the willing subject exists'.[5] For though it would be absurd to depict man as a being which surveys the world from a vantage-point outside the world, it seems to me misleading to assert that there is no thinking subject. At the same time man as subject is an active subject, a willing subject, as Wittgenstein puts it. Man finds himself in a world, a world in which he has to act. And it is arguable that he seeks knowledge of his environment and of himself in order to be able to act as a human being, that is intelligently for conceived ends or purposes.

Now from the point of view of the active agent himself, considered precisely as such, he is a free agent. From the psychological point of view at any rate, when a man is faced with an important decision, he feels that the decision rests with him, within, that is to say, the limits set by external circumstances and by his own capacities. If we say with Spinoza that the persuasion or feeling of freedom is equivalent to ignorance of the determining causes, this judgment is passed from the external point of view, that of the spectator. When I am actually faced with the taking of a vital decision, I am for myself the free agent. And this is as true of the theoretical determinist as of anyone else. From the internal point of view one is immediately 'aware' of freedom, as Bergson, for example, held. It is when we take the external point of view that doubts about freedom tend to arise.

4

What I have been saying represents more or less the point of view of Karl Jaspers (1883-1969), one of the leading existentialists. After studying law he turned to medicine and received the doctorate in this subject at Heidelberg. He then turned to psychology and psychiatry. The fact of the matter was that legal studies disgusted him. He wished to study man, not merely man's body but man as a totality, the human personality as a whole. As a lecturer in psychology, however, he became more and more involved in philosophical reflection; and in 1921 he obtained a chair of philosophy at Heidelberg. As a philosopher, he insisted and continued to insist on the great importance of the sciences as representing objective impersonal knowledge (or at any rate the search for it). But he also insisted that man is more than the content of his self-understanding by means of science. Science is man's creation; and man exists in the world as a being which reaches out towards its possibilities and creates itself through its free choices. As for philosophy, this is not another science. That is to say, it does not *prove* freedom; nor in general, is it concerned with the objective impersonal truth, in the way in which science is concerned with impersonal truth. Philosophy aims much more at drawing attention to what a man knows from within as it were, at illuminating man's possibilities of choice, and at thus facilitating man's actualization of his possibilities in an authentic manner. To put the matter in another way, philosophy aims at enabling the individual to attain *his* truth, the truth, that is to say, by which he can live and orient himself in the world of ordinary experience and of science.

In his philosophical reflection Jaspers was influenced by both Kant and Kierkegaard. Kant had grappled with the problem of reconciling or harmonizing the outlook of the classical Newtonian physics with man's moral consciousness. In Kant's view the scientist cannot help extending the idea of causal determinism from the physical world to man himself and his actions. The consciousness of moral obligation, however, presupposes freedom. To act morally was, for Kant, to act with the conviction of freedom. 'You ought; therefore you can'. To deny freedom is to deny morality. But how can we reconcile these two points of view? As we probably all know, Kant tried to effect a reconciliation by describing human actions (the actions which we ordinarily think of as free) as phenomenally determined but noumenally free. From the outside, spectator point of view, the point of view of the scientist, actions are determined by their causes. From the inside point of view, that of the moral agent as such, these actions are free. Kant's solution of the problem was perhaps hardly satisfactory. But my point is that his distinction between 'outer' and 'inner' reappears in the thought of Jaspers.

One great difference between the two men seems to me to lie in the fact that Kant's approach was predominantly ethical, whereas Jaspers' approach was predominantly religious. Perhaps one might express the matter by saying that Kant was obsessed by the idea of moral obligation, of the categorical imperative, whereas Jaspers was obsessed by the idea of man's self-relating to the Transcendent or ultimate ground of existence and saw in Kierkegaard and Nietzsche symbols of the two poles of human existence, two opposed possibilities of man.

Kierkegaard (1813-1855) had no sympathy with the view of man which he took to be characteristic of speculative philosophy, as represented by Hegel, namely that man realises his true self in so far as he transcends his particularity and becomes a member of a greater whole, whether this is the state or reality, the Absolute, coming to know itself in and through the human mind in the course of man's cultural development. To Kierkegaard, to exist as a human being meant realizing oneself through free choice between alternatives, through self-commitment. For him authentic existence did not mean merging oneself in the group and identifying one's will with the ends of the group. Nor did it mean understanding reality and the historical process. Man does not realize his true self by thinking, but rather by choice and self commitment. And as self-commitment is something personal, we can say that authentic existence means becoming more and more the individual, instead of more and more a member of the group.

Kierkegaard outlined several possibilities of human existence, on the aesthetic, ethical and religious planes. But throughout his discussion he emphasized the fact that the transition from one level to another is a matter of choice, of a 'leap'. The truly existing individual is the actor, rather than the spectator. The spectator can understand everything and *be* nothing. A man becomes something, makes himself, gives form and direction to his life, only through self-commitment. And the truth in which he is interested, when he is considered precisely as the self-making individual, is not the impersonal objective truth of mathematics or science, but *his* truth, the truth by which he can live.

This sort of idea of man reappears in Jaspers. But whereas Kierkegaard laid the emphasis on Christian faith, Jaspers laid the emphasis on what he called 'philosophical faith', man's self-relating to the unobjectifiable ground of existence, of which we can form only symbolic representations, none of which can be final or of universal validity. In other words, Jaspers might be described as Kierkegaard turned into a university professor of philosophy.

5

With an existentialist such as Jean-Paul Sartre (b. 1905), the religious aspects of the picture of man given by Kierkegaard and Jaspers naturally tend to disappear. For Sartre is an atheist, who maintains that the idea of God is self-contradictory. But the notion of man as making himself through his own free choices and by self-commitment remains. So does the distinction between authentic and inauthentic existence, which can be found implicitly in Kierkegaard, explicitly in the writings of Jaspers and in the famous work, *Being and Time*, by Martin Heidegger (1889-1976), which exercised an obvious influence on the reflections of Sartre. Heidegger, as is well enough known, repudiates the label 'existentialist' and insists that his primary concern has always been the problem of Being. The fact remains, however, that his analysis of man in *Being and Time* had become a kind of *locus classicus* for the existentialist concept of man.

To return to Sartre. In a certain sense he seems to be committed to denying that there is any such thing as a universal concept of man, if, that is to say, we mean by a universal concept of man a mental represent- ation of a definite, fixed human essence or nature. For Sartre has defined the thesis that existence is prior to essence. There is no eternal essence of man, it were, which human beings instantiate. Man first exists and then defines himself. He makes or creates himself through his free choices. And what the individual becomes depends on himself. He is responsible for what he makes of himself.

Well, if we assume atheism, it is obvious that there cannot be an eternal idea of man existing in the divine mind. Nor of course can man throw on God the responsibility for what he is or becomes. At the same time it hardly needs saying that Sartre is as able as the next man to dis- tinguish between Africans and the lions in Africa. Further, his analysis of 'the for-itself' *(le pour-soi)* can perfectly reasonably be described as an analysis of the essence of man. Suppose that I say with Sartre that consciousness is always ahead of itself, that man is always reaching out towards his possibilities, that he is not determined by himself as some- thing already made (by his *facticité*), that he is defined by his *projet* or operative ideal (which may be different of course from his professed ideal), and that it is only with death that man relapses into being-in-itself *(l'en-soi)*, am I not giving a description of the nature or essence, as I see it, of man, the human reality? The fact of the matter is that Sartre tried to show that freedom follows from the very structure of man. And if an analysis of this structure does not involve a concept of the human nature or essence, I do not know what does involve it. The absence of a theological background does not seem to me to affect the issue. Nor does the fact that one man can become St Francis of Assisi, while another becomes Adolf Hitler.

As for Sartre's picture of the scope of human freedom, it may seem at first sight that the scope is unrestricted. For example, in answer to objections drawn from the influence of early environment and upbringing and from that of physiological and psychological factors Sartre has replied that a human being is himself responsible for the effect which such factors have on him, for his reaction. But we also find Sartre maintaining (in a manner somewhat reminiscent of Schelling) that the way in which a man reacts to such influences depends on his original life- project, on a sort of basic act of free choice, of which all particular choices or decisions can be regarded as consequences.[6] At the same time Sartre admits that a change in a man's life-project is possible, though this would demand a total 'conversion'.

One of the features of Sartre's concept of man is the idea of man as conferring meaning on things, an idea already present in Heidegger's *Being and Time*. The world has no determinate meaning or goal, for Sartre, a meaning which can, so to speak, be read off it. It is man him- self who confers meaning on things. To be sure, human beings have some common ends or purposes. Hence there can be and is a common world. But human beings also have different purposes and different points of view or perspectives. Things can thus have different meanings for different people. The earth can have one meaning for the farmer, another for the geologist, another for the military strategist, another for the artist. The world of the poet is not precisely the same as the world of the nuclear physicist. The Christian interprets the world and history rather differently from the Marxist.[7]

Man is also the creator of values. There are no such things as absolute values. Nor is there any universally-obligatory moral law. Man chooses his own values. Of course, as Kant saw, to adopt a value-system is in a sense to legislate universally. If I opt for love as the supreme value, I necessarily desire that others too should value love. But there is no way of *proving* that love is the supreme value. If a man were to say that for him hatred was preferably to love, I could try to make clear to him the probable or possible consequences of this position. And if they were unacceptable to him, he might change his value-judgment. But if he recognized the consequences of his position and yet was prepared to stand by his value-judgment, there would not be any neutral standpoint from which he could be proved to be wrong.

This point of view is similar to that of, say, Bertrand Russell. Indeed, Sartre's talk about 'anguish' and so on may blind us to the extent in which a good deal of what he says can be presented without the use of emotively-charged words and in a manner which would be acceptable to a good many philosophers who are not existentialists. To be sure, it is not so easy as some people may think to avoid implying that there are in fact objective values. For example, Sartre frequently gives the impression of thinking that authentic existence is objectively better or more admirable than inauthentic existence. For instance, it is objectively more admirable to embrace Communism and all that it stands for deliberately than to vote for the Communist Party simply because 'one' does it, because, that is to say, fellow-workers vote in this way. And it is objectively better to commit oneself wholehartedly to Christ than to profess Christianity simply out of social conformism or because one is too lazy to do anything else. But Sartre can reply of course that the distinction between authentic and inauthentic existence is, in itself, simply an analysis of two possible types of human existence, and that if he prefers authentic to inauthentic existence, this is a personal judgment of value, which presupposes his own choice of a set of values and is not supposed to be an absolute judgment, passed from a valuationally neutral standpoint.[8]

When writing of the existentialists Professor Ayer remarks that 'to be told to live authentically is not really to be told how to live.[9] This is obviously true. It must be rememberd, however, that the existentialist does not undertake to provide a map of the ethical life which would be valid for every individual. He might perhaps claim that he is concerned with clarifying possibilities, and that he is no more committed to telling people what moral decisions they should make than the philosopher who regards moral philosophy as concerned simply with the language of ethics. It must indeed be admitted that if the last-mentioned type of philosopher were to exhort people to live morally, without giving any clear indication of what is meant by living morally, we would be inclined to object to such vague generalization. So Professor Ayer certainly has a point. And it applies perhaps especially to Jaspers, who regards philosophy as appealing to human freedom. But Sartre might possibly reply that he is concerned with analysis rather than with exhortation. In any case Sartre himself does not hesitate to commit himself socially and politically, though he would doubtless admit that this self-commitment is the result of personal option and not the result of a logical deduction from existentialism as such.

6

Mention of social and political commitment brings me to consideration of a feature of existentialism which is likely to arrest the attention of any social scientist, namely the existentialist tendency to dwell on the individual as such, the lonely individual. Kierkegaard fulminated against the influence of 'the crowd' and the crowd-mentality; and, as we have seen, he laid emphasis on the individual. As for Heidegger, he has indeed said that the distinction between authentic and inauthentic existence is not intended to be a moral distinction; but it is clear that in his view a man lives inauthentically to the extent in which he is merged in 'the one' and that he lives authentically to the extent in which he rises above the level of 'the one'. As for Jaspers, he has indeed written a good deal on social and political matters (on the question of German guilt, for example); but in his more philosophical works he dwells more on what he calls 'communication', a mutual self-revealing between two human beings, than on general social-political relationships. Sartre has even gone so far as to say (in *Huis-Clos*) that hell is other people. And he seems to hold the rather pessimistic view that human beings can achieve real unity and solidarity only in face of some external power, such as an exploiting class. If the external cause or occasion of cohesion is removed, the centrifugal forces of individualism prevail. There can be no real 'we' except in the presence of a 'you' or 'they'.[10] Even love between two human beings is doomed to frustration. For love seeks a union which, if achieved, would automatically exclude love, inasmuch as there would no longer be two distinct persons.

Of course, if one says that the existentialist philosophies do not provide any sound basis for social-political theory,[11] this is not equivalent to suggesting that existentalist philosophers *as men* must remain politically uncommitted. In the early thirties Heidegger made an excursion into politics in favour of the Nazis, an excursion of which the least said the better, as far as the reputation of that philosopher is concerned. And Sartre has certainly committed himself, in the Resistance and later in favour of Marxism.[12] It is not necessarily a question of accusing the men themselves of aloofness from our social-political problems. It is rather a question of suggesting that even when a given existentialist is obviously committed, as is Sartre, this commitment has little, if any, clear connexion with his existentialist philosophy. Some writers have tried to establish a connexion between Heidegger's Nazism and his philosophy; but the attempt does not seem to me to have been very successful. And even if Sartre has lately been attempting some sort of synthesis between his brand of existentialism and Marxism, I think that any real fusion would demand considerable modifications in one or the other or in both.

It must be remembered, however, that even if the political views of certain existentialists are not deducible from their existentialism, their situation in this respect is by no means exceptional. Nobody would suggest that Bertrand Russell is uncommitted. But he has never pretended that his social and political views are deducible from his theoretical philosophy. On the contrary, he has asserted the very opposite. Indeed, he does not regard the treatment of concrete social and political problems as being, strictly speaking, part of philosophy at all.

Yes, it may be said; but the trouble is not that the social and political convictions of a man such a Sartre cannot be deduced from his phenomenological ontology. Why should they be deducible? The trouble is rather the question of compatibility. A man may very well hold two positions, neither of which is deducible from the other. But if he wishes to retain both of them, they should be compatible. Insistence on social and political self-commitment presupposes a social view of man or, better, a view of man as a social being, as essentially a member of society. But the whole weight of existentialism is directed to emphasizing the individual, who is said to 'exist' in so far as he stands out not only from infra-human things but also from society. Obviously, no existentialist would deny that man is a member of a society. For this is simply a plain fact. But the emphasis is placed on the lonely individual. And though this may be understandable in terms of the situation obtaining in Germany and France after the second world war, at the time when the popularity of existentialism reached its zenith, it will certainly not do as a philosophical anthropology or theory of man.

There is, I think, a good deal of truth in this point of view. So by way of conclusion I propose to make some further general remarks about the existentialist concept of man.

7

In the first place it would be a great mistake to think that the existentialists look on man as an isolated subject of consciousness, confined within the field of subjectivity (of 'ideas' or, as Hume might say, of 'impressions'), so that the problem arises, how is it possible to prove the existence of the external world and, in particular, of other selves? Heidegger has said[13] that the scandal of philosophy is not that adequate proofs of the existence of an external world and of other selves have not been found, but rather that such proofs should ever have been sought or deemed necessary. The cognitive relationship, the subject-object dichotomy, arises within the world. And man becomes self-conscious only by separating himself, as it were, *within the world* from other things. He could not even raise the question of proving the existence of material objects and of other selves, unless he were already well aware of their existence. *Mitsein*, being-with, is a constituent factor in *Dasein*, the human reality. We cannot therefore understand man except by seeing him as a member of society. It is all very well to talk about man as a thinking subject or as a *res cogitans*. Man's very thought presupposes society. We have only to consider language to see this.

Sartre has argued in the same sort of way. And he has given graphic examples to show that it is untrue to say that we know other people only as objects and are thus compelled to infer that they are selves or subjects. Suppose that I am squatting down in a hotel corridor, looking through the keyhole of a room. I think that I am alone and unobserved. Suddenly I become aware that someone is standing watching me, an employee of the hotel or a fellow-guest. I am the object of *le regard*, the look. I experience myself as object and the other as subject. His look invades my world. Well, we are always subject to the look. My world is always being invaded, as it were, by another's world. Indeed, my world is *my* world only through being distinguished from the other's world. I do not start with *my* world and then have to argue to the existence of the other's world.

Or consider the thought of Merleau-Ponty (1908-1961). In opposition to a dualistic view of man he spoke of man as the 'body-subject', unity which is reflected in the unity of thought and language, language of course being a social phenomenon.[14] And he insisted that man, the body-subject, awakens the actual, explicit consciousness through appropriating, as it were, an already existing situation. That is to say, we start our personal lives, as individuals, by entering into a common natural world and a common cultural world. Indeed the natural world is in a real sense given to us only through the cultural world. For example, we learn to think about the natural world, to conceive it, only by appropriating or entering into language, which belongs to the cultural world. In fine, individual personality presupposes a common historical situation. Of course, we come to have ideas, points of view and convictions of our own. But the body-subject is unintelligible apart from its historical environment, the natural and cultural world which personal consciousness and life presuppose.

At the same time it is clear, I think, that the impression that existentialists are concerned with the lonely individual is caused by the writings
of certain existentalists themselves. The impression, in other words,
certainly has a foundation in fact. And it has several causes or grounds.
For one thing of course talk about such themes as dread or anguish, guilt
and death naturally suggests the idea of the tortured individual.[15] Again,
though Kierkegaard did not deny the existence of impersonal objective
truth, as in mathematics and science, what he was chiefly interested in
was the religious faith by which, in his opinion man relates himself to the
God whose existence cannot be proved. Faith was for Kierkegaard a
venture or risk. And it is of course the individual who ventures out over
the deep waters and affirms what for Kierkegaard is an 'objective
uncertainty'.[16] Again, in existentialism as a whole there is a marked
reaction against any tendency to identify the individual with his social
function or to see him simply as part of a totality. Man is, by his nature,
a free agent; and free decision is an act of the individual. We are all
rooted, as it were, in 'the one'. We tend to think as 'one thinks', to feel
as 'one feels', to act as 'one acts'. But man can rise above mere social
conformism, not totally but to some extent. And to the extent in which
he does so, so that his life is an expression of his basic freedom, he lives
an authentic human life.

8

Any philosophy of man is likely to exhibit to some extent a personal
perspective, namely that of the philosopher himself. But it can also
express some features at any rate of what we might describe as man's
self-understanding. So of course do the sciences which deal with man.
Indeed, science can perhaps be regarded as inheriting the Greek idea of
objective knowledge. But it is man himself who creates the sciences; and
man's self-understanding need not be confined to the sciences. There is
room, for example, for a basic phenomenology of human consciousness
or experience, such as we find attempted by some of the existentialists.
Again, any tendency to conceive human beings simply as exemplifying
the characteristics of a class or simply in relation to their social functions
is likely to give rise, sooner or later, to a counter-emphasis on the free
individual, or man considered from the point of view of the creative
agent rather than as an object of scientific research and classification. To
be sure, counter-emphases, such as we find in existentialism, are apt to
produce exaggerations. But it not infrequently happens that it is
precisely by means of its exaggerations that a philosophy draws attention
to something to which it is worth while paying attention. A philosophy
of man, such as we find in existentialism, may not be of much obvious
use *within science itself*. But a scientist, whether he is aware of it or not,
is apt to have an implicit philosophy. And reflection on it in the light of
ideas expounded by the existentialists might contribute to the avoidance

of an over-narrow concept of man. As I said at the beginning, we can see things in various ways. And existentialism expresses one way (or, more accurately, several ways) of seeing man.

Notes:

[1] I am thinking for example, of remarks by Wittgenstein (Lectures and Conversations on Aesthetics, Psychology and Religious Belief, p.44), Sir Karl Popper (British Philosophy in the Mid-Century, ed. C.A.Mace, pp. 161-2), and Professor Eysenck (The Scientific Study of Personality, p. 16).

[2] Metaphysics and Common Sense (London, 1969,) p.220.

[3] Whether it is appropriate to speak of 'methological determinism' in this connexion is doubtless open to discussion. But whether the description is apt or not, I do not think that it is very difficult to understand what is being referred to.

[4] I do not mean to imply that the physical scientist actually sees all the 'particles' of which he speaks. I mean that his attitude is that of the external spectator.

[5] Notebooks, 1914-1916, ed. & trans. G.E.M. Anscombe (Oxford, 1961), p. 80.

[6] When Sartre was asked for advice on an important issue by a young man, he declined to give it, saying that it was up to the youth to make his own choice. When told by a Marxist that he ought to have given advice, Sartre replied that he knew very well how the young man would choose, and that he did in fact choose in this way. This reply becomes intelligible, if we bear in mind Sartre's theory of a basic life-project.

[7] In view of the activity which Sartre attributes to le pour-soi it is difficult to take seriously his interpretation of consciousness in negative terms, as a privation of being.

[8] Obviously, if a human being is necessarily free (condemned to be free, as Sartre puts it), choice of inauthentic existence is as much an exercise of freedom as choice of authentic existence.

[9] Metaphysics and Common Sense, p. 218.

[10] It appears that for Sartre human beings in general could be united only in the presence of a God. But for him there is no God.

[11] With Gabriel Marcel relationships between human beings form a prominent theme. But Marcel repudiates the label 'existentialist'. And his thought in some respects is much more similar to that of Royce than to that of Heidegger or of Sartre.

[12] The Russians' intervention in Hungary repelled Sartre. But he would make a distinction between Marxism and Russian imperialism.

[13] Being and Time, trans. by J. Macquarrie & E. Robinson (London, 1962), p. 249.

[14] One might compare Maurice Merleau-Ponty's view of man with that of Gilbert Ryle in The Concept of Man. Both philosophers are opposed to Cartesian dualism.

[15] Obviously, an examination of the actual use of these ideas in the writings of the existentialists is required in order to estimate the extent to which we can justifiably speak of the 'tortured' individual. My point here is simply that the words ('anguish', for instance) inevitably suggests this notion.

[16] Something of the sort can be found in the philosophy of Jaspers, but in a less specifically Christian framework of thought and, in my opinion, with less exaggeration.

CHAPTER 14

ORTEGA Y GASSET AND
PHILOSOPHICAL RELATIVISM

S OME YEARS AGO I gave a talk in the Third Programme on some
Spanish philosophers, including Ortega y Gasset. The talk was
meant to be simply informative and explanatory: I did not wish to take
sides either for or against the philosophers of whom I spoke. But the
talk was not well received, I believe, in certain quarters in Spain. And
soon afterwards one of Ortega's principal Spanish critics sent me a copy
of a small book he had written against this philosopher. One of his chief
points of criticism was Ortega's relativism; and this point is stressed by
some other critics too. According to these critics, Ortega is involved in a
flat contradiction. All philosophies are relative. But the philosophy
which says that they are relative is supposed to be the absolute *truth*.
Hence Ortega says at the same time that all philosophies are relative and
that at least one is not. And this is a contradiction. This is more or less
the burden of the criticism.

It has always seemed to me that this criticism is somewhat 'simpliste'.
I mean, it smacks of the text-book refutation of the thesis that there is
no absolute truth, but that all truth is relative. This does not render the
criticism necessarily false, of course; but it suggests that there may be
something more to be said about the matter. And to a historian of
philosophy the matter is of some interest. For a historian of philosophy
is very apt to be struck by the elements of relativity in philosophical
systems. And it was largely for this reason that I chose the subject for
my lecture today.

Ortega y Gasset (1883-1955) is a great figure in modern Spanish
literature. So far as I know, nobody, whether friend or foe, has questioned his literary ability. Indeed, it seems that one of the points in the
writings of his critics which most annoyed Ortega was their tendency to
praise him as a writer of Spanish and to belittle him as a philosopher.
For he not only occupied a chair of philosophy but also looked upon
himself as the philosopher of our time. And his more fervent admirers
accepted and propagated this judgment. Thus in his *Historia de la
Filosofia* Professor Julián Marias starts with the pre-Socratics and ends
with Ortega y Gasset, as if his system were the culmination of philosophical thought up to date.

However, though considered by some to be the greatest philosopher
of our era and by others to be little better than an intellectual charlatan,
Ortega's thought is not well known in this country. Hence I propose to
begin by outlining some of his ideas and leading up gradually to this
theory of perspectivism, which is the main ground for the accusation of
relativism. Perhaps I should remark at once that many of Ortega's ideas

can be paralleled in the philosophies of other writers. In some ways, I suppose, Ortega was profoundly Spanish; but he was also a great European, and he had a remarkable flair for expressing ideas which either had or would come to the fore in other European countries. But I propose to abstain from constantly making remarks such as 'This theory seems to come from Nietzsche', 'This idea recalls Bergson', or 'Here Ortega's ideas resemble those of Heidegger'. For, though such remarks may serve to show that the speaker is not entirely ignorant of the history of philosophy, they would be irrelevant in the present context.

2

The centre of Ortega's attention is the human being in his concrete, historic life. The point of departure for reflection is myself and my world. That is to say, Ortega does not begin with an abstract epistemological subject, as in some forms of idealism. Nor does he begin with 'things', as if they were the ultimate reality, to which the idea of man is added in the course of time. In his view the bare epistemological subject is an abstraction. And so are 'things', considered entirely apart from the subject. The fundamental reality is for him 'life'. And 'life' means a dialogue with the world, a treating or occupying oneself with the world. Life is an activity; and it is on the basis of this activity that I come to know myself and things. This activity is the radical or fundamental reality, an active intercourse between myself and my world.

We can, of course, say that the point of departure for philosophical reflection is the self. But it is not the bare epistemological subject, a kind of timeless spectator set outside the world. In *Adán en el Paraiso* (1910) we are told that Adam in Paradise signifies I in the world, this 'world' being not so much the sum of things as the scene or horizon in which the drama of life takes place. In *Meditaciones del Quijote* (1914) Ortega enunciates his famous proposition: 'I am I and my circumstance'. This circumstance or situation includes not only the external world of nature but also other human beings, society. It also includes the past, as bearing upon the present.

Whether man likes it or not, he cannot help participating in the dialogue between himself and his situation with constitutes life. He has before him a limited field of possibilities, within the framework of his 'circumstance' or situation. And life consists in choice between these possibilities, in actualizing them. By these choices a man makes himself. For he is not something already made: he is a *quehacer*, something to make. Man, as Ortega puts it in *Historia como sistema*, goes on accumulating being . . . the past: he continues to create a being (himself) in the dialectical series of his experiences.

3

It is in the light of this insistence on the fundamental reality of 'life' that we have to understand Ortega's doctrine of 'vital reason'. It may appear at first sight that there is an opposition between reason and life. Reason apprehends, for instance, changeless mathematical truths, whereas life means change and movement. But the so-called pure reason is only one particular function of reason, and reason in general is a function of life. Indeed, Ortega sometimes speaks as though reason and life were the same thing. He means apparently that it is living, the active dialogue between me and my world, which brings things within my perspective, so to speak, and renders them intelligible for me. In any case reason is a function of living: it is the servant or instrument of life. I do not live in order to reason; I reason in order to live.

This should not be understood in the sense that Ortega intends to belittle the mind and its work or that he denies value to the striving after intellectual clarity and conceptualization. He is not an irrationalist in this sense. Speaking of Hegel (in *Meditaciones del Quijote*) he remarks that reality is too rich to be reduced to the concept, to thought. But we cannot live without thought. And 'each concept is literally an organ by which we capture things. Only vision by means of the concept is a complete vision; sensation gives us only the diffused and plastic material of each object: it gives us the impression of things, not the things'. Intellect or reason gives us mastery over things; and it is necessary for life. But the words 'for life' need to be emphasized.

Insisting, as he does, on the vital function of reason, it is only natural that Ortega applies this conception to philosophy. Life means activity, choice. And in order to be able to choose and to act, I require some knowledge of myself and of my situation. Life is insecurity; it is a drama, an adventure. And in his radical insecurity man seeks for certainty, for something to hold on to, as it were. His desire for knowledge is thus a function of life. He seeks to know in order to be able to live. This is the root of philosophy.

But we can give a more concrete and accurate account of the nature of philosophy. In *Ideas y creencias* (1940), for instance, Ortega distinguishes between ideas and beliefs. An idea is something which occurs to us, which we think about and which we know we hold. If we are asked for our ideas about some subject, we may indeed have to say that we have no ideas on the subject. But if we have ideas on the subject, we know what they are, even if for some reason or other we are unwilling to say what they are. A belief, however, is something on which we count, whether we think of it or not. For instance, that the earth is firm in spite of occasional earthquakes is something on which I count in my activity. I do not normally advert to this belief at all; I simply presuppose it and act on this presupposition.

Now, in each culture there are a number of beliefs which began as

ideas and then became beliefs or presuppositions. They became incorpor-
ated, as it were, into the background of the culture in question, and they
were then taken for granted. In other words, in each culture there is a
certain tradition or way of life which rests on or presupposes certain
beliefs. But these beliefs are not, of course, immune from doubt. Men
can begin to question the fundamental beliefs on which a given culture
rests. And when this happens, it is necessary for life that the mind
should endeavour to overcome the ensuing state of doubt and uncertainty. This it does by working with a system of ideas to replace the
beliefs which have been subjected to doubt. Obviously, different attitudes towards the past are possible. The mind may attempt to give an
explicit rational basis to the formerly presupposed beliefs. Perhaps, if we
allow for necessary qualifications, we may say that Socrates and Plato
in the fifth century B.C. and Descartes in the seventeenth century A.D.
were partly engaged in such an activity. Thus Socrates and Plato endeavoured to give a firm rational basis to moral and religious ideas which had
been called in question during the intellectual ferment of the Sophistic
period, the Greek Enlightenment. Obviously, they sought to substitute
clear, distinct and purified ideas for what had gone before. But the
Platonic philosophy rose, partly at least, out of a period of questioning,
and Plato was opposed to the intellectual revolutionaries, to men such
as Thrasymachus and Callicles for example, who maintaned that the
traditional moral convictions should be thrown aside. Again, Descartes,
in the face of the Renaissance scepticism of Montaigne, Charron and the
free thinkers, endeavoured to place certain traditional beliefs on a firm
foundation of clear and distinct ideas and unquestionable demonstrative
argument. But the mind can also set itself against the past, endeavouring
to substitute for former beliefs a new and revolutionary system of ideas.
It is not, I think, unreasonable to class Nietzsche as one of these thinkers.
But in either case philosophy presupposes doubt and uncertainty. It is an
endeavour to overcome this doubt and uncertainty, an endeavour inspired by the need to act with understanding, to attain some security,
something to hold on to. Here we have reason displaying its vital
function.

It may be said, of course, that philosophy, as we know it, is by no
means always this. But Ortega is well aware of the fact. He emphasizes
the fact that philosophy, like so many other things, becomes conven-
tionalized. Thus it may become a game or a learned pursuit of academic
thinkers or a means for gaining a livelihood. For Ortega this is not what
he calls genuine philosophizing. The member of a philosophical School,
for instance, who spends his time interpreting the Master and patching up
his system here and there, is not a genuine philosopher. The genuine
philosopher is one who is inspired by a passionate desire to understand
himself in his situation, in order to live, to act, with clarity. Genuine
philosophizing is borne out of doubt and uncertainty and of the felt need

for emerging from this state, so that one can live with a recognized purpose and set of values. We can, of course, find genuine philosophers in any epoch; but they are most likely to be found at a time when there is widespread questioning of the beliefs and values on which a former culture rested or which were accepted by a former 'generation'. For Ortega was much given to thinking in terms of 'generations'. Each generation is a new social body, consisting of a dynamic compromise between the minority, the intellectual leaders, and the mass. And each generation has its own historic task to perform, to which it may be faithful or unfaithful.

4

Now, inasmuch as philosophy strives to substitute certainty for uncertainty and doubt, clarity for darkness, and a rational system of ideas for the unquestioned beliefs which preceded the state of doubt, it can be said to aspire to transcend tradition. A philosopher such as Plato did not set out to describe the Greek tradition; he set out to find and expound *the* truth. This does not necessarily mean that he considered that all he said was certainly true. We all know that he made deliberate use of 'myth' and hypothesis. But he aimed at the truth. Nothing but *the* truth, transcending traditions of time and place, would provide a secure foundation for human life and action. Similarly, when Descartes set out to overcome the scepticism of the Renaissance and the uncertainty within himself, he aimed at establishing, not his private truth, but *the* truth, a system of truths which woluld be universally and necessarily true. He aimed at establishing a timeless philosophy which would transcend the tradition of any given cultural epoch.

But though philosophy aspires to transcend tradition and the limiting conditions of time and place, it inevitably falls, against its own will, within a tradition. Philosophy is tied in some sense to a given historical situation, the situation which it tries to clarify.

One can put the matter in this way. Ortega was in one sense a realist. Though educated in Marburg, he reacted strongly against neo-Kantianism. He says, for instance, that it is not the mission of the intellect to project its form on the chaos of received data, but exactly the contrary. The characteristic of thought . . . consists in adopting the form of objects, in making them its principle and norm *(La 'Filosofia de la Historia' de Hegel y la historiologia)*. At the same time each philosophy is what he calls 'perspectival'. 'Two men look at the same landscape from distinct points of view. However, it is not the same (thing) that they see' *(El Tema de Nuestro Tiempo,* 1923). Similarly, each philosophy, if it is a genuine philosophy, is an interpretation of the world by a particular vital centre. 'Spinoza's *species aeterna,* the omnipresent and absolute point of view does not really exist: it is a fictitious and abstract point of view' *(ibid)*. It is true that 'the perspective is one of the components of reality' *(ibid)*, in the sense that a man's perspective or point of view is a constitutive part of what reality means for him. But it is none the less *his* perspective. God may enjoy all possible points of view; but man certainly does not. Different points of view converge, indeed, towards a mobile or receding horizon; they may very well be complementary rather than mutually exclusive. But they resemble the distinct views of a landscape as seen by different persons from different points. No one particular point of view is uniquely privileged. That is, we cannot say of any one particular view that it is the only true one. Nor can we say that there is an absolute point of view distinct from all partial points of view. At the same time we cannot say of any particular point of view that it is false. It is simply partial and inadequate. And the different possible views are complementary. So it is with philosophies.

5

Now, some of Ortega's Spanish critics have fixed their attention on this doctrine of perspectivism and have equated it with pure relativism. They have then objected that pure relativism is self-contradictory. For the relativist states as an absolute truth that all truth is relative. And here there is a contradiction. But before I discuss the relevance of this objection to Ortega's thought, I wish to indicate briefly what he himself has to say about relativism in *El Tema de Nuestro Tiempo*.

Knowledge, according to Ortega, consists in the acquisition of truths. And in truths the transcendent (that is, the transsubjective) universe of reality manifests itself to us. The 'rationalist' maintains that knowledge is possible only if reality can 'penetrate into' the subject without the least deformation. The knowing subject must therefore be a transparent medium, without any peculiarity or colour, the same, yesterday, today and tomorrow. In fine, the subject must be outside life and history. For these mean change and peculiarity. Relativism on the other hand maintains that reality, on entering the subject, is deformed; and it is this deformation which the subject takes to be reality. On relativistic principles, therefore, reality can never be known. In fact, according to Ortega, there will be no transcendent reality, but only a number of supposed realities.

Neither extreme is tenable. Rationalism is untenable because the subject is not outside life and history. Relativism is untenable because it makes knowledge impossible, and because it should end by denying the existence of any transsubjective reality. Yet both theories express certain truths. Rationalism expresses the truth that there is a transsubjective reality. Relativism expresses the truth that the subject is a historic subject with a particular point of view. What we need is a combination of these truths. For they are really complementary.

Ortega tries to indicate the line which this combination should take by using an analogy. If we place a net in a stream, it lets some things pass through it, but not others. One can say that it selects, receiving some things, rejecting others. But it does not deform what it receives. 'This is the function of the subject, of the living being with regard to the cosmic reality which surrounds it'. It does not retain everything, nor does it create any illusory reality. It selects. Out of the infinity of elements which compose reality the individual lets pass or receives those things which fit the meshes of the net. The others remain unperceived, unknown. One can take an elementary example from physiology. The eye and the ear receive light-waves and sound-waves of varied velocity and intensity. But there are upper and lower limits beyond which sounds, for instance, are not perceived. Thus the structure of the subject is a determining factor in determining what is perceived; but it does not follow that what is perceived is deformed, in the sense that it is illusory, an hallucination. Again, the psychic structure of the individual permits the understanding of some truths, but makes a man blind to others. 'Similarly, each people and each epoch has its "typical" soul, that is, a net with meshes of definite size and shape which gives it a strict affinity with certain truths and an incorrigible inability for arriving at certain others. This means that all epochs and peoples have enjoyed their own "congruous" portions of truth; and there is no sense in any people or epoch pretending to oppose itself to others, as though it alone enjoyed the entire truth'. Indeed, according to Ortega, if the universe presented itself in exactly the same way to an Athenian of the time of Socrates and to an inhabitant of New York in the twentieth century, this would indicate.that it was a question, not of an external reality, but of an imaginary conception which happened to be identical in two subjects.

6

Now, it seems to me to be fairly clear from the foregoing that Ortega does not intend to say that all truth is relative, in the sense that every truth is true only for a given individual or for a given epoch or generation. Philosophical reflection presupposes some truths. Or let us put it this way. Perspecitivism already presupposes some truths which are universally valid. For example, there is a transsubjective reality. This is presupposed by the doctrine of different points of view. If I take up my position at Geneva on a clear day, I see Mont Blanc from a particular point of view, in a particular perspective. If I go to another place, I see the mountain under a different perspective. But I should not see the mountain under any perspective unless there were a mountain to see. And if I go on to say that no one perspective or point of view is uniquely privileged, in the sense that it gives the true view of the mountain and that all other views are false, this statement does not deny, either explicitly or implicitly, the truth of the statement that there is a Mont Blanc. I think that this is sufficiently obvious.

Nor have I any reason to suppose that Ortega intended to say that there are no abstract and analytical propositions which are universally true. He would say, I presume, that such propositions do not reveal historic reality, that they are hypothetical rather than existential or descriptive of existent reality. They are necessary conditions of historic reality, and in this sense they are *a priori*, though they are not *a priori* in the sense that they are known *a priori*. They are known by analysis, the point of departure for this analysis being my life.

However this may be, I do not see that Ortega can justifiably be interpreted as saying that all truth is relative, in the sense that no truth is universally valid, that is, for every life. It is in function of my own life, from my own point of view, that I discover, for example, that there is a transsubjective reality. But I can then see that the presence of trans-subjective reality is a necessary condition of every life. Hence I do not see that we can legitimately say that Ortega contradicts himself by saying that all truth is relative and that one truth is not.

7

Ortega's Spanish critics might perhaps retort on these lines. 'Very well, let us talk, not about propositions in general, but about philosophical systems. Now, philosophical systems consist of propositions, philosophical propositions. You may wish to say that when Ortega speaks of points of view he is speaking of the central vision or fundamental and inspiring idea which is expressed in each system rather than of particular propositions or sets of propositions. But this vision or inspiring idea does not really enter into philosophy until it is expressed or made articulate. And it is expressed or rendered articulate in the form of a proposition or of propositions. Therefore it is still true to say that philosophical systems consists of propositions. Hence in saying that philosophies are relative Ortega is saying that philosophical propositions are relative. But the statement that they are relative is itself a philosophical proposition; it is part of his philosophical system. It follows, therefore, that Ortega is contradicting himself. For he says at the same time that all philosophical propositions are relative and that one at least is not. And this is a contradiction. Or we can put the matter another way. If no philosophical propositions are absolutely true, there is no criterion by which we can judge between the degrees of truth attained by different philosophies. All will be on the same level. And philosophy will be reduced in the end to the history of philosophy. Yet in undertaking to make evaluative statements about philosophies in general Ortega places himself to this extent outside the flux of history; he sits in judgement on history. Yet this is the very thing which he says cannot be done. Hence he contradicts himself'.

The stock answer to this stock objection is this. If I say that all judgments of taste are relative, I do not involve myself in any contradiction. For the statement that all judgments of taste are relative is not itself a judgment of taste. It is a statement *about* judgments of taste. Similarly, if I say that all philosophical systems are relative, my statement is not itself a philosophical statement. And if I say that all philosophical propositions are relative, my statement is not itself a philosophical proposition. It is a statement *about* philosophical propositions. It is a meta-philosophical proposition, a proposition of a different order. Hence I do not involve myself in any contradiction.

That the statement that all judgments of taste is not itself a judgment of taste seems to me to be obviously true. And it seems to me to be also sufficiently clear that the statement that all philosophies are relative need not be itself a philosophical statement. For it might be interpreted, for instance, as an historical statement. It would then mean that in looking back on past philosophies I can discern the influence on them of contemporary cultural factors which serve to 'date' them. And if I say this, I am making an historical rather than a philosophical statement. At the same time it is not clear to me that the statement that philosophies are relative *cannot* be a philosophical statement. For it may be the expression of a decision about the nature of philosophy: and it is not immediately clear to me that a decision about the nature of philosophy necessarily falls outside the class of philosophical statements. It might do so, of course. For it might be an historical generalization. Or it might be a mere recommendation to understand the word 'philosophy' in a certain way. But it is not clear to me that it could not be something more, namely the expression of a philosophical system.

Perhaps I am wrong in thinking this. But in any case I doubt whether we can get very far by means of slick objections and slick answers of the type to which I have just alluded. For Ortega's doctrine of perspecitvism, as I have described it, is not clear. And unless we know what he means, we are scarcely in a position to decide whether a given objection is relevant or not.

8

In the first place it seems to me possible that Ortega's critics have been hypnotized by words such as 'perspectivism', which suggest Nietzsche's description of truth as a biologically useful form of error, and that they have paid insufficient attention to his analogies, treating them as merely casual illustrations.

Consider the landscape-analogy. If I look at Mont Blanc from Geneva, my view of the mountain is relative to my position, and it differs from the view which a man would enjoy who was standing on the other side of the mountain. But it does not follow that either view can properly be called false. So reality as a whole can be seen and interpreted from different standpoints in the movement of history and in the light of different cultural beliefs and problems: but it does not necessarily follow that any particular interpretation can properly be called false. In so far as it is not the only possible point of view, it can be called inadequate or partial; but 'false' is not the right word to apply to it. The mediaeval thinker, for example, encountered the world as a system dependent on a Creator and shot through, as it were, with final causality. The teleological interpretation of nature, which formed the cultural background of his thought, was a component part of the world as it appeared to him. That is to say, his perspective entered into, or was a component of reality. The perspective of the rationalist philosopher of the seventeenth and eighteenth centuries was, however, somewhat different. Living in a different cultural epoch, and after the rise of Renaissance science, he saw nature as a mechanical system, ruled by efficient rather than by final causality. Here we have points of view. But it does not necessarily follow that either point of view is false, though both points of view may be partial. Reality is seen from different angles, so to speak; and nature as a teleological system is not incompatible with nature as a mechanical system. The two views are complementary rather than mutually exclusive.

Moreover, in both cases it is reality which is seen. When John looks at Mont Blanc from Geneva and William from the Italian side they both see Mont Blanc. Their visions differ; but neither is an imaginary and purely subjective construction. So with the mediaeval thinker and the seventeenth- or eighteenth-century philosopher. Both apprehend reality; both have some vision of the truth. But neither sees the complete truth. Nor can any finite mind do so. For any finite mind must occupy some particular point in history: he does not, and cannot, stand outside history, occupying a timeless and absolute standpoint. But it does not follow that his interpretation of reality must be a purely imaginary and subjective construction simply because it is partial.

It may be objected, of course, that I have given a carefully selected example. There is ultimately no incompatibility between the mediaeval vision of the world as a system dependent on a provident Creator and the later vision of the world as a mathematical-mechanical system. True, the transition gave rise to special problems, with which Descartes, and later Kant, were faced. And these problems could hardly arise apart from the historical and cultural context in which they did arise. But the general points of view are complementary rather than mutually exclusive. At the same time it would be easy enough to mention points of view and interpretations of reality which are obviously mutually exclusive − theism and atheism, for example, or spiritualism and materialism. They cannot all be true. Yet how can we judge between them if all philosophies are relative to different cultural epochs? To do so, do we do not need an absolute norm or standard of judgment?

Ortega's answer appears to be that we evaluate past philosophies in the light of our own philosophy. That is to say, we evaluate past perspectives according to our own perspective. This is what we do in fact. And what else can we possibly do? The past, including past thought, forms part of our world. And in interpreting our world we interpret past thought. But our interpretation of past thought will form part of the world of thinkers in the future. And they will evaluate it from their own point of view. No one point of view is uniquely privileged.

Now, this is obviously one of the main points to which Ortega's critics take exception. On his view, they would say, philosophy becomes the same as the history of philosophy, not so much in the sense of a descriptive historical account of the development of philosophy as in the sense of the actual development of philosophy. We are in the stream, so to speak, and we cannot put our heads outside the water to take a view of the stream from outside. At the same time, by talking about philosophy in general and its nature, Ortega clearly implies that one can lift one's head above the water. In other words, he asserts that there is not, and cannot be, a perennial philosophy; and at the same time his own reflections inevitably imply that there is such a philosophy. To call it a meta-philosophy and not a philosophy is to juggle with words. We must conclude, therefore, that Ortega is involved in self-contradiction, at least by implication.

But the matter is not quite so simple. If I understand him rightly, Ortega does not deny, for example, that there is a fundamental human situation, which recurs in all concrete historic situations. And we can therefore make universal statements, which apply to man and his world in all epochs. In this sense we can get our heads above the water. At the same time this fundamental and universal human situation is an abstraction. It never exists as such. We never have man as such, but only primitive man, Greek man, mediaeval man, the man of the eighteenth century, and so on. Similarly, we never have the world as such, things as such. Thunder as such, for example, is an abstraction. The fact, so to speak, is given to us with a certain interpretation or meaning. Thunder was one thing for primitive man; something else for us. It is quite true that we can recognize the character and causes of different interpretations. And we can form abstract ideas of the conditions of possibility of all concrete situations. But we approach these abstract ideas from our own point of view, from the point of view of our own situation. How can we possibly avoid doing so? And in this case perspectivism has the last word.

9

One could doubtless carry on the debate on these lines indefinitely, and, perhaps without reaching any very clear conclusion. But I prefer to leave the matter there and suggest instead that the controversy between Ortega and his critics depends to a large extent on the different ideas of philosophy which they severally hold. The critics who accuse Ortega of a self-contradictory relativism and who defend the concept of a perennial philosophy seem, if I do not do them an injustice, to think of philosophy as a science which is already formed, in the sense that certain arguments and conclusions need only be learned and handed on. One can learn philosophy in a manner analogous to that in which one can learn the results of chemical analysis up to date or the facts about the life of Julius Caesar. And if one conceives philosophy in this way, it is quite natural that one should speak of a perennial philosophy in the sense of a body of true propositions which can be taught and learned. But Ortega's idea of philosophy is quite different. He looks on philosophy as something to which human beings — that is, some human beings — are driven by the felt need for attaining clarity about themselves and their world in order to live. Philosophy is therefore, not a body of propositions which can be handed on, but a personal activity, the activity of the striving after clarity about the human situation. And, as a personal activity, it is, and must be, constantly renewed. Each genuine philosopher must do the work again, so to speak. But there is no genuine philosopher-in-himself. He is a particular man, living in a particular historic situation. And it is this particular situation which impels him to seek for clarity, and about which he seeks clarity. He seeks, indeed, *the* truth; and, so far as he is a successful philosopher, he attains it. But he necessarily sees it from a particular point of view, from a particular point in history.

There is another difference between Ortega and his critics. The latter are inclined to think of reality as something which has, as it were, a constant and unvarying physiognomy, which can be reproduced in one philosophical theory or system, so that all other theories or systems are *eo ipso* ruled out as false. But Ortega does not think of reality in this way. He would say, for instance, that Mont Blanc does not possess one 'absolute' physiognomy, one which is independent of every point of view taken of it. Reality is rather the infinity of possible perspectives. Ortega's critics doubtless understand this as leading to the conclusion that there is no objective reality; that what we call reality is a name for a multiplicity of different points of view, these points of view being subjective. But this is not, I think, what Ortega means. As we have seen, a man's perspective of reality is, according to Ortega, a component of reality for that man. And we must not understand this as meaning that the man projects a subjective point of view or perspective on objective reality. The perspective is reality revealing itself to a man in a definite situation. Once more reference to Ortega's analogies is relevant. When I look at Mont Blanc from Geneva, the view of the mountain which I enjoy obviously depends on my position. But I do not project on to the mountain the view which I have of it. Rather does the mountain reveal itself to me in a particular way because of my particular situation. And what I see is the mountain, not an illusion.

10

Perhaps this chapter has sounded like a defence of Ortega's position. And it has, indeed, been a defence in the sense that I have argued that Ortega did not intend to say that no objective truth is attainable. But I doubt whether the doctrine of perspectivism is really very informative. To say that all philosophies gives us different perspectival views of reality sounds very well. But what is meant by it? After all, we cannot say that all philosophies, as recorded in the writings of philosophers and described in histories of philosophy, are, as they stand, complementary. For it is only too obvious that they frequently contradict one another. We have first to determine what elements in each we consider to be true. And to say that different true propositions about reality give us partial but complementary views of reality does not tell us much.

It may be objected perhaps that in trying to rescue Ortega from the charge of sheer relativism I have over-emphasized his analogies and so misinterpreted him. The analogy of a landscape or, as I have given it, of Mont Blanc suggests an unchanging reality, even if Mont Blanc is not, physically speaking, unchanging. And this is, indeed, what his critics had in mind. I mean, they were thinking principally of God and of our knowledge of God. And they thought that the theory of perspectivism was incompatible with the maintenance of definite religious beliefs. But when Ortega spoke of reality, he was not thinking primarily of God, of whom he speaks very little.[1] He was thinking primarily of historic reality, historic man in the changing cosmos. And this fact is concealed by speaking about Mont Blanc.

There is a lot of truth in this contention. I think that some of Ortega's critics did not perhaps pay sufficient attention to this point. At the same time, if we understand 'reality' as meaning history in a wide sense, something like the perspectival view becomes almost a truism. For it is obvious, for instance, that the historic 'circumstance' of the Athenian in the fifth century B.C. was not the same as the historic 'circumstance' of the twentieth-century European or American. Their points of view are bound to differ.

My own objection, therefore, against Ortega's theory is not so much that it is relativistic as that it is ambiguous. He does not make it sufficiently clear what it is exactly that he wishes to say. And this is, I suppose, the reason why some have been able to maintain in all good faith that he is a sheer relativist, while others have replied with warmth that he is nothing of the kind.

Notes

[1] In *El Tema de Nuertro Tiempo* Ortega says that God is "the symbol of the vital torrent". In later writings he spoke of the necessity of transcendence and of absolute Being. But, so far as I know, he did not develop this theme.